BETTER THAN SCHOOL

BETTER THAN SCHOOL

One Family's Declaration of Independence

by Nancy Wallace

INTRODUCTION BY JOHN HOLT

LARSON

International Standard Book Number (cloth) 0-943914-05-1
International Standard Book Number (paper) 0-943914-04-3
Library of Congress Catalog Card Number: 83–11333

Manufactured in the United States of America

Illustrations by Barbara Holtermann
Design by George Whipple

Published by
Larson Publications, Inc.
4936 Route 414
Burdett, New York 14818

Distributed to the trade by
Kampmann & Co.
9 East 40 Street
New York, New York 10016

10 9 8 7 6 5 4 3 2 1

To my family

Contents

Introduction

BY JOHN HOLT

I am not in the least bit unbiased about this book. Ever since I met Nancy Wallace, her husband Bob, and their children Ishmael and Vita some three or more years ago, they have been among my very closest and dearest friends. I feel myself a member of their family and I think they feel me as one. When Nancy first showed me some of what she had written about the children, I was very enthusiastic and urged her to continue, and though she would surely have gone on even without my urging, I like to think that my encouragement and occasional advice were helpful. I felt from the beginning that this would be a very valuable book to have in print and I am more pleased than I can say that it has now appeared.

This is by no means the first book about home-schooling. Others have taken their children out of school, taught them themselves, and written interesting and intelligent books about the experience. What then makes this book so special, and why is it likely to be so useful right now to so many families? For one thing, some of the best of the other books were written some years ago, or in other countries. This book is about what has just happened and is happening, here and now. And no other book I have read takes us so deeply into the day-to-day thoughts and concerns of a parent, or the day-to-day lives of parents with their children. More than any other book about home-schooling, this tells us what the experience of home-schooling was actually like, in one family at least. Not that the Wallaces are a typical home-schooling family—but then, there are no "typical" home-schooling families; the home-schoolers are a very varied group of people. And their children are no more all alike than they are, especially the two children brought so vividly to life in this book. Except for their love of music and theater and their great affection for each other—I have rarely known brother and sister who enjoyed each other's company more—these two childen are about as unlike as two people could possibly be.

When I think of them, already at age eleven and seven the kind of people that the schools wish—no longer with much hope—that all their graduates might (after twelve to twenty or more years of schooling) turn out to be, intelligent, capable, self-motivated and self-reliant, responsible, energetic, active, happy, and at ease in the world around them, I am quite literally filled with terror when I think of what would have become of them if they had been made to stay in school. Ishmael would probably have been labeled Emotionally Disturbed, Vita Severely Learning Disabled (because of letter reversals which in her own good time she is clearing up), Hyperactive, and eventually also Emotionally Disturbed. These children would not have been stars in school, but dismal failures and indeed serious problems. This is not to say that, given enough time, they could not have adjusted to the realities of school—as they could even now adjust if for their own reasons they chose to go—but only that they would not have been given the time. Ishmael would probably have been pushed, as in one year he had already been pushed, into deep depression, Vita into furious rebellion. No average classroom or school could ever have understood or contained her boundless energy, enthusiasm, or joy in life, far less tolerated her indignation and sometimes volcanic rage at anything she sees as contemptuous or unreasonable or unfair treatment, which she now hardly ever meets but would have met every day in most schools. In short, with the best will in the world, trying at least much of the time to do what it thought was best, the average school would have destroyed these children.

We must all be thankful, as the Wallaces are thankful, that the schools in New Hampshire and Ithaca, N.Y., the first perhaps a bit grudgingly and the second enthusiastically, supported them in their intention to teach their own children. We can only hope that, as indeed seems to be the case, more and more school districts all over the country will take this cooperative position. For there is a great deal that the schools can learn, to their own long-run and even immediate benefit, from the experience of these and other home-schooled children. One of the most important things the schools can learn is that their efforts, now of long standing, to force on all children a uniform curriculum, timetable, and methods of learning is a disastrous error. Reading about Ishmael and Vita, we can only be struck by how very personal, idiosyncratic, and unique are their ways of learning. It is tempting to think that most children have rather more orthodox ways of exploring and making sense of the world. But it is not so; all children move into the world in personal and idiosyncratic ways, and no two do it alike.

I use the word "idiosyncratic" here for a particular reason. It is a word that Supreme Court Justice Byron White used, in rather guardedly supporting in his concurring opinion in *Wisconsin v. Yoder* the right of Amish parents to take their children out of school after eighth grade, to say that he was emphatically not supporting the right of parents to put their own "idiosyncratic" philosophies and methods of education over those adopted by education authorities. No greater mistake could possibly be made, by the Court or by the schools themselves. The beginning of wisdom for our hard pressed and critically ill schools is to realize that all children's ways of learning are and in the nature of things *must* be idiosyncratic, if their learning is to be real, lasting, and useful, and not, as is now the general rule, something to be discarded after the exams are over and the grades are in.

Still another point I would like to make. You will gather from the book that the Wallace children love to make music and do it well. But in my opinion they are even more talented than this book suggests. If Nancy Wallace understates this talent a little,

it is perhaps partly because she doesn't want to boast about her
own children, and partly because she doesn't want to seem, to
them or to anyone else, to be pressuring them into a musical
career. She isn't; one thing I have learned in many years as a
teacher and an observer of children is to recognize pressure on
children when I see it, and I can assure you that these children
are not in any way being forced into music. What they do with
music, they do because they love it. Music bubbles out of them
like water from a spring—Ishmael can hardly walk by a piano
without playing *something* on it. If one day they choose to take
other paths into the world, perhaps theatre, perhaps literature,
perhaps who knows what, that will be fine with their parents.
One thing we can already be sure of—whatever the children
choose to do, music will always be a rich source of pleasure in
their lives, which is what their parents really care about.

That said, let me say again that these children are amazing
young musicians. I visit the family every few months, and the
changes I see and hear in the children's playing in that short
time are simply astonishing. This is not to say they are on their
way to Carnegie Hall—there are probably quite a few other
children of their age who are more technically advanced. But
many far more advanced and much older muscians, even students in top conservatories, do not play with the freedom, ex-
pressiveness, and conviction that these children show. Further-
more, they are much more than performers; both are very
interested in the theory and history of music, and both like to
compose, Vita at a beginning level—she is not yet a young
Mozart—and Ishmael at a remarkable level of skill and sophisti-
cation. They are, in a word, not just skilled performers but true
musicians.

What all this is leading up to is that, as musicians usually
judge the talent of young beginners, these children were not at
the start unusually talented. I know some of the tests by which
musicians try (to no useful purpose) to measure and judge musical talent in young children, and by these tests and measures I
don't think either of the Wallace children would have been

called more than average. They have gone as far as they have not because they began with unusual talents but because they have the good luck to have parents who love and make music, because their mother is herself a very sensitive, understanding, patient, and skillful teacher, because they have been much encouraged without being in the least pressured, and because— since they don't go to school—they have *time* to work on music as much as they like.

And other things as well, like plays. You may want to know how Ishmael's second play (in which both he and Vita acted) came out. It was a great and well-deserved success, and in the Cornell University paper and one of the Ithaca papers got the kind of reviews that most adult playwrights would give an arm to get. I saw the last three performances and have rarely enjoyed myself more in the theatre. It was a very well constructed, lively, interesting, and funny play, and I hope I don't have to wait too long before I see his next.

One last point. I often see in public places ads for an organization raising money for colleges and universities. They all show a photo of a forlorn looking young person, usually black, with these words: "A Mind Is A Terrible Thing To Waste." The snobbery, dishonesty, and threat in that ad always infuriate me—it says, in effect, everyone who didn't go to college is some kind of idiot, and if *you* don't go to college you're going to be one yourself. And yet, for all that I understand and detest this way of thinking, I often slip into it myself; when I meet exceptionally intelligent and articulate people, I assume that they have gone to college. So one day, chatting in the Wallace's kitchen, I said to Nancy without thinking, "Did you and Bob meet when you were at college?" She laughed and said, "College? I didn't even finish high school—I got my high school diploma later from a correspondence course." A good lesson for me—and for us all.

Educators insist that nobody can teach who has not endured, not only four years of college, but two or three years of graduate school as well. This book is one more proof among many that it is not so. Intelligence, competence, and the ability to share with others what you know, have nothing whatever to do with time spent in school, above all in schools of education. In fact, if we abolished *all* requirements of training and certification, and let public schools do what private schools do right now—hire as teachers people they like and trust, without having to worry about their credentials—it would probably do more than any other single thing, including raising teacher's salaries, to improve the quality of public school teachers and teaching, since many more of those people who truly love teaching and have a real gift for it, but cannot stand the thought of spending years in schools of education, trying to pretend to believe what is taught there, might then be attracted into the schools.

Unfortunately, that's not going to happen for some time. Meanwhile, enjoy and learn from this lovely book. What the Wallaces (and many others) have done, you and your children —if you want to—can also do.

BETTER THAN SCHOOL

Chapter 1

A Day in
Our Life

It is 8:15 in the morning and I am in the kitchen doing morning chores. I hear the sound of the school bus as it grinds up the hill. It stops, and creaking doors summon the four or five children waiting at the Four Corners. The doors close, again with a creak, and the bus roars off along its morning route. As always, I breathe a sigh of relief as the roar grows fainter. My two children aren't on that bus, and they won't ever have to be.

Although of school age, they are still eating breakfast. Vita, who is five, is smearing peanut butter on her bagel and Ishmael, who is nine, is making rivers in his yogurt with his spoon. They can usually linger over their breakfast, because they don't go to school. They learn at home and in the wide world around them. They spend their days reading about things that matter to them, making scenery for their plays and operettas, playing the piano, going to various classes in the community, and, of course, doing what we still call "school work"—math, science, and other academic subjects.

Today is Wednesday, and we have our piano lesson this morning. Feeling a bit rushed, I decide that it's time they stop their dawdling. "If you kids want to do the dishes you'd better hurry up! Vita, you really ought to copy over your story soon so

17

we can send it to Grandma . . . and Ishmael, I'd like it if you'd get a couple of lines of math done before we have to leave."

I go off to get the dirty laundry, but before I have finished dumping it into the washer, Ishmael has cleared the kitchen table and Vita has dragged the piano stool over to the sink to stand on while she rinses and stacks the dishes.

I leave the kids splashing about, floating plates and playing navy in the soapy dish water, and sit down for a minute with the book on physics that Bob has been reading to Ishmael. They keep telling me how good it is, but I never seem to have time to listen when they are reading it at night. I hate to be left out, though, so I snatch glances at it whenever I have the chance.

Bob, meanwhile, is already working in his study. We have an "understood" daily schedule that we try to keep whenever possible. I look after the kids until three and then he takes over. This arrangement leaves me time to myself before supper and then afterwards, when he reads to the kids before bedtime. Today, though, includes an exception: we have a French lesson that lasts until four.

While the kids perform their daily task of feeding breakfast to their dolls and sending them to work, I make the best of my last chance to play the piano before our lesson. Yes, being involved in the kids' interests and seeing their eagerness to learn has inspired me, too: I'm also taking lessons. My fingers try to coax a Mozart sonatina (which I've finally memorized) from the keys, but they'll need to play it another dozen or so times before they really begin to feel comfortable with it. I only have time to play it through once, though, and do my scales, before it's time to brush Vita's hair and get rolling. I hope she doesn't want some ridiculous hair-do, and fortunately she's satisfied with a pony-tail. I grab the music books, a pad and some pastels for Vita, call to Ishmael to bring a book, kiss Bob good-bye, and then we're off.

The drive to the music lesson is a long one. Ishmael keeps his nose deep in an anthology of Ogden Nash's poetry, and he reads passages aloud to entertain Vita:

> The song of canaries
> Never varies,
> And when they're moulting
> They're pretty revolting.

Vita is only listening with one ear. Mainly she is concentrating on what is going on outside her window. Unlike Ishmael, she likes to keep track of where she is and what everybody else is up to.

Finally, we arrive at our lesson. Greeting us at the door is Maxie, our teacher's oversized, overly shaggy, and overly child-like dog. He is as big as Vita, and at least as spoiled. Is Maxie going to quit barking today and back away from the door so we can get in, or are we going to have to squeeze around him? We squeeze. Ishmael goes straight to the piano and starts plunking away, not even taking time to remove his coat, while I arrange all our music and help Vita get her jacket off.

In a minute Bob Fraley, cup of coffee in hand, arrives from upstairs. Maxie barks another boisterous greeting, and our lesson begins. Altogether it lasts for two hours. We take turns at the piano, and while they're not playing, Vita draws and Ishmael reads. Maxie spends his time chewing rags under the piano.

Vita likes to have her lesson first, and today she is bursting with excitement. Bob Fraley asks, "Do you have a surprise for me?"

"Yes," she says, "I can play my minuet both hands together!" She smiles, crawls under the piano to find a footstool, and climbs onto the piano chair. Fraley adjusts it, makes sure it is in the center of the piano, and then Vita plays.

I always find myself holding my breath as Vita begins. She is *such* a flibberty-gibbet! You never can tell if this will be one of

her good days or one of her bad ones, where she forgets everything. But the Bach minuet is going smoothly. A few slips, but
all in all, well done—especially when you consider that she is
only five. Fraley is impressed. He didn't expect her to be able
to put both hands together for another few weeks and he tells
her so. But still, in his usual manner, he also has suggestions to
make.

First, he asks Vita to play the piece hands separately, so he
can help her iron out some rough spots; then he claps the 1-2-3
beat to help her even out her tempo. Next, he works a bit on
her opening note, showing her how to curve her pinkie as she
presses down, and then lift off gently. The sound is so much
nicer than when she bangs down on a key with a sort of karate
chop! Finally, Vita plays some old pieces and she and Fraley
work on reading music. As Vita steps down from the piano, he
thanks her for playing so well.

Then it's Ishmael's turn: he puts down his book, scrounges
around for a lower footstool, and begins by playing his Clementi sonatina straight through. Ishmael does a good job—
in fact, he plays the first movement, which is quite fast, better
than I do. Once again, Fraley is visibly pleased, but he has all
kinds of little things he wants to work on. First he helps Ishmael to even out the rhythm of his long runs in the first movement, explaining how Horowitz seems to play faster than he really does only because he keeps his tempo so incredibly exact.

Although Ishmael manages to learn all kinds of things on his
own, he often gets confused when other people try to teach him
things because he's not sure what they expect. So it has taken
Ishmael and Bob Fraley a long time to get to know and understand one another. But now Fraley is taking pains to explain
himself carefully and Ishmael is remaining fairly relaxed.

Next, they work on the trills in the second movement. Fraley
wants them speeded up, and he shows Ishmael some new trill
exercises. This time he sprinkles his advice with anecdotes
about Arthur Rubinstein. By now, I can see that Ishmael is
getting impatient. He wants to play, not to learn exercises, and

he is beginning to grimace and tense up. Fortunately Fraley senses this, and turns to the Diller-Quaille book, from which he and Ishmael can play duets together.

Shyly, at the end of his lesson, Ishmael shows Bob Fraley the new compositions he has recently written down on his music pad. Fraley studies them for a few long seconds and then sits down to play. Ishmael beams contentedly. The musical process seems so miraculous to him. Only a few days ago the notes were his alone, in his mind and on his fingers; but thanks to a grand staff and a pencil, Fraley is now able to play them back. He ends with a flourish. "Good! There are just a couple of little things we should go over." They both huddle happily over the music, discuss, erase, correct, and discuss some more.

By the time it is my turn, our two hours are almost up. I play my scales and my pre-Czerny exercises and then a Mozart rondo. Too soon, it is time to go. We gather up all our stuff, say good-bye to both Fraley and Maxie and head for the grocery store to do our weekly shopping.

When Ishmael was in school, he lost track, naturally, of what I did during the day. I think he assumed that the floor never got dirty, that the beds made themselves, and that there had always been food in the pantry and always would be. Now that he is out of school, I try to involve him—and Vita, too, of course—as much as possible in my day. This is partially for the selfish reason that I want both kids to know that even though I don't get paid for what I do, I still work hard. But also, and more importantly, I find that Vita and Ishmael are happiest when they are allowed to be productive members of the family. They enjoy washing dishes (if they are allowed to splash a bit), they like making their beds (if I help them with the hard spots and don't smooth out the wrinkles when they're done), and they enjoy running errands.

Likewise, they enjoy helping me shop for food. Today I send Ishmael off to pick out a good bunch of bananas and some canta- loupes while Vita picks out some crackers. Then she spies some grapes and jumps up and down begging, "Couldn't we get some grapes today?" And Ishmael chimes in with, "Oh yes, please!" Grapes are awfully expensive, but why not? The more healthy things they pick out, the less they'll take notice of the doughnuts in the bakery section. Then I suggest that perhaps they'd each like to pick out a few vegetables and make a stir-fry for supper tonight. Delighted by the idea, they wander up and down the produce department pinching, feeling, and enjoying the richness of all the vegetable shapes, colors, and textures. Finally, after some prodding from me (I'm always impatient in grocery stores), they decide on a small purple cabbage, a bag of carrots, some red peppers, and broccoli.

Then we move along, past the bread, the dairy section and the bakery. Finally we reach the checkout counter. It feels good when Ishmael groans along with me as the cashier rings up our weekly total. I hand over the money and then we're on our way.

At home, Bob makes lunch while I put away the groceries. After lunch I help the kids chop up the vegetables. If they get a head start now, we can get dinner over with at a reasonable hour and then they'll have more time to read with Bob. Right away, though, they start squabbling. "Ishmael got the knife with the pretty green handle. And you gave him the best carving board." "No she didn't!" "Yes she did!" "All right, you do the whole thing yourself!" Ishmael yells and stomps away.

I sigh my regrets and wish that Ishmael didn't always seem to overreact to Vita's little bursts of temper. With Bob's help, we settle everyone down and begin again. Vita gathers herbs in the front yard—as many different kinds as she feels like—while Ishmael chops onions and garlic. Both kids are pretty handy with kitchen knives. They are well aware of how dangerous it is to be careless with them and in any case, they are working slowly and meticulously now, trying to cut their vegetable pieces as evenly as they think I do. Every five minutes or so, Ishmael wanders over to the kitchen piano and thumps away at a catchy little tune he is currently obsessed with. This drives me crazy because he's getting garlic all over the keys. In time, though, the vegetables get chopped and put away.

Vita and Ishmael barely have time to feed the dolls lunch before we have to leave for our French lesson. Fortunately, our teacher, Anna, lives only about a quarter of a mile down the road and it's a lovely walk. Up our dirt road, across the big road, and down Anna's road, past woods and hayfields we go. The kids aren't enjoying the scenery though: they're playing some kind of ridiculous game that involves running around and jumping into the bushes. "Hurry up!" I shout, "We're already late!" Obediently, they catch up with me; but somehow the game manages to begin all over again. Once more I yell, and so it goes until we get to Anna's.

In Anna's kitchen, Ishmael, Anna, and I sit around the table while Vita disappears with Anna's four-year-old son, David. Sometimes she hangs around listening to our lesson. She enjoys it when we read *Babar* or *Le Ballon Rouge* aloud, but today David is more enticing. After an initial little chat about the weather—"*Bonjour Anna, il fait froid, n'est-ce pas?*"—we get to work ironing out our latest snafu, "*de, de la, du,* and *des.*" Anna has a worksheet ready for us and we begin filling it out: "*La centre* de la *terre, La voiture* de *l'homme, La queue* du *souris.*" Poor Ishmael and I have a tough time, especially since we rarely remember the genders of the nouns in the first place. Afterwards we read a few pages of *Babar et son ami Zephir.* French has been fairly frustrating for us since we only have lessons once a week and we just don't hear the language spoken enough between times. But Ishmael loves to read French. It's like deciphering a code, and he's always amazed and delighted by the number of French words that are similar to English ones.

In the middle of page three David storms in crying, "Vita's locked me out of my room!" I jump up and everyone follows me to David's room where we find Vita at the door looking as innocent as ever. "Vita, please," I beg, "find a game to play with

David or look at books with him or something. You know it's not nice to lock a person out of his own room." She gives me a defiant look, but then Ishmael offers to read to both of the little kids. All is quiet.

Back in the kitchen, Anna and I have our weekly ten-minute gossip. "Did you know that Becky had her baby?" "How's your mother feeling?" "Who are you going to vote for?" Too soon, the clock strikes four and it's time to go. Anna likes to meet Billy, her older son, at the bus after school and all of us walk down to the main road together.

As we arrive, the neighborhood children are tumbling out of the bus. Timna, small and perfectly organized, heads straight for home without looking in either direction or greeting us. The bottom of Bojo's crayon box comes open just as he's on the last step of the bus, and all of his crayons fall to the ground—to be trampled on by the other children. He gives Anna a despairing look, and she responds by securing the bottom of the box for him while he does his best to collect the crayons.

Last to emerge is Billy. "Where's your coat?" Anna asks. "Don't know," says Billy. He's tired. He is dragging a sweater and a lunch box and hanging over his shoulder is a fat roll of electrical wire that he probably took to school for "Show and Tell." We wave good-bye to Anna, wade through the crowd of children, cross the road, and head for home. I hear the *thump, crack* of Bob splitting wood. There's Purry Pot arching her back and meowing for us on the rail fence. The kids run off to the woodpile while I go into the kitchen and flop down comfortably in the armchair by the stove. It's been a full and exhausting school day.

While mine has hardly been a typical mother's day, I imagine that its end has been much like that of many other mothers. They, too, are flopped on chairs in their kitchens. Probably most, though, haven't been fortunate enough to have spent the entire day enjoying their kids. They may be just back from work—having stopped off at the grocery store on the way home

—and they are now faced with several bags of groceries demanding to be put away. They know that the laundry hamper is overflowing, and they can just imagine the mess that the kids and their friends have made gobbling peanut butter sandwiches and cookies after school. Although what these mothers really want to do is to hug their children and play and talk with them for an hour or two, most likely, in their exhaustion, they will end up haranguing them for leaving their lunch boxes and jackets on the floor, tell them to clean up their cookie crumbs, and then start figuring out what to make for supper, do a couple of loads of wash, and worry about when to find time to take the kids to the dentist.

Of course other mothers, also flopped on their chairs after a long day, *have* spent it with their children. These are most likely mothers of preschoolers who plan to go back to work when their kids reach school age. Meanwhile, they spend their days changing diapers, wiping runny noses, watching soap operas while folding laundry, and worrying about unpaid bills.

Obviously, I am one of the lucky few. And as you read on, my good luck will become even more apparent, although it should become obvious, too, that my life has had its "downs" as well as its "ups." It has not been my intention, though, to write a book about my good fortune, oblivious of the hard realities of others' lives, in order to make other parents jealous. My purpose is very much to the contrary. Although this book is most directly relevant to home-schoolers, or to people who are interested in home-schooling and are able to undertake it without great economic hardship, I hope that anybody who deals with children will be stimulated, by reading about our experiences living and learning with our children, to find more meaningful and fulfilling ways to live with theirs—even if it can only be during the evening and on weekends, or (for that matter) in classrooms.

I could have written a "how-to" book: *How to Teach Your Children at Home*, or *How to Live With Your Children*, or *How to Turn Your Classroom into a Home-Like Environment*; but one of the most important lessons that Bob and I have learned as home-schooling parents is that we have to be our own "experts" in making decisions about how we live: we have to rely on our *own* judgement and knowledge of ourselves and our family. Consequently, it would be presumptuous of me to set myself up as an expert on how *other* people should raise *their* children or live *their* lives. For too long, it seems to me, we have *all* been encouraged, pushed, or even compelled (in the case of schooling, for example) to go to "professionals" with formal training and "expertise" for advice about how to do even the most ordinary tasks—to doctors, lawyers, dentists, teachers, experts telling us how to lose weight, eat right, or have happy or well-behaved children. We even seek out experts to help us decorate our houses or organize our closets. But the more we rely on these experts, *the more helpless we become and the more useless we feel*. This is a syndrome that I don't want to be a part of, any more than I can help, on either end.

Bob and I were as helpless as anyone when we first sent Ishmael to school, and much of this book, while on the surface about our home-schooling experiences, is really about how we have increasingly learned to trust our own instincts and "know-how" in order to raise Vita and Ishmael in ways that make sense to us, even in the face of disapproval, interference, and distrust. I hope that our successes will encourage other parents to develop the self-confidence they need to find ways to share more of their lives with their children, despite the obvious obstacles—whether it is by taking their kids out of school, by bringing their little ones with them to work, by cutting expenses and finding ways to earn money at home so as not to have both parents working elsewhere full-time, and, in general, by not underestimating the importance of the time that they actually spend with their kids.

Of course many parents feel (as I have sometimes felt, too, especially when Vita and Ishmael were younger) that it is lonely and boring to spend so much time at home alone with children, no matter how much you love them. Mothers often go back to work, not because they can't afford to stay home, but because they find their homes isolating and they are afraid they'll go crazy with only babies or young children to talk to all day long. Certainly the way we tend to live can be terribly lonely, and no one can claim that children are always the most entertaining people to be around. In fact, when we lived in Vermont, I used to hear about mothers committing suicide when the phone lines were down during blizzards.

If we want to spend more time with our children, then, it's obvious that we have to find ways of doing that without cutting ourselves off from the rest of the world. One important step would be to find interesting and exciting (though not necessarily "paid") work to do at home, rather than always assuming that one must look elsewhere for that kind of stimulation. In other words, we have to bring more of the "world" back into our homes. Traditionally, homes were busy, productive places where people grew, cooked, ate and preserved wholesome food, doctored and were doctored, taught skills and learned them, produced goods for sale, and even made their own music and entertainment. If we didn't rely totally on doctors, schools, psychologists, outside employers, television, or possibly even little things like electric can-openers, homes could once again become real living centers, satisfying and nurturing places not just for children but for all of us.

Just as important, though, we have to find ways to raise our children to be our friends, so they can help to fill the void as early as possible. Bob and I have done this in many ways, although at first we weren't clever enough to realize what we were doing. We thought we were being selfish when we insisted on reading aloud to Vita and Ishmael only books that we enjoyed, and when we took them along to the movies we wanted to see but seldom if ever took them to children's movies. Of course we were being selfish, in a way; but on the other hand, we gradually gained two extra people that we could discuss books and movies with, and the kids, of course, enjoyed being treated like equals—or at least not like "babies." When

Ishmael, at age eighteen months, drove us crazy by tearing apart our two-room cabin in Vermont during a severe winter, Bob began taking him to work occasionally just to protect the house; and we began making a point of including him in as many of our adult activities as possible, hoping to distract him from his overeager curiosity by letting him help with tasks like cooking, cleaning, and carpentry work. Better to let him measure the flour and break the eggs, no matter how many shells went in, than to let him take the phone apart or break all our chess pieces, we reasoned. It was only later that we realized that by including him, and in time Vita, in our own work and interests, they not only learned to be helpful around the house but they became our closest friends. Home-schooling, for us, has only strengthened this relationship as we share more and more of our favorite books, ideas, music, and other activities with each other.

At this point, it may be useful to give some background information with regard to the whole issue of home-education. We were ignorant of most of these facts when we began our own home-schooling adventure, but knowing them would have given us a better sense of perspective. We would have felt a little less daring and a lot more self-confident.

Home-schooling, despite all the publicity it has gotten recently, is nothing new. Obviously it was a way of life far back in the days of cave men, but even as late as the eighteenth and nineteenth centuries, middle- and upper-class children were often taught at home by their parents or by paid tutors. Schools were felt to be, and were created, as such, primarily for so-called common children, and yet even these "common" children were often mostly home-schooled. During the American westward expansion movement, for example, many children grew up in sparsely populated areas where there were no schools, or they were needed at home to help clear the fields or bring in the harvest. They learned their lessons during spare moments at their mother's knee, or at night by the light of the fire, like Abe Lincoln. Many parents, too, in those days, kept their children out of school for religious reasons; but home-education then didn't create the legal hassles that it sometimes does now, because few states had compulsory schooling laws.

With the advent of these laws and the establishment of free public schools throughout the U.S., the number of home educators dropped dramatically, and yet the types of people who teach their children at home today are just as various as they were a hundred years ago. This diversity never ceases to amaze and delight me as I read John Holt's newsletter, *Growing Without Schooling*, which draws most of its material from letters that parents have written to him about their home-schooling experiences. Many, as in the past, write that they have taken their children out of school for religious reasons—they are disturbed by what they often call the "secular humanism" that is dominant in the public schools. Some parents find schools too rigid, while others find them too loose in regard to discipline; some families live too far out in the country to reasonably send their children to school, while others travel too much to allow regular school attendance. Many parents are disturbed by the competitive and even cruel social environment that schools foster, and others, like us, take their kids out initially because they are just plain miserable. But whatever reason families have for choosing to home-school, they share an honest concern for their children.

Unfortunately, not everyone agrees with this view. Eighteen states ban home-education altogether—although parents have discovered ways to circumvent these laws, mostly by forming private schools on paper—and some states severely restrict home-education by requiring, for example, that parents teaching their own children be certified teachers, or, as in the state of New Hampshire, that parents prove to their local school authorities that their children would suffer an educational or physical "hardship" by being in school. At the same time, though, in court cases and even in one or two state legislatures, home-schooling families are winning important decisions that are opening the doors for others and making it increasingly difficult for school officials to act arbitrarily or to interpret their state compulsory education laws too stringently.

John Holt estimates conservatively that there are currently 10,000 families across the country who are teaching their own children; others put the figure as high as 40,000, which might be a reasonable guess if you include all the home-schoolers currently operating "underground" and those using correspondence courses with loose ties to private and religious schools. Certainly the home-schooling movement has been gathering momentum over the last five years or so, and for us, and others like us, this is very exciting because it means that for the most part we no longer have a sense of isolation or a feeling that we are pioneers in a wilderness. Even more importantly, and of broader significance, it seems quite likely that as our numbers grow, we may begin to have some impact on the schools. Serious educators may begin to think of home-schools as unique research centers—places where they can learn more about how children learn and discover more about the kinds of environments that nurture children's learning.

Nowadays, unfortunately, with their tight budgets and "back-to-basics" approach, most schools feel that they can no longer afford to offer educational researchers and dedicated teachers opportunities to experiment. Also, most parents feel increasingly distrustful of the kinds of educational experimentation that went on in the '60s and '70s. They just want to be sure that their children learn enough in school to be able to find jobs and earn a decent living. As a result, teachers and schools are allowed little or no flexibility to explore educational alternatives.

Because of the experimental nature of what they do, then, home-schoolers have a great deal to offer the schools. Being such a diverse group of people, though, with such a variety of uniquely different children, we are not likely to ever point the way to the one best or magical approach to teaching. Instead, by observing families like ours, educators may eventually come to realize "that there *is* no one best way, and that it is a waste of time and energy to look for it; that children (like adults) learn in a great many ways; [and] that each child learns best in the ways that most interest, excite, and satisfy him or her. . ." (John Holt, *Teach Your Own*, page 331).

No doubt it will take a long time before these ideas are widely accepted, but I like to think that home-schoolers, by their very existence and determination, will someday help to bring this about. In the meantime, I hope that this book can be a contribution toward opening up a useful dialogue between parents and teachers, teachers and teachers, and parents and parents.

Chapter 2

School Days

Our school troubles with Ishmael started during his very first week in first grade. He was told that he couldn't go to the bathroom without first raising his hand and getting permission, and apparently he sat there for a long, long time with his hand raised before he finally wet his pants: not a very auspicious beginning. Then he was upset because all they seemed to do was to color in mimeographed papers, but when he went up to the teacher and explained that he already knew how to color and wanted to learn something else, she told him to go back to his seat and work on coloring more neatly.

I watched Ishmael struggling to resign himself to school, to the boredom and seemingly arbitrary rules. But as the weeks passed, the teacher still didn't give him a reading book although he literally craved reading. In desperation, he began gluing himself to books at home, from the moment he stepped in the door after school until bedtime. It was frightening to watch him droop in and head straight for a bookshelf—not even giving himself time to say "hi" to me or to Vita.

Finally, after about three weeks of this misery, I decided to talk the situation over with his teacher. I drove over to the school at the end of the day. It was such a lovely little country school that I immediately felt hopeful—surely the teacher would understand our problems. So, after asking Ishmael to look after Vita on the swings, I walked over to the first-grade classroom. Inside, Mrs. R. was correcting papers. The room itself was much less pleasant than the gay paint job, rolling fields, and trees outside the building. I was a bit disconcerted by its bare walls and crooked rows of desks. Hoping that Mrs. R. would look up, I cleared my throat and walked all the way around her desk. Finally, despite my insecurity about interrupting her, I leaned over and said, "Mrs. R., I am Ishmael's mother." She looked up hesitantly, with what seemed to be an anxious look.

Before I could say anything more, she began nervously reassuring me.

"Ishmael's doing fine," she said. "He gets all of his papers done, he's well behaved, and the other day when I was showing the class the relationship between $5 - 2 = 3$ and $5 - 3 = 2$ he was one of the few children that caught on. Now I always tell the children that math is hard. In fact I failed it one year in school myself. So I explain that we'll go over things many, many times, and if someone doesn't get it the first time, he'll have lots of chances to get it later. But Ishmael seems to be quick with numbers."

Before I became too inflated, she continued, "Ishmael does seem to have a problem with listening skills, though. I've been playing a record that gives the children instructions on how to follow specific directions, and Ishmael invariably gets lost. His hearing appears to be normal, so I'm just not sure what to do. He also has a problem grasping 'whole concepts.' For example, if I read the class a paragraph, he can't tell me the main idea. He gets too involved with all the little details. I'm thinking that maybe we should have Ishmael tested, just in case we discover some kind of developmental problem. Then we can send him to the resource room for, say, ten minutes a day, so they can help him."

When Mrs. R. had finished, I stood there, blank, for a moment. What was I supposed to say to all that? We must have talked a little in greater detail about Ishmael's supposed "listening skills" problem or something, but then I finally managed to ask her about reading books.

"Oh well," she said, "I won't start dividing up the class into reading groups for another two or three weeks. I am still getting to know the children, and of course I have the problem that some of the children don't even recognize their letters. . . . Yes, I have noticed that Ishmael can read, but that's a problem, too. Nobody else in the class is reading yet—well there are a few who are on the verge—but I'm afraid that I'll have to put Ishmael in a group by himself. And I really don't know where I'll be able to find a book. Perhaps I could borrow one from the second grade . . ."

I left feeling extremely confused, and it took me a long while to sort out our conversation. I had thought that Ishmael would have been an easy child for the teacher to deal with. I had imagined her giving him a stack of books, some paper and a pencil and letting him enjoy himself. But her problem seemed to be that she felt it was her responsibility to *teach* Ishmael something, and, at the same time, she had thirty other kids on her hands—all with very individual needs.

A few days later, Ishmael told me that he'd been given a third-grade reader and the corresponding workbook. "That's great, Ishmael!" I exclaimed, although he certainly didn't seem thrilled. Before long, Ishmael started coming home a nervous wreck. At first he wouldn't speak, he'd just drop his jacket and lunch box on the floor, grab a book, and flop onto his bed. Then, if I spoke to him—told him supper was ready or asked if he'd like to take a bath—he'd burst into tears. As I comforted him, rocking him back and forth on my lap, I'd wonder, "Why can't Ishmael be like other kids? Why does he have to be so difficult?"

Finally, one day, his troubles just tumbled out. The workbook was too hard, he didn't know what prepositions were, he couldn't divide words into syllables, and he hated suffixes and prefixes. Worse yet, he kept forgetting to do his workbook

pages and instead would read ahead in his reader by accident—
something his teacher had asked him *not* to do.

What had happened, I guessed, was that Mrs. R. had confused my desire to have Ishmael do something interesting in
class with what she thought was a request for her to challenge
him. But she was wrong about the desirability of challenging
Ishmael. Because he appeared to be so smart, she assumed that
he enjoyed tackling difficult work; but in fact, quite the opposite was true. Having to do something "hard" made Ishmael
tense, and often he'd just fall apart, miserable and mad at himself for finding the task too difficult. Ishmael hadn't *tackled*
reading, for example; he had just *learned* without really being
aware of what he was doing; and because he loved books, he
had gradually learned a lot about letters, words, and language.
He had accumulated vast stores of historical knowledge for *fun*,
not because he *had* to. So to expect him to delight in the challenge of learning grammar was just a mistake. Perhaps Ishmael
just didn't fit the stereotype of the "smart kid."

Anyway, I went back to speak with Mrs. R. She was as unhappy as I was. If Ishmael could read so well—at a fifth-grade
level, really—why couldn't he cope with third-grade grammar,
she asked. She just couldn't seem to understand that Ishmael
was totally self-taught and that all of the third-grade grammar
was new to him. Sure, he could write complex sentences correctly, but that didn't mean he knew the parts of speech; and
sure, he could add "*ed*" to the end of a word or "*un*" to the beginning of one, but that didn't mean he knew what suffixes and
prefixes were. Couldn't she put Ishmael in a first-grade workbook, I asked.

Mrs. R. said that she couldn't possibly do that since, for some
obscure reason, the reading book and the workbook were inti-
mately connected. Then there was another problem: Ishmael
kept reading ahead in his reader. She just couldn't tolerate
that, she said, since she needed to be sure that Ishmael com-
prehended one story before he went on to the next one. With
all those other kids on her hands, she just didn't have the *time*

to spend with Ishmael discussing so many stories. And if she put him in a second-grade reader, which would mean that he'd be using an easier workbook, he'd be more tempted than ever to read ahead.

Finally, though, she did decide to use the second-grade reader and workbook with Ishmael. Although he soon became as bored as he had been before, he didn't seem quite as agitated when he came home.

It seemed obvious to me that what I had been asking of Mrs. R. was outside her professional experience, and that she just hadn't known what I wanted. Unfortunately, Ishmael ended up suffering a lot more through my meddling than if he'd merely been bored. But I couldn't really blame myself, either. After all, a child has a *right* not to be bored in school. Occasionally, Mrs. R. really did blossom as a teacher. She spent a few exciting hours teaching the kids about Pilgrims, and in the spring the class spent a week learning about plants. But, for Ishmael, that simply wasn't enough. What could *I* do?

Realizing that I wasn't doing much good interfering from the "outside" with Ishmael's education, I thought that perhaps I could be useful as a volunteer in Mrs. R.'s classroom. If I worked with some of the other kids for a few hours a week, maybe she'd have more time for Ishmael. This was not to be, however, because Mrs. R. couldn't think of any way I could be useful. Instead, I volunteered in the fourth/fifth-grade classroom, where the teacher was young and considered experimental. She set up learning centers that the kids visited while she was holding reading groups.

Vita and I trundled off to the fourth/fifth grade twice a week with a bagful of crayons, paper, books, and snacks for Vita, who was barely two, while Ishmael trudged off to the first grade. I felt better having a "foot in the door" at school, but life didn't get any better for Ishmael.

About this time, he started suffering from severe headaches. Frequently he'd write entries in his diary like, "It's Monday and I hav a head aik. My head does not feel good. I feel like I poot too much sap in my ear." I took Ishmael to the doctor, but the doctor told me not to worry. "The headaches are probably caused by the strain of reading too much," he explained.

Still, Ishmael seemed so exhausted by the end of the week that we often kept him home on Fridays. What a pleasure to have him around more often! Of course, Vita loved it. She had someone to play Lego with, someone to help her build block castles, and someone to play with her out in the snow. And Ishmael would wake up on these days so much more relaxed. He wouldn't fly for a book because he knew he could read any time. He could leisurely immerse himself in all the subjects he was fascinated by: sailing and navigation, Greek mythology, knights and the Middle Ages, and so on. If only school could have been like that!

By spring I was desperate. I was enjoying my work in the fourth/fifth grade, but I was feeling more and more depressed about the school. There weren't enough textbooks, the kids seemed to spend too much time watching lousy television programs in class, and the Public Service Co. was always hanging around extolling the virtues of nuclear power during science class. Even the smartest kids were being taught "advanced" phonetics in the upper grades. If you knew how to read, why couldn't they just let you read, I kept wondering.

Gradually, Bob and I developed the habit of getting into bed as soon as the kids were asleep (bed was the warmest place in the house) and being miserable together—a sort of nightly sob session where I poured out my heart to Bob and he tried to be as supportive as possible. "What's wrong with Ishmael?" I used to despair. "Why can't he be like other children?" Other times it was myself I worried about. "What's wrong with me, anyway? Why don't other mothers feel the way I do?" How often, at the school, at the library, and even at the grocery store I had searched the faces of the mothers I saw, looking for even a trace of the misery I was feeling over Ishmael's life at school. But everyone seemed so complacent, so accepting of their children's situations. It was lonely for me, and I needed Bob to tell me I was right: Ishmael was shrivelling up before our very eyes.

Finally, in a more constructive frame of mind, Bob and I began seeking advice about our problems with the school from friends who were teachers. One friend, who taught special education, tried to convince us to get Ishmael tested. If his I.Q. turned out to be above a certain point, it would prove that he was "gifted." Maybe then I could force the school district to provide Ishmael with a "team" (composed of his teacher, perhaps a gifted specialist, the school psychologist, etc.) that would make up a special program for him. I just couldn't get excited. In the first place, what if Ishmael didn't turn out to be gifted—what if he missed the mark by one point, even—then what? Would that mean it was alright for him to be bored in class? And what if he really did turn out to be gifted and the school was generous enough to make up a "team" for him and provide him with a "special program"? Where were the books going to come from, and the teacher time? But above all, I knew that Ishmael was happiest when given the freedom to learn about the things he wanted to learn, and I'd never heard of a "team" leaving a child's education up to himself.

Then we became interested in the idea of tuitioning Ishmael to a school in a neighboring district. It had a special program for gifted children, an organized parent volunteer program, and—since the district was much richer than ours—lots of fancy equipment. I called up the principal and he seemed delighted to have me visit.

When I arrived, he greeted me warmly and assigned his assistant to show me around. But already I was depressed. The school, a vast brick structure with a huge asphalt playground, just didn't seem to have been built with children in mind. It contrasted sharply with Ishmael's tiny, one-story, brightly-painted school, where the children played in a field surrounded by woods.

The principal's assistant led me through dark, hospital-green corridors; I peeked through doors to see children sitting at shiny new desks and using modern textbooks. In the sterile cafeteria, I was shown how the hot lunch program worked. The well-balanced meals were cooked at the high school and trucked over in styrofoam boxes: no fuss, no muss. The library, or rather "resource center," really did look great, though, and there was a room entirely devoted to math materials, with shelves piled high with math games. The school even counselled pre-delinquent kids (how were they picked, I wondered) and it was the principal himself who taught the gifted children.

I visited a first-grade class (with learning centers at the back) where the teacher was giving a lesson on suffixes (I couldn't seem to escape them anywhere!). Afterwards, I talked to her and asked her why she taught those things. Unlike the teachers at Ishmael's school, she actually gave me a coherent answer.

"We are trying to help the children increase their vocabularies," she said, "by showing them that by adding a suffix or a prefix to a word they can make an entirely new one."

I couldn't help thinking to myself, though, that suffixes and prefixes had, if anything, only encouraged Ishmael to hate words. His vocabulary, on the other hand, was impressively large because he read a lot and was often talking with adults.

Still open to the possibility of sending Ishmael there, though, I went and talked to the principal about his classes for gifted children. He raved about them enthusiastically, but when I asked specifically how Ishmael could fit in, he clammed up. Ishmael would have to be tested thoroughly before we could even begin to discuss any kind of special program for him.

"All parents seem to think their children are gifted," he said, "and that simply isn't so."

With that, he went back to his work and I went out to my car.

By the middle of June, first grade was over and we began to relax. Ishmael played in the back field with Vita, built forts out of scrap lumber in the woods, and waded in our little brook. And whenever he felt like it, he read and read and read. Miraculously, his headaches disappeared—despite the doctor's warning that it had been reading that had caused them—and Ishmael's face glowed with happiness. That summer he revived his neighborhood newspaper from the year before; he and Vita tramped around collecting news from all the neighbors, and Bob ran off copies on a duplicating machine in the office where he worked. Meanwhile, I weeded the garden, planted fruit trees and, trying to forget about the future, helped in the woodpile. The present was too nice to spoil with worries I thought I could do nothing about.

In August, we saw a tiny ad placed in the newspaper by a woman who was thinking about starting a private school in her home in the town next to ours. Were there parents out there who would be interested, she wondered? We were, definitely, and a few days later we went to visit her. Her home instantly appealed to me—with its beamed ceilings, book-lined walls, and grand piano—and she herself was wonderful with Vita and Ishmael. When we settled down to talk about her proposed school, though, she sounded like all the rest, only more sophisticated, perhaps, since she was a Ph.D. from Harvard. The words flew past me: "gifted, diagnostic testing, bad habits, special programs," etc. God, I was so sick of experts telling us what would be good for Ishmael. We knew. We had been watching him grow and absorb knowledge since he was born!

Not knowing what else to do, we sent Ishmael to school again that fall. Maybe his teacher would turn out to be great and all our problems would be solved, we hoped dimly. In a way, Miss B. did turn out to be great. She was a plain-spoken country woman, with brown skin from working outdoors and a Gertrude Stein haircut. She wore men's pants and she always lit up a cigarette the minute school was out. We talked about the farm she lived on, about gardening and maple sugaring. She told me about the Iroquois longhouse she built in her back yard and the dried apple dolls she made.

But she brought none of her enthusiasm for these things into the classroom, and Ishmael wilted like an unwatered flower.

She decided that Ishmael needed to be part of a group and not be as isolated as he had been, academically, the year before. So she put him in the same reading book as the rest of the second graders, even though that meant he ended up repeating the work he had done in first grade. He continued to do stacks of mimeographed papers, and math was a constant ordeal, since Miss B. was preoccupied with timed drill. Ishmael's headaches returned more painfully than ever, and now we knew we had to do something quick. This school was not going to work out —ever.

While I was moping about miserably, keeping Ishmael home a lot and pampering him like some sort of invalid, I began entertaining the idea of starting a parent-cooperative school. At first it seemed like the answer to all our problems. I imagined five or six sedate children working on math with cuisenaire rods at our dining room table or peering through a microscope at some amoebas and intelligently discussing what they saw. If I moved the blanket chest out of the living room, I dreamed, I could put an old oak file cabinet in its place to keep the school records. And it would look great with a plant on top!

Fortunately, my good sense got the better of me. I remembered the free schools I had visited, with all their noise, clatter and excitement, splotches of paint and clay on the floor and walls, raisins and half-eaten sandwiches gathering mold on messy bookshelves, and books, paper and crayons scattered all over the place. And Bob, who never showed much enthusiasm for my idea, described graphically his years in a small progressive school, where his mother had spent evening after frustrating evening worrying about the school's meager finances and hashing out her philosophical differences with the other parents. No, we soon agreed, we just weren't the type of people to handle that kind of situation comfortably.

Then, in early October (1978), I happened to read an article that had just come out in *Yankee* magazine about two families in New Hampshire who were educating their kids at home. I devoured the article on the spot and was particularly impressed with one of the families, the Sandoz's. Peggy Sandoz, who later became a friend of ours, explained, "Most people simply assume that children should be in school when they are five years old. This seems quite arbitrary to me. A large gathering place for children is not natural. I don't think young children should be away from their families all day long."

As she went on to describe the class her daughter had previously attended, it sounded exactly like Ishmael's. "The days were too long, all ditto sheets and busy work. There was little time for game playing and fun things that really allow children to learn. I thought the teacher, an elderly woman, was delightful, but the curriculum was not delightful. I don't think the children were encouraged to use their own minds."

The article then examined Peggy's home curriculum. It read,

> She spends only two hours a day with the kids doing solid academics. "You get as much done in that time as a teacher with a roomful of kids gets done in a day." Then too, the Sandoz children avoid the long arduous, unproductive bus ride to and from school each day. Instead, Peggy explained, "They spend that time playing games, composing or reciting poetry and immersing themselves in real life."

Playing games, composing or reciting poetry, and immersing themselves in real life . . . those were the things Ishmael had been aching to do! Later, talking about the article with Bob, I found that so many loose ends seemed to fall into place. Not just in Ishmael's school, but in every school we had seen, the students had done so much busy work and were drilled in so many minute skills that they had had very little time to read, write, draw, or figure—much less to think or enjoy learning. In contrast, it had been at home or out in the community that Ishmael had learned almost everything he knew—by reading books, exploring the countryside, conversing with friends of all ages, and going to museums, concerts, and movies.

Although we had once hoped that school would provide Ishmael with a community of peers that he could learn and share with, that simply had not happened. As the months rolled by, he only became more and more withdrawn and unhappy.

The more Bob and I talked, the more relief I felt. It was as though a great weight had been lifted from my heart. Teaching Ishmael at home seemed like the obvious solution to all our problems and Bob wholeheartedly agreed. Still, it was important that Ishmael be involved in such a big decision affecting his own life. But, talking the idea over with him the next day, we were amazed at his instant enthusiasm. He had no doubts at all. He wouldn't miss his teacher or the other kids, he assured us. He had had enough of school, forever, or at least for a very long time.

The *Yankee* article implied that home-schooling was perfectly legal in New Hampshire, but it had been so vague that we felt we really needed to educate ourselves about the legal ins-and-outs of the compulsory attendance laws before we took any steps towards getting Ishmael out of school.

A couple of days later, while talking to a friend, I learned that a family that Bob knew slightly had just received permission to teach their eight-year-old son at home. They could tell us all about how they had gotten their son out of school. I rushed back to the house to tell Bob and he phoned them that night. Bob talked to Sally for a long time, and later that week we drove over to visit them at their hilltop farm about forty-five minutes away.

Bill and Sally lived amidst chickens, goats, and rusty farm machinery with their two sons, Dilly and Gwyn. Dilly was a little older than Ishmael, and Gwyn wasn't yet of school age. While Vita and Ishmael went off to tinker with scraps of metal and a soldering iron, watched over with an eagle eye by Dilly, Sally brought down a sheaf of material sent to her by the State Department of Education. It included the compulsory attendance laws, regulations for the approval of non-public schools, and a five-page mimeographed document entitled, "Advisory

Memorandum for Discussion Purposes Only; Subject: Requests from parents to teach their own children at home."

Basically, this memorandum was the initial attempt by the State Board of Education to clarify the appropriate statutes that were relevant to home-schooling and to establish some general guidelines for dealing with home-schooling requests. Sally explained that the unfortunate words in the title, "advisory" and "for discussion purposes only," were there because the state board was in the middle of writing some definitive guidelines to insure that requests from parents to do home-instruction received some kind of "due-process." But in the meantime, this document was the only advice local school boards and parents had to go on; if they chose to overlook it, they ran the risk of being overruled at the state level.

On glancing through these pages, what struck us right away was the requirement that parents prove to their local school boards that the attendance of their child in school would create a "manifest educational hardship" for that child. I remember sinking into a chair, feeling completely hopeless, and asking Bob, "How are we ever going to prove *that*?"

But Sally was a great help. She explained that she and Bill had taken Dilly out of school partly because his behavior had deteriorated. He had rebelled against the strict authority at school and had caused all kinds of problems at home. But also, they didn't feel that it was right to send him to a place for six or seven hours a day that did its best to instill values in him that were totally contrary to their own. Where they were trying to become as self-sufficient as possible, cutting down drastically on their use of energy, the school taught about the wonders of nuclear power; and where they raised their own organic meat and vegetables and ate no sugar, Dilly was always being given candy at school parties and in a science class he was taught that you could get a wholesome, well-balanced meal at Mac-Donalds.

Sally argued that it was a "manifest educational hardship" for

Dilly to remain in school, when what he appeared to need was the nurturing environment of their home, which was much more flexible and geared toward his needs. And her school board had agreed.

In our case, she seemed to have no doubts that it was a hardship for Ishmael to have to go to school if he was unhappy and had headaches, and likewise, if he craved the time to read and his teacher didn't give it to him. "In fact," she went on, "it's a hardship for any child to go to school if his parents are offering him all the advantages of learning at home. What school can offer such individualized instruction, after all?"

At first I had a hard time grasping her notion of "manifest educational hardship." Did she really believe that all those kids who were bored and restless and all those kids who were trouble-makers were suffering a hardship? "Yes," she said vehemently, "at least if their parents are offering them a viable alternative." Gradually I began to see her point and to understand her vehemence. Of course I had a right, as Ishmael's mother, to do whatever I could to alleviate his misery, to keep his mind open and inquisitive, and to protect his health; and although it was a new way of looking at things, it did make sense to say that for the state to deny us those rights would cause Ishmael to suffer a "manifest educational hardship."

While we were sorting out all this information, and later, as we were discussing Sally's curriculum with her, I kept glancing at Ishmael, who was making rings for all of us out of nails. He and Dilly acted as though they'd known one another forever. They were so casual, so content with each other, and they seemed to speak the same language. If Ishmael mentioned Daedalus or Medea, Dilly knew what he was talking about; and if Dilly mentioned Iroquois longhouses, Ishmael likewise understood.

Sally agreed that once Ishmael was let out of school it would be nice to get the kids together once a week to play and do special projects. Not only were we now ready and determined to teach Ishmael ourselves, but he had found a friend who was available on weekdays!

Figuring that our school superintendent would be the most influential person in our approval process, since the school board almost invariably went along with his recommendations, I decided that I'd better get to know him and explain our plans as soon as possible. Sally had told me that all the superintendents in the state had been given copies of the home-schooling guidelines, and since we needed one to help write our letter requesting permission to teach Ishmael at home I figured I'd ask our superintendent for one. It would provide a good excuse for us to get together and talk.

The day after visiting with Sally, I called him:

"Hello, Mr. F. This is Nancy Wallace calling. I understand that you have some new guidelines regarding home-schooling. We are considering teaching our seven-year-old son at home and would like to look them over. Could we have a copy?"

"I don't think I have a copy," he replied coolly.

"But I understand that the state sent all the superintendents copies," I said.

"Oh well," he muttered, "let me look and see . . . Yes, here's a copy, but I couldn't let it out of my hands. Its addressed to superintendents."

"O.K. then," I said, "I'll come over to your office and look at it there. I'll be over in half an hour."

When I arrived, I discovered that the superintendent had apparently had second thoughts, because his secretary presented me with a freshly xeroxed copy (with the words "for discussion purposes only" heavily circled as though to warn me that he wouldn't feel bound by them). I was then ushered into his office, where he greeted me and introduced me to his assistant.

I think both men were relieved that I appeared to be a normal human being, with brushed hair, clean, conventional clothes and the ability to speak correct English. I, in turn, was relieved to find that they were polite and eager to talk. The first

question that Mr. F. asked me, when we had finished discussing the weather was, "Why don't you move to a more afflu-
ent school district?" Carefully and politely I explained that we'd
lived in town for five years, we loved our house, Bob's work
was here, and we'd made good friends among our neighbors.
Moving was out of the question. Mr. F. softened after that. He
began to understand that I was serious and not just an intellectual snob fresh from "the city."

Then I began to recount Ishmael's school experiences: his
boredom, his headaches, and his misery. I could see that Mr.
F. and his assistant felt a certain sympathy with our situation.
They asked lots of questions about Ishmael, about his teachers,
about my volunteer work, and about our plans for teaching Ishmael at home. Finally, Mr. F. said brightly, "Why don't you
take some long trips during the school year, Mrs. Wallace? I'm
sure Ishmael and your whole family would benefit from getting
a look at the rest of the country." And his assistant added, "Yes,
and you could also keep Ishmael home occasionally for special
enrichment."

But they hadn't thought of the problem of the attendance
records, and no doubt they weren't prepared to defend me in
front of the truant officer. Besides, I was sick of enrichment,
and with a three-year-old, a husband who worked, and a shed-
full of chickens, the last thing I was prepared to do was travel.

Finally, we agreed that I'd write up a formal request to teach
Ishmael at home—including a description of his hardship and a
proposed educational plan. Meanwhile, they'd visit with Ishmael and his classroom teacher to see if they could devise some
sort of special program within the school that would allow Ishmael to be happier and more productive. While I doubted that
they could come up with anything acceptable, I saw no harm in
letting them try.

Mr. F.'s assistant visited the school about a week later. From
what Ishmael told me, they really got along. Ishmael showed
him a story he'd written and a little march he'd just composed,

and since Mr. S. was an organist in church and loved music, they had a lot to talk about.

Meanwhile, Bob and I wrote our "request" and sent copies to the superintendent and to all five school board members. First we outlined in detail the state guidelines. We emphasized that home-schooling was a legal alternative to school and pointed out that while the guidelines did say they were "for discussion purposes only," it was important to take them seriously since the State Board of Education had put its weight behind them.

Then we gave lots of background information about Ishmael and the rest of us. We defined Ishmael's "manifest educational hardship" by focusing on educational benefits he'd get at home. "Because we have the time, the motivation and the ability to meet Ishmael's educational needs, which the school's teachers are unable to do under present circumstances," we wrote, "we feel that it is a manifest educational hardship to send him to school." Finally, we outlined all the community resources we planned to use, like libraries and museums, included a brief curriculum, and explained that we would keep complete files of Ishmael's work.

Rereading this letter three years later, with a good deal of experience behind me, I still think it's pretty good. But it was Ishmael who wrote the best letter. I remember finding it on the kitchen table when I came in from the woodpile. It went:

To the Schoolboard:

I write (or print) books; and I print poems. I like to climb trees. I like to invent things. My teacher tries very hard to teach her class. We like her. I am too creative to stay in a class where I don't have time to read. I have a bicycle. I even have a math book at home. Now I am not boasting.

Ishmael Wallace

As much as it delighted me to read Ishmael's letter, it made me very sad, too—not just because I realized how much he wanted to learn at home and how aware he was of the difficulties we were having in getting permission for him to do so, but because, by his distinction between printing and writing, he had innocently exposed an absurdity of the school's attitude towards education. You see, the only time the kids had a chance to put a pencil to plain lined paper was during handwriting lessons when they either printed or wrote in script. It was only "script" which they called "writing," and technically, the school didn't consider that Ishmael had started "writing" yet— although at home he kept a diary, put out a neighborhood newspaper, and wrote letters and stories.

We expected to be notified of the school meeting at which the board members would act on our request, but we never were. Fortunately, we heard about it by chance from the wife of one of the board members, whom Bob happened to run into at the hardware store. Naturally, we were furious, but it just made us more sure than ever that we had to get Ishmael out of there and back into the center of our family.

The meeting was a gruelling affair that lasted over three hours. As we walked in, I wondered if the school board members were surprised that we'd actually discovered where and when the meeting was to take place. I do know that they were surprised when four or five of our friends showed up to watch. Judging from the difficulty in finding room for everyone to sit down, they didn't have audiences very often. The board members were distinctly uneasy when we plugged in our tape recorder. We didn't like that formality either, but we felt we had to be prepared for the worst. It wouldn't do to go to court without a record of the meeting.

There was a tense and forbidding atmosphere in the room as the chairman opened the meeting. First Mr. S. passed out a two-page document he'd written up, suggesting ways in which Ishmael's school curriculum could be enriched. I had thought that Mr. S. planned to show this to us before the school board meeting so that we would have time to react to it. Since he hadn't, we were pretty nervous as we read it. Fortunately, it was immediately clear that most of Mr. S.'s plan was unworkable within the inflexible structure of the school. And, considering the inadequacies of the school library and the very limited availability of even basic textbooks, much of the rest of it was absurd. Fortunately, too, the school board members understood the resource limitations at the school and realized that Mr. S.'s proposal would not be feasible without the expenditure of a great deal of money—something they were not eager to do.

Then it was our turn, and we launched nervously into our presentation. Bob spoke for about fifteen minutes about the state guidelines on home-schooling, and I elaborated in detail on our proposed educational program. I kept watching the stony eyes and restless bodies of the school board members. Finally the feeling that I was boring all of them became so powerful that in desperation I blurted out, "Do you want me to stop?" But, stifling their yawns, they answered, "No, no, finish what you have to say." So I did.

Three of the board members were teachers or school administrators, and I could see that it was difficult for them to take us seriously. After all, we weren't certified experts, merely parents. One of them said later, "Well I am a book-addict too, just like Ishmael, and I'm sure my son will be one as well, but, after all, I survived school and so will he. Parents just can't make up for the peer group learning experiences that school provides." And another, the chairman of a social studies department in a neighboring high school, was so used to pushing paper, filling out reports on teachers, and writing elaborate curricula and program evaluations that he appeared to have dismissed us as hopelessly amateurish even before we opened our mouths.

Two of the board members had no interest in children. They were on the board only to keep their tax bills as low as possible. Neither of them, I felt, was likely to be able to sympathize either with Ishmael's misery or with our concern. One board member, though, had two bright kids in the school, and she was well aware of the boredom we were talking about. Once, at the local beach, she had told me that in school her daughters were given stacks of papers to do for the week on Mondays and since they usually finished up by Wednesday or Thursday, they had to spend the rest of the week reading at their seats. Actually, I would have loved it if Ishmael had been allowed to read at his seat, but I didn't say so. Now, I could see that she felt threatened. We were proposing to do something for Ishmael that she either felt she couldn't do or didn't have time to do for her daughters. It was to her that I was most concerned about explaining myself.

Immediately after the question-and-answer period started, the board members revealed their primary concern: "socialization." It was the job of parents to "enrich" their children and to "remediate" when necessary, the board's chairman explained, but it was the role of the schools to teach the basics and to socialize children into society. How would Ishmael ever learn to get along with others, he wanted to know. Weren't we just proposing to shelter him from the hard, cold world in the name of education? And he said, almost outright, that he'd rather see Ishmael stultify in school than to allow his social development to be irrevocably damaged by not being in school.

Soon the questions became more personal, more accusatory, and more contradictory. Weren't we "permissive" parents for wanting Ishmael to learn at home because he wanted to, they asked each other. And in the next breath I had to fend off the accusation that most likely we'd keep him home even if he expressed the desire to go to school. They accused us of pushing Ishmael too hard at home, of forcing him to learn to read at an advanced level—and yet they tore my curriculum to pieces because it was full of things he wanted to do.

As the evening progressed, I was struck forcibly with the realization that here were five arbitrarily chosen people, none of whom knew Ishmael or were particularly interested in him, with the power to make a crucial decision about his life—a decision that Bob and I and Ishmael should have had the right to make in the privacy of our own home. I felt as though that right was being taken away from us, or as if it had never been our own. It was frightening.

The meeting dragged on, and everybody's tempers grew shorter the more exhausted they became. Finally, around 10:30 P.M., the chairman of the school board asked the superintendent for his recommendation. He responded as I guess we knew he would: "I recommend against allowing the Wallace boy to be taught at home." And he went on to say how he regretted ever showing us the guidelines. He rambled about the bad precedent we'd be setting and justified his decision by saying that, after all, Ishmael was only in school for seven hours a day and we could "enrich" him for the remaining seventeen hours at home.

At last the school board voted. As the chairman said, "All those in favor, raise your hands," I closed my eyes. I couldn't bear to see all those hands sitting idly in their laps. But then I felt Bob clutch me. I opened my eyes again and, my God! I saw five hands raised in the air. It was amazing. I gasped with relief. I would have jumped up and down, but the board members looked so pained and harassed that we felt it would be best to get out of there as quickly as possible. Out in the dark night, Bob and I hugged each other. We had won! Ishmael was free!

Chapter 3

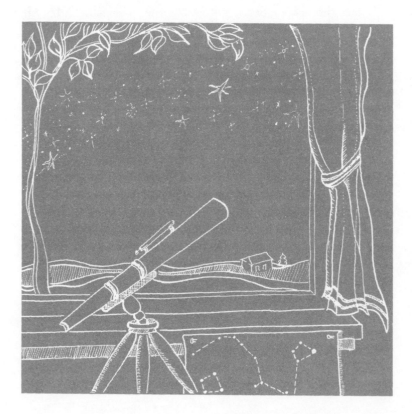

The First Six Months

The school board's vote was mighty hard to understand, but after hashing it out with our friends in the parking lot after the meeting, we finally agreed that the board had probably voted for us out of fear. After all, we had given the impression of being so knowledgeable about the law and so clearly determined to go to court rather than send Ishmael back to school, that the board, with its shoestring budget, really felt its hands were tied. The last thing it could afford was to hire a lawyer to meet us in court. But it was no time to look back. Ishmael was free!

Bob and I took him to school the next morning, and he cleaned out his desk and said good-bye to his teacher. I had the same sort of weepy feeling inside that I used to have every summer when I left camp. Of course I was homesick and wanted to go home, but still . . . I wondered what Ishmael was feeling as we carried our armload of papers, pencils, and crayons to the car. Did he have any twinges of regret? If he did, he sure didn't show it.

A few days later there was a light knock on the door. As I opened it, one of the kids from school handed me a fat manila envelope. I was amazed to find a bundle of letters inside addressed to Ishmael from his entire class. They reminded me uncomfortably of the time I had had pneumonia and my fourth-grade classmates had been assigned to write me get-well cards. But Ishmael was understandably excited. He dumped the letters on the floor and began reading:

Dear Ishmael,

We are having a party. I wished you was hear. I hope you will come back. Are you sick or Not. The hole class misses you.
                                                    Yours,
                                                        Chris

Dear Ishmael, Im whanten to see you. I am having a good time. We got our Class Journal. You shood of hard the joks that were in them. Your friend, Mark.

Dear Ishmael,

We are having a good time. Wish you cood be here. We are having a party Friday. I will save sum of the stuf I get. We got are pichers. Your fren, Jason

As I watched Ishmael, I think I half-expected him to change his mind and decide to go back to school. How could he fail to soften to all those expressions of friendship? But apparently his hurt had gone too deep for that, and his only response was one of distrust. "I didn't know everyone liked me. If I went back to school I don't think they'd be nice." He gathered up all the letters, stuffed them back into their manila envelope and went back to his game with Vita.

Before our school-at-home could really get rolling, I had to figure out just what kinds of learning materials I wanted to use for the year and incorporate them into a lengthier, more elaborate curriculum than the one we had presented to the school board, since the board chairman had asked us to send in more details about what we actually intended to teach Ishmael. I spent a couple of exciting days in libraries and bookstores with the kids. We looked primarily at social studies and science materials, and I managed to accumulate quite a heap of interesting books and pamphlets. I also bought fancy little notebooks for Ishmael to write in—satisfying both of our paper fetishes—and restocked our art shelf with paints, paper, pastels, glitter, and crayons. Actually, I was embarrassed to discover just how low we were on art supplies. Had I just assumed that forty-five minutes of art a week was enough for a young child?

Finally, I bought myself a large spiral notebook in which to keep a daily log of all our school activities. I knew that the school board would want reassurances that we were actually carrying out our proposed program, and I figured that my daily notes, including lists of all the books Ishmael read and all of his paper work would be more than adequate.

So that took care of acquiring books and paper. Now I had to settle down to actually write the curriculum. This was much more troublesome since I knew I had to include as much detail as I could, and yet I didn't want to tie Ishmael down to a specific schedule or group of books and workbooks. I ended up with only two typed pages, but it looked professional. The subject matter was divided into English, mathematics, social studies, and science. I also included a tentative schedule that went as follows:

> *9:00–11:00* —Structured learning, including all the things Ishmael does not do naturally: math, language skills, structured writing and handwriting.

> *Afternoons* —Less structured learning encouraging Ishmael's natural inclinations: free reading, creative writing, science experiments, nature study, social studies, sports, cooking, etc.

I felt quite pleased with my efforts and sent the curriculum in to the school board. Now I, too, was free (at least I thought I was), and I settled down to teach Ishmael. Every morning, after breakfast, he recorded the outside temperature in Fahrenheit and Centigrade in his notebook and listed any new birds he saw at the bird feeder. He looked up the ones he couldn't identify. Then he got to work on math and other little sticklers like handwriting and "language skills." At first, I was afraid to deviate too much from the school curriculum—partly because I was hesitant to incur the wrath of the school administration and partly because I viewed our home-schooling project as experimental. I wanted Ishmael to be able to fit back into school easily if that ever became necessary. But also, although I had developed a pretty radical philosophy of education by that time, I hadn't yet talked to many people or read any books that agreed with me. Assuming that I was an oddball, I was quite uncertain of myself.

I tried my best to make subjects like handwriting more interesting than they had been in school. Once again, Ishmael was so grateful (and at the same time so accepting of school work as an inevitable part of his day) that he went along with me fairly cheerfully. He kept a handwriting notebook into which he copied his favorite poems in script and then illustrated them with colored pencils; we used little wooden cubes—similar to the ones in the "Spill and Spell" game, only with words instead of letters printed on the sides—to learn the parts of speech. For dictionary "skills" we used a *real* dictionary, which was quite a change from the boring mimeographed worksheets on alphabetizing and "guide words" used in school. As Ishmael and I worked, Vita liked to sit up at the table, too, and play school. She began learning how to make her letters, and she drew and painted happily.

The afternoons were much more fun. After a break during which we walked, skied, or just played in the snow, the three of us snuggled up on the couch and read about New England Indians from some wonderful books we found at the library. I made little charts to help us distinguish between all the smaller tribes from our area, and we were fascinated by descriptions of village life, early agriculture, hunting, and so on.

One of the most interesting things we read was about the infiltration of the fairly advanced Adena Indians from the West into New England. The more primitive New England Indians soon adopted much of the Adena culture, including both the ability to make ceramic pots and the cultivation of maize. The foraging ways of the past gave way to intensive agriculture and women assumed the crucial tasks of farming and pottery making. Left with less and less to do, the men—former stone craftsmen—turned to warring and plundering.

This reminded Ishmael of the Vikings, and how, during the long cold winter months in Scandinavia, with no farm work to do, the men often set off across the ocean to rob and plunder, returning home in spring to till the soil. In his excitement, Ishmael then read all the books he could find on the Vikings, and then quite naturally he became obsessed with explorers—Champlain, Cartier, Vasco da Gama, and the like. I tried to keep up with him as best I could, because I too was interested and with my mediocre education, knew practically nothing of history. I think Vita listened in on our reading sessions just because it was so nice to be where Ishmael was.

Then by chance, we discovered a book called *America B.C.* by Barry Fell, a Harvard professor and amateur linguist who had recently been able to decipher and identify numerous ancient inscriptions on granite slabs in the New England area—some of which had mystified the local people for generations. The key to the mystery was a medieval Irish manuscript giving samples of an ancient Celtic alphabet known as Ogam. Fell's theory is that Celts, whom Julius Caesar knew as great sailors, crossed the Atlantic several centuries before the time of Christ. As Fell writes in his introduction (page 5), "The hundreds of inscriptions among the ruins (in Vermont and New Hampshire) attest the vitality of Celtic civilization in pagan times." This book completely captured our imaginations, particularly since we lived near two of the ancient sites. We were eager for the snow to melt so we could go exploring ourselves! Meanwhile, we read all we could on the Celts and other early travelers like the Phoenicians. Ishmael enjoyed himself thoroughly, but I was the one who was most enthusiastic. It was delightful to have such a good excuse to spend long hours educating myself!

In the evenings Bob took us star gazing and read us books on astronomy, and I discovered a book that explained how to make simple navigational instruments like astrolabes and primitive compasses, some of which Ishmael built in the shed. Soon he had dreams of building a raft and, charting his path by the stars, sailing out to sea. By accident, I ordered enough brine shrimp eggs from a science catalogue to entertain a class of thirty and so we raised thousands of shrimp in jars all over the kitchen piano. Ishmael kept a journal describing their development and gradual demise—I think their living conditions became too crowded—and then he filled the rest of the notebook with descriptions of various science experiments he did with Bob.

Every Thursday Ishmael got together with Dilly. Soon two other home-schooling families that Sally knew with girls, Melissa and Vanessa, joined us. We encouraged the kids to do special projects together like writing and printing a newspaper, making baskets, painting, and hiking. Mostly though, these Thursdays were times for boisterous play.

For the past year or so, I had been operating a marginal egg business, and now I discovered that two of our neighbors were interested in spending a couple of hours a week teaching Vita and Ishmael various skills in exchange for eggs. John, up the hill, was a potter. The kids helped him to build a kiln and fire his pots and he taught them how to make various kinds of hand-built pots, how to use a potter's wheel, and how to mix glazes. Anna, a former French teacher from New Zealand, offered to teach Ishmael French. Not only was he delighted, but so was I, since I had always wanted to learn French. As it turned out, Vanessa and her mother, Jenny, were also interested in joining our little class, and they paid for the lessons with homespun wool.

It was Jenny who introduced us to John Holt's newsletter, *Growing Without Schooling*. John Holt, who was to help us with many of our school battles in the coming months, had already written numerous books on education and school reform. Recently he had become more interested in the varieties of learning experiences that take place outside institutions. He concluded that because most learning best takes place in the world at large, schools—except perhaps purely specialized ones like medical schools—are unnecessary. *Growing Without Schooling* grew out of these ideas. Its primary purpose was (and is) to provide a place for an exchange of ideas and experiences about home education and ways of acquiring skills and knowledge in the everyday world.

Bob and I were happy to discover through this newsletter that there were many people across the country educating their kids at home. It was especially good for us to read about how these families directed (or didn't direct) their children's educations. Some, for example, used elaborate correspondence courses. But many left their children totally free. This was reassuring, because gradually our structured mornings had begun to peter out as we realized that although Ishmael was polite about the teaching we imposed on him, his real learning was mostly taking place through his own reading and explorations.

For example, believing that the sooner Ishmael learned how to acquire knowledge independently of us the better, we had originally planned to spend a few minutes every day teaching him how to use an encyclopedia and a dictionary. My aunt and uncle had recently given us their old Compton's encyclopedia, and for one of our very first lessons I decided to help Ishmael get acquainted with it. I wrote down three words—botany, butterflies, and Brazil—handed him the "B" volume of the encyclopedia and showed him that the subjects were arranged in alphabetical order. Then I asked him to see if he could find botany. He was polite. He gave me a weak smile and opened up the encyclopedia at the beginning. Then, with new eagerness, he started reading about baboons. But I wasn't teaching him about baboons, I was teaching him alphabetical order and how to find specific information in an encyclopedia! I reminded Ishmael of this and he started flipping through the pages in search of "botany." Then I went to do some chores, but when I returned, he was guiltily reading about birds. Well, it was the first week of our school; wanting to be nice, I didn't press my point but talked about birds with him instead.

The same thing happened when I asked Ishmael to look up words in the dictionary. He was polite, and dutifully looked up the words I asked him to, but I only saw a sparkle in his eye when he had a free moment to explore the pages on his own.

We soon dropped our formalized plans to teach him how to use these basic tools, thinking that perhaps he wasn't old enough yet. Before long, though, I noticed that he had begun to read the encyclopedia and even the dictionary for pleasure.

One day, not long afterwards, Dilly came over to visit Ishmael, and they set about preparing for a big battle out in the field. They gathered sticks for swords and guns, trained Vita as a soldier, and then disappeared inside the house. I soon discovered them in the living room: Ishmael was sitting in an armchair, Dilly was on its arm, and both were hovering over that same "B" volume of the encyclopedia. They were looking up Bunker Hill, they explained, so that they could figure out how to make their battle an accurate re-enactment of the original. I left them busily advising each other on how to wade through the morass of "B" words to get to B-u-n-k-e-r. By then I had learned that it was often best to let them continue their struggles on their own.

After that, Dilly and Ishmael often read the encyclopedia together to look up subjects like automobile, Civil War, explorers, and so on. What eventually happened, of course, was that they taught *themselves* how to use the encyclopedia because there were things they wanted to know, and the encyclopedia was the place to find out about them.

I wasn't the only person learning how to do less teaching—Bob had his little troubles too. Ishmael wanted to learn about electricity, so Bob went out and bought a bunch of electrical equipment and suggested that they begin by building an electric motor together. Bob had meant to let Ishmael do all the work, of course; but, in the typical adult manner, he began giving advice, and then more advice, and finally, without even realizing it, he began to do all the work himself. Soon, out of sheer boredom, Ishmael slunk away and started reading. Naturally enough, Bob felt rotten. That afternoon Ishmael spent hours secretively building something in his room. When he emerged, we were amazed. Eyes glowing, and overflowing with pride, he showed us his new invention: an electric car, similar to one he had seen at Dilly's house, made out of a flashlight battery, tinker toys, and rubber bands! Ishmael wanted to learn about electricity but, once again, in a way that made sense to him.

So the weeks flew by. We had just begun to settle into a routine and were happily learning how to let Ishmael learn when we heard, once again from a relative of a school board member, that our curriculum had been rejected: "Mrs. A. took one look at your first line, 'For reading we will let Ishmael pick his own books from the library,' and said, 'You can't call that education!'"

Sure enough, about a week later we received a letter from our superintendent explaining that we must provide curriculum instruction in mathematics, science, language arts, reading, social studies, fine arts, and socialization. The letter went on to instruct us to send in "Topic Outlines" for each subject, filled out according to an enclosed form. I think I almost blanked out when I looked at it, and looking over the form now, I don't blame myself in the least. It went on and on in "teacher-ese" about unit-titles, statements of unit-scope, topic limits, behavior, attitudes, specific objectives, long-range goals, culminating activities, and so on. Finally, the superintendent asked us to describe at least one sample lesson plan for each major unit of study in each subject area and to include our aims, methods, resources, and evaluation.

This little mailing from the school really strung me out. I lost all interest in Vikings, French, and astronomy and just wandered around for days in a haze. I didn't know what to do, particularly since I had no idea what words like "behavior," "attitudes," and "subject fields" were supposed to mean, and I couldn't imagine filling out that form for a subject like "socialization." It was sheer madness! Most important, tying ourselves down to "units of study" and lesson plans would only interfere with Ishmael's education.

But although we knew that Ishmael learned best in an unstructured environment, we were tired of fights with the school authorities. Obviously, we'd have to compromise; but how were we to do that without jeopardizing the very essence of our school at home? In a state of aggravation and confusion, I finally decided to write to John Holt. I thought maybe he could give me advice or at least a little reassurance, and he was kind enough to do both. He wrote:

> Don't be in such a tizzy about the curriculum for the school people. I realize it's a nuisance, but it doesn't need to be more than that. They may be partly interested in making things hard for you, but they are also timid bureaucrats and they want to be sure that their own rear-ends are protected, so they need papers in the file to prove to someone that they are paying attention. Tell them whatever stories are needed to keep them happy.
>
> Stories don't even have to be lies. To another parent who is in much the same situation, I said that the thing to do was to take the most ordinary events of daily life and dress them up in fancy school language. Thus I suggested that in going to the store, the kid could be called "participating in consumer experience." I'm dead serious! As for what to *call* the business of having kids learn according to their own curiosity, I suggested, "intrinsically motivated thematically interconnected organic learning." She has actually tried it on them and finds that some of them are quite impressed. Think of all the things you do, all the things you look at, all the things you talk about, all the things you are interested in. Turn each one of them into a fancy school subject and you will have a curriculum three times as fancy as anything they have in school. As far as schedule goes, you can dig your heels in about that. You can say that the time and order in which the various subjects are going to be taught will depend very

much on the interests of the children. You could probably add that this, of course, is what the schools would do if they had as small a pupil-teacher ratio as you do at home, that only the necessity for dealing with large numbers of children forces them to make schedules, that there is no strictly speaking *educational* justification for that, only an administrative one, which does not apply to you. In other words, say you are teaching and evaluating in the way that the schools would do if they could afford to.

One more word. The curriculum *can't* be too long. I know that it's a nuisance to write, but each additional page will be more intimidating than the one before. It's a shame we have to play such games, but for a while we probably do.

Although phrases like "intrinsically motivated, thematically interconnected organic learning" were a bit far out for our purposes, John's letter was full of important ideas and practical suggestions and it restored our self-confidence.

I also went and talked to a teacher friend in hopes that she could translate some of the "teacher jargon" on that miserable "topic outline" for me. She explained that "language arts" meant writing and grammar, but she advised me to ignore "behavior," "attitudes," and "subject fields" since even she had no idea what they meant. Basically, she agreed with John that I should include some "fancy school language" in order to appear more professional, and she told me about the latest educational rage—"uninterrupted silent sustained reading" (which was actually plain old reading) and "uninterrupted silent sustained writing" (commonly known as writing). She suggested that I incorporate them into our curriculum, preferably in a prominent place for all to see.

Feeling much more relaxed, I sat down with Bob and we were able to write our revised educational plan in a few hours. The worst part was the typing job since the curriculum filled eight single-spaced sheets of paper and I am an excruciatingly slow typist. Although we skipped "socialization" entirely, as well as some of the other crazy categories required, we did

present our program in terms of units, approaches, and resources. But we worded every sentence carefully to allow ourselves latitude and at the same time give the impression that
our program was highly structured. We changed phrases like
"Ishmael will pick his own reading books from the library" to
"Ishmael will spend at least one hour daily reading fiction works
from the library"; and we filled the first page with detailed lists
of math skills that we planned to cover—making for such boring and formidable reading that I doubt anyone read far beyond
that. It was even difficult for me to proofread and fortunately
Bob, who is adept at reading insurance policies, took over that
job for me.

John was right when he said, "The curriculum can't be too
long. . . . each additional page will be more intimidating." We
never heard another word from the school people on the subject of curriculum.

As the snow gradually melted and the buds swelled on the
trees, Ishmael began reading less compulsively. His cheeks
were rosy and his eyes were full of life. He rode his bike up and
down the road and even explored seldom-used dirt roads without his usual timidity. He and Dilly began planning a long
white-water canoe trip (imaginary, thank goodness) and pored
over maps discussing all the provisions they'd need.

The Thursdays, which included spending time with Dilly as
well as Melissa and Vanessa, were going less well. The carefully
planned projects that the parents had contrived gave way almost immediately to play. More than anything, the kids had
needed a chance to play with each other, especially since other
children were the main ingredient lacking for each of them at
home. Melissa could *always* make baskets—she didn't need a
special Thursday meeting for that—and Ishmael put out a
weekly neighborhood newspaper on his own anyway. But after
a few months, when the first excitement of getting to know each
other began to fade, the kids began to play less and less together as a group. Vanessa and Melissa played with dolls and
Ishmael and Dilly played Indians. It became obvious as time

went by that this group of kids was very artificially formed. It reminded me strongly of school, where kids are plunked together because they are kids, not because of any special interests or pleasures they may have in common.

For a while, it was hard for the parents to admit this; but as spring planting began, our schedules became erratic, and the Thursdays gradually died out. Ishmael did continue to see Dilly, since their friendship continued to be strong, and he saw Vanessa every week at French. Occasionally he visited over at her house, too, since he enjoyed climbing all the big trees in her yard and felt at home with her family.

As for his academic life, he was bursting with knowledge. At supper he rambled on about the explorers he was currently reading about; he was beginning to sprinkle his sentences with simple French words; and he had even gotten the hang of arithmetical borrowing and carrying.

Too soon, though, we received another bombshell from the superintendent's office—once again in the form of a letter. After a few introductory remarks, it got right down to business:

1. Your child is to come to school on May 1, 1979, 3:15 P.M. to meet with those staff members having teaching assignments commensurate with the level of instruction in your child's curriculum outline. At that time the staff will confer with your child through written and/or oral procedures as determined by each staff member. You will be informed of the room and staff member upon your arrival. If, at the end of this conference, the staff member feels more time is necessary in making this assessment, another appointment will be arranged with you.

2. On Tuesday, April 24, at 9:00 A.M., you are requested to bring your child to school for the administration of an appropriate Standardized Test as a means of providing some measure of achievement in the areas of reading, language usage and mathematics. This procedure may require two or more days during that week to complete; we appreciate your patience and understanding in this matter.

Bob and I were neither patient nor understanding. We wanted our home-schooling program to be evaluated for itself. Ishmael was reading Samuel Eliot Morrison on the explorers and would have been delighted to talk with any of the school people about his reading. His science notebook was full of notes about the experiments he was doing. Best of all, he had made a close friend that he was always eager to play with. Gone were the headaches and the sullenness. Instead, he was relaxed and happy. These were the kinds of things we wanted the school people to look at. As for the standardized test, our program was not geared to a standardized child and we didn't want either to be judged as such. I was also worried about how it would affect my own teaching. With that test looming over our heads every spring, I couldn't help imagining that I'd cave in and start "teaching to the test" just like a classroom teacher—making sure Ishmael knew his math facts, his punctuation, his consonant blends, or whatever, at the expense of all the truly exciting things we were doing.

This time I was so desperate that I *phoned* John Holt in Boston. I was afraid that maybe we were crazy to be upset about this type of evaluation procedure. After all, there was really no question about Ishmael passing. As I should have guessed, though, John was quite understanding and was outraged at the insensitivity of our school administration. He gave me some advice over the phone but also sent a more detailed letter the next day. He wrote:

> I enclose some quotes about testing from a couple of books. Dr. Fine's may be out of print, since I got it from a remainder house. They both make the same point, the Fine book very insistently—that how a child perceives the tester and the test situation can have an enormous effect on the test results themselves.
>
> This is common knowledge among psychologists, even otherwise fairly conservative or traditional ones. Indeed, the knowledge is so common that it is hard to believe that anyone with any claim to competence in education could make

the kind of proposal, or demand, which the school has made to you—that your child be tested in an environment and before people that the child will see as unfamiliar and in all probability hostile and threatening. I think you could say that to have your child tested under these circumstances would in the deepest sense of the word constitute a "Manifest Educational Hardship," and that you can have only the gravest doubts about the professional competence of educators who would suggest such a thing.

Some such statements as the above, along with plenty of quotes from that book should go in a letter to the Superintendent and probably members of the School Board as well.

I understand and support very strongly your wish to stay out of court. Any really honest lawyer will tell clients that the best thing to do is to stay out of court if possible, but I think it is also true, and that most lawyers would say, that the more you are ready to go to court if you have to, and the better prepared you are for a court battle if it comes to that, the greater your chances that you will not have to go. It is important in your case that when the school people read your letters, they always have in mind the question, "How would a judge respond to this?" The more things you can put into your proposals, and your justifications for these proposals, which a reasonable judge would be likely to support if he saw them, the greater your chances of not having to see that judge. You see my point.

To some extent you are in a battle of mutual intimidation with the schools. They are trying to use the threat of the law to scare you into doing what they want. You must in turn use the threat of an adverse court decision to make the schools let you do what you want. You can't afford to let the schools think that you are determined at all costs to avoid legal action, because if they think that they will drive you right into a corner.

Aside from the question of who tests your child, and where—and here I think you must insist on doing the testing yourself, and in your own home, with some impartial third party for a witness if the school wants that—I think you can also make the point any tests or other evaluative methods that you use must reflect your "curriculum" as well as the school's. It is a matter of the plainest common sense that the evaluative instruments and/or methods must be fairly closely matched to the materials being taught, or they are meaningless, and again, one has to wonder very seriously about the professional competence of people who don't understand this.

Meanwhile, keep the correspondence flowing. Don't talk to these people in person or on the phone, but keep a stream of letters crossing their desks, asking them all kinds of questions. The one family in Utah made it a practice, *every time* somebody in the schools asked a question or proposed something, to ask them to quote the statute that gave them the authority to make that proposal. This kind of talk makes them nervous and is a bother to them. Here's the Superintendent in his office, baskets full, phone ringing, people rushing in and out. He doesn't want to have to call up his lawyers, who may not be in the office or may be busy with something else, asking them to look up this statute or that. Aside from anything else we do, we have to make sure that these folks know that harrassing unschoolers is in the long run just going to be more trouble than it's worth. If this means that for a while you are going to have to spend a lot of time at the typewriter, so be it. Too bad, but that's the way it is.

Once again, with John's help and the assistance of Peter Kelman, a sympathetic education professor whom we met through a friend, we were able to formulate our answer to the superintendent. Our letter began:

> Thank you for your letter of April 2nd laying out a schedule for the evaluation of Ishmael's educational progress. Ishmael will not be able to keep the appointments you have made for him at this time, because we do not feel that we can comply in full with the policy adopted by the school board.

Sprinkling the pages with quotes from John and other educators, we detailed at great length our objections to the school's proposed evaluation procedures. Then we went on to suggest an alternative method of evaluation. Although we felt that Ishmael's work, activities, and state of mind more than spoke for themselves, we knew that the school people were anxious to have Ishmael tested, and we proposed a compromise.

What we suggest is that, with the help of Dr. Peter Kelman, we should make up our own test for Ishmael, based on the curriculum we are presently following and using the state Board of Education's suggested competency requirements as an additional point of reference and comparison. We feel that we can do an adequate job that will be helpful both to the school district and to ourselves in evaluating Ishmael's educational progress and in helping us to assess our home-schooling experiment thus far.

Rather than going into a classroom which is now foreign to Ishmael (and possibly even threatening, given the possible consequences of a negative evaluation), and rather than taking a standardized test with very little relationship to most of what he has been learning since December, Ishmael would then be taking a relevant test in a comfortable environment —our home. In addition to the help this test would afford us and the school board, it could also be a learning experience for Ishmael, by involving him in a comprehensible way in assessing his progress towards the goals we (and he) have set for his education.

We never had a chance to "keep the correspondence flowing" as John suggested because, right after receiving our letter, the superintendent set up a meeting for us with the school board. This time he was decent enough to notify us of the place and time. The details of the meeting itself have escaped me. It was so horrible that I must have blotted it out of my memory entirely. The only images that remain are cartoon-like, in exaggerated TV colors. The five board members raged and raged—I see them all in a red haze shaking their clenched fists at us. They spent an hour accusing us of destroying Ishmael, and when their lungs were tired out they voted—not just unanimously against us, but unanimously to make the testing situation as demanding as possible. Not only did they insist that Ishmael be tested, but they wanted him to take the test in the second-grade classroom with all the other children and without me anywhere around.

What they were saying, in effect, was: "Not only do we regret our decision to allow you to teach Ishmael at home, but we feel so crummy about it that we are going to make sure, from now on, that we don't give an inch on anything else." What shook us more than their vengeance though—their insistence on punishing Ishmael because they disapproved of us—was the inescapable realization that the state, in this case represented by the school board, had the authority to make crucial decisions about Ishmael's welfare. That was something that we could not accept.

Fortunately, we didn't have to take any drastic steps because the superintendent's assistant, who had been given the job of making arrangements for Ishmael's evaluation, had some sympathy with our feelings. In a garbled and tentative way, he quietly suggested that for administrative simplicity it would be best to administer the test during a school vacation, and he offered to let me help with it. Of course I didn't like the idea of the test at all, but I was so tired and confused that his offer seemed to be the most we could hope for under the circumstances. So I went along with it. And when I suggested that he and Ishmael's former teacher (who was the designated "staff member having teaching assignments commensurate with the level of instruction") should come to our house for their evaluation, he was agreeable.

So, at the end of April, testing day arrived. Ishmael, Vita, and I went back to the school, only this time it was silent and empty. Vita carried her bag of crayons, books, and paper like in the old days, and Ishmael was in his old apprehensive state of mind. I carried a huge lunch since we expected to spend the entire day there. Mr. S. showed us to a room, went over the testing instructions with me and then left us alone.

The test was too long. It was boring and irrelevant, but Ishmael zipped through much of it. Then he hit a section on phonetics and really goofed up—at least he and I thought he had—and he felt rotten. I could see him thinking, "Here I am, totally confused and hating this stuff, but it must be important or it wouldn't be on the TEST. Maybe there's something wrong with me because I don't understand it." Of course in reality, phonetics weren't important, at least not to Ishmael. He had taught himself how to read, bypassing most of the phonetic rules, and although I could never figure out his method, it must have worked, since he could read anything.

We ate a picnic lunch and took a walk through the woods before attacking the math sections of the test, since numbers still made Ishmael nervous. Although I had worked patiently with him for months and had gradually begun to succeed in helping him to relax around numbers, this test amplified all his troubles. He was confronted with pages of problems, many of them too difficult, and he began trembling and sweating, making mistakes from sheer nervous tension, and progressively feeling more and more inadequate.

After Mr. S. scored the test late in the day, we found to our surprise that Ishmael had scored in the seventy-eighth percentile in both math and phonetics. Hence, although he had made so many mistakes, he was performing above his grade level and Mr. S. congratulated him heartily—especially since he had done even better on the rest of the test. Although I was relieved, it disturbed me to realize that it's just the expected thing for average kids to get lots of answers wrong on tests. In school, they are constantly confronted with their own failure, and then told that they are really doing fine, just as Ishmael had been on *this* test!

The visit at our house with Mr. S. went quite well. He was interested in the books we were using and was overwhelmed with the stacks of Ishmael's stories, poems, and other written work that I showed him. It was interesting though, that one of his first questions was about handwriting. I think he wanted to know if I was really getting down to the nitty-gritty of teaching Ishmael, as opposed to just letting him learn. Handwriting was a subject that a child wouldn't ordinarily just "do"; most often it had to be taught. Anyway, I hadn't totally given up teaching, and fortunately I was able to whip out Ishmael's neat little handwriting notebook which was full of poems written in a rather awkward script.

Mr. S. also asked me whether I gave spelling tests. It was a question I was glad to answer. I explained that Ishmael learned how to spell by reading books, in which he always saw words spelled correctly, and through writing, where he strove to match with his own pen the words he'd seen in books. Occasionally, I admitted, I would point out a misspelled word to him; but that wasn't really very necessary, since his spelling improved all the time anyway. (As I write this, I think it's safe to say that he is a better speller than I am.) Mr. S. seemed thoughtful as he started glancing again at Ishmael's written work, but almost immediately his face gave a startled look. As luck would have it, his eyes had fallen upon a poem Ishmael had written in an Irish brogue and Mr. S. figured it was entirely misspelled! Fortunately, I was able to explain.

Miss B.'s visit went less well, partly because she didn't know what the school board wanted her to do. She, too, was impressed with Ishmael's writing; but she felt pressured into giving him a series of mimeographed "papers" to do, just to see if he was keeping up with the rest of her class. Ishmael struggled through them but finally came to one he just couldn't figure out. Miss B wasn't too happy—was Ishmael really falling behind, she wondered? Looking the paper over, I discovered that it was about "guide words," something Ishmael hadn't studied yet. Fortunately, I had the presence of mind to ask Miss B., "Aren't you really trying to find out how well Ishmael can use a dictionary?" And when she admitted that yes, she was, I had him find a dictionary and look up some words for her. I wasn't altogether certain that he could use an English dictionary, since he had mostly had reason to look up French words in our

Larousse de Poche; but I hoped for the best. And actually, although Ishmael was a bit slow, Miss B. admitted right away that he could use a dictionary better than anybody in her class. What a relief!

After that she gave me a little lecture about math, which was the real low point of her visit. But no matter how often she told me that Ishmael needed to spend an hour a day on math, I knew she was wrong. In her class, Ishmael had suffered from severe headaches, thanks in part to all the math drill she had pushed on him. At home, those headaches had disappeared, and that was of primary importance to me. I wasn't ready to even consider forcing Ishmael to do math, and besides, an hour a day of nothing but borrowing and carrying would drive anyone crazy. But I didn't say so. I didn't want any more battles.

The next week we went before the school board again—this time to hear the evaluation report on Ishmael from Mr. S. and Miss B., to submit our own unasked-for evaluation, and to request permission to teach Ishmael at home for the following year. Both Mr. S. and Miss B. gave glowing reports of our educational program and Ishmael's progress, although they did mention regretfully his lack of "peer contact." And no one could dispute Ishmael's scores on the standardized test. For the "total basic battery" (that means the whole test) his average score was 96%.

Then we submitted our evaluation. It was rather understated since I knew the school board wouldn't find us credible if we seemed too enthusiastic. Mostly we focused on the day-to-day details of how our school at home worked. We also included a few paragraphs about Ishmael's social life—not that we really thought it was any of their business, but we wanted to appease them if at all possible.

Here is part of what we wrote:

In assessing Ishmael's social experience, we have looked at his individual social needs, how well school met those needs, and how well we have done along the same lines. In first and second grade, Ishmael had trouble adjusting to the large group of children he met in the classroom and on the playground and he made few friends—certainly no one he felt like playing with after school, on weekends, or during the summer. He came home from school unhappy, withdrawn, and frequently on the verge of tears.

During our six-months' experiment we have not only satisfied Ishmael's craving for reading so that he now feels he has time to play, but we have found that he plays best in small groups, where he feels he has a chance to get to know individuals. He has become very close to an extremely bright and active eight-year-old boy, and they see each other once a week.

Ishmael has become more socially outgoing and self-confident because of this relationship, and he now plays with other kids around the neighborhood and with children from other towns—whom he has gotten to know because he wants to know them and has made the effort to do so. That is the way we, as adults, form friendships and it has worked well for Ishmael.

Certainly Ishmael's days are happy, busy, and full, and his general outlook and behavior have improved remarkably. As parents, it has been wonderful to see Ishmael transformed from a moody, silent child into a cheerful, eager child, bubbling over with information he has gathered from books and friends.

Finally, we submitted a letter written by Ishmael's pottery teacher which was quite persuasive—to us anyway. Part of it read as follows:

I have found Ishmael to be an excellent balance of serious student and playful child. We have serious talks together. We make jokes. He has an outstanding sense of humor. We play together and physically rough-house together. He is equally at home climbing a tree (which he loves to do) or taking instruction.

As usual, the school board ranted. They seemed primarily to be disgusted that Ishmael was doing so well. "You must push Ishmael too hard," one board member accused, and others seemed to be outraged that we allowed Ishmael to make choices about what he wanted to learn. We just sat there. After all, there wasn't much we could say.

They did finally grant us permission to teach Ishmael at home for another year. They knew they had no other choice. It wouldn't have looked good to say, "Ishmael has been learning so much and appears to be so happy at home that we have decided to deny him permission to learn at home again next year."

For Ishmael and the rest of us, the school board's decision was a tremendous relief. And even more so, for Bob and me, was the prospect of having the summer absolutely free to settle down to the real business of home-schooling. For at least three months we'd be able to relax and enjoy Ishmael and Vita without the constant interference of the school people.

To celebrate, we packed a lunch and our book, *America B.C.,* and, together with Dilly, drove out to the Vermont hills to explore a Celtic underground stone-slab chamber complete with Ogam inscriptions on the walls. It was a lovely day and a fitting beginning for what has turned out to be real freedom for the kids and ourselves to learn about and explore the world around us.

Chapter 4

School at Home

Our first summer as home-schoolers was lovely. Bob took a month off and we spent the time at home—gardening, cutting hay in the field, swimming, and walking.

Vita and Ishmael had their own tiny organic garden plot where they raised corn, tomatoes, peas, pumpkins, and potatoes. As well as vegetables, they nurtured all kinds of bugs, most of which were pests. Still, they were fun to watch. We observed gold and yellow striped potato beetles laying piles of tiny orange eggs on the undersides of potato leaves. Then we counted the days until the eggs hatched into hideous sluglike larvae and finally matured into adult potato bugs. They almost demolished the kids' potato patch, but a few plants managed to bud and flower. Vita got very excited because she noticed that the purple potato flowers looked just like the yellow flowers on her tomato plants and she discovered a vine growing near the back porch with similar deep blue flowers. I got out my book of New England wild flowers and helped the kids look up and identify the blue flower. It turned out to be Bittersweet Nightshade. With the help of the encyclopedia, we discovered that potatoes and tomatoes are also members of the nightshade family. Once we had the encyclopedias out, we couldn't stop ourselves. We read about the history of the cultivation of potatoes and tomatoes, about potato bugs, and about the evolution of plant families.

Meanwhile, Bob and Ishmael, with help from Vita, built a raft. Ishmael and Dilly had been dreaming of water-travel all winter long. When the snow finally melted they built a series of scrap-lumber rafts that they launched in our little brook. Unfortunately, though, the rafts always seemed to sink as soon as any weight was put on them. Worse yet, a raft would sometimes just fall apart, with the individual boards floating downstream and out of reach forever. Building a raft that really worked, then, was an adventure for Ishmael. Since he was pretty good at sawing, hammering, and nailing, he could do most of the work; but Bob helped enough with the design and some of the trickier carpentry so that the final product was sturdy and trustworthy in the water. Since Ishmael had a passion for sailboats, I helped him hem a triangular-shaped piece of cloth for a sail. Then he and Bob fixed up some complex rigging so that the sail could be raised and lowered. Once the raft was finished, Ishmael painted and varnished it until it looked shiny and new. Every few days we tied it onto the roof rack on the car and took it to a nearby swimming hole, where the kids paddled around happily.

Later, Ishmael wrote an article about how he built this raft. This article, when published in *Mother Earth News*, was actually the first to appear in a newly created (now regular) feature in the magazine. Pat Stone, one of the editors, had been thinking for some time about running "how-to" articles by children for other children. When he casually mentioned this to John Holt, John suggested that he write up the idea for *Growing Without Schooling* to see if he could interest any home-schooling children. Ishmael was definitely interested. Describing the article he wanted to write, he sent a query to Pat. Pat wrote back an encouraging letter, requesting photographs with the proposed article and cautioning Ishmael, as he would have cautioned any adult writer, that he would only use the piece if it were well written. Ishmael worked hard, Bob and I carefully shot a few rolls of film, and, fortunately, Pat Stone was pleased with the results. He sent Ishmael a check for $80. Later, when they put a picture of Vita and Ishmael sailing on the raft on the cover, Pat sent Ishmael an extra $20. One hundred dollars was more money than he had ever seen in his life, and I took him to the bank where he opened his own savings account.

Starting in July, I began canning fruit and vegetables. In the past, I had always made sure that Ishmael and Vita were out of the way before I began canning. But that summer, with Vita now four and Ishmael almost eight, I decided to let them help. The season started with blueberries. Both kids got sick of picking when their bellies got full, since it was tiresome to work in the hot sun; but they enjoyed the kitchen part of the job, which involved rinsing, measuring, stirring, and sterilizing. We canned peaches next, and that was even more fun, since Vita and Ishmael got to use paring knives to peel and pit the peaches before we put them into the jars.

Ishmael still found time to read. He especially enjoyed Greek and Roman mythology and narrative poetry. Altogether, he managed to read close to a hundred books, including at least ten volumes of the Lucy Fitch Perkins' "Twin Series"—*The Chinese Twins, The Dutch Twins, The Belgian Twins,* and so on.

In August, with school right around the corner, we were faced with the daunting task of writing another year's curriculum for Ishmael. This time we were struck with a clever idea: why not base it on everything he had done that summer? It would look impressive, and besides, not only would we be focusing it on Ishmael's current interests, but he would have completed most of the "work" already, which would free him to go on to other things as his interests changed.

The typed curriculum looked impressive, too. Although we took the liberty of combining "Units," "Approach," "Methods," and "Resources" into one heading, our curriculum was long and full of content. For "Reading and Language Arts" we included "dramatic reading" (Ishmael loved reading Lord Macauley's *Ho-*

ratius aloud) and "story-telling," as well as mythology, silent reading, creative writing, and French. Our topic for third-grade social studies was "Foreign Children and their Life Styles," which incorporated (you guessed it) the Lucy Fitch Perkins books. For science, we planned to carry on with our chemistry experiments with a book Ishmael enjoyed called *Science Experiments You Can Eat*. Jenny Wright had offered to give the kids nature lessons, and Bob and Ishmael wanted to play around with various metals and a propane torch. For good measure, we listed all the science magazines we subscribed to and some books that we hoped to read from the library. Our "Science Unit" looked good. During the summer, I had finally laid my hands on some decent math textbooks and, once again, we described them at the greatest length imaginable. We planned to start Ishmael on piano lessons that fall, too; and, as Ishmael and Vita were signed up for art and drama lessons in town, that took care of Art, Drama, Music, and even "Socialization."

I mailed the curriculum to the superintendent's office at the beginning of September, and we opened our "school" a few days later. With art and drama classes on Mondays, piano and French on Wednesdays, and nature lessons on Thursdays, we soon settled into a fast-paced schedule. When people I met for the first time asked how I ever managed to teach Vita and Ishmael, I laughed and said, "Oh, I'm not the teacher, just the chauffeur."

In reality, of course, I was doing far more than driving. Besides the housework and gardening, I spent a great deal of time with the kids—reading to them, talking to Ishmael about his writing, working with him on math, and helping Vita with her letters. And I liked to be available for as much time as possible to answer their questions and to chat with them about the things that they were interested in.

But despite the fact that I was now much more than a full-time mother to Ishmael and Vita, I discovered that I had more time to myself than I had ever had before. I hadn't realized how much time I had spent dragging around worrying about Ish-

mael when he had been in school. My whole life had been consumed with his problems, and I had been drained—emotionally and physically—by watching him suffer. Being so preoccupied with Ishmael's troubles had allowed me little energy
to do much more than a minimum of household chores and
babysitting. By comparison, my life now was a breeze. With
Ishmael back to his normal, cheerful, healthy self, I had far
more energy and became far more efficient and organized. By
afternoon, I found that I was able to sit down for an hour or so
and read, or even do some writing.

Although we had originally planned to have just Ishmael take
piano lessons, Vita and I impulsively decided to take them, too.
By winter, we were all spending a great deal of time practicing,
playing tunes like "Twinkle Twinkle Little Star" and "Go Tell
Aunt Rhody." Ishmael spent the fall learning mime and sign
language with a group of about ten other children. At Christmas, they "sang" carols in sign language for a crowd of parents,
friends, and relatives. Meanwhile, in their drama class, the
children wrote their own play and produced it—complete with
costumes and scenery they'd designed themselves.

Every Thursday we got together with Jenny and her daughter, Vanessa. Jenny took the kids on nature walks, and in return
I gave Vanessa piano lessons. Although I (obviously) was only a
beginner on the piano, I really wasn't such a bad teacher. In
fact, it was just *because* I was such a beginner that I was able to
be unusually receptive to Vanessa's difficulties. If she had problems with the rhythm of "French Children's Song," for example, I certainly understood why, since most likely I'd just had
the same trouble. And since I remembered just what I'd done
to overcome my problem, I was able to help her in the same
tried-and-true way. Then too, I had learned a lot about teaching piano from our piano teacher; so, for much of the time with
Vanessa, I just passed along all the musical ideas and skills he
had taught us.

On her walks with the kids, Jenny helped them to identify
trees, and later, when the snow melted, flowers and other wild

plants. Sometimes, instead of walking, they all pruned fruit trees with little pruning saws. When there was a fresh snow, they tracked animals in the woods. When it was too cold to go outside, Jenny read to them or showed them how to use identification keys in various books about trees and plants; and sometimes they pasted pressed leaves and flowers into scrapbooks.

Ishmael enjoyed the nature walks, but it was Vita who was most enthusiastic. She became a veritable walking encyclopedia, continually dropping the names of obscure flowers, trees, or insects and telling us anecdotes about them—prefacing her remarks with a predictable, "Jenny said," or "Jenny told me."

Ishmael and Vita occasionally went to work with Bob, who was putting in long hours as a community organizer. When he was on the phone in the office, the kids typed or drew. But what they liked best was to go "door knocking" with him, walking from door to door in neighborhoods about town and listening to him talk with people about how to take action on problems that concerned them in the community. Bob liked to take the kids along because their young faces always made people more cheerful.

That winter, though, he decided to quit his job. There were many reasons for his decision, but high on the list was his desire to spend more time with Vita and Ishmael. He had been working fifty or sixty hours a week, much of that at night or on weekends, and he hated being gone at suppertime and not being able to put the kids to bed at night. But mostly, he wanted to be an integral part of their lives, not just an occasional treat.

Ten years before, he had translated a fat, and in his opinion, important, German philosophy book. Over the years, he had tried to get it published—without success. But now he became determined to find a publisher. There were other books he hoped to translate, and he wanted to do some writing of his own. So we went out on a limb, and he set up shop in our bedroom. In a few months, he not only found a publisher, but he was asked to translate two other equally fat books. With four to six years of work ahead of him, we were able to relax—about money anyway.

For a while, we worried that it would be difficult for Bob to work at home, with the inevitable noise that the kids made and their inevitable invasions into his study during working hours. But he actually found his study quiet in comparison with the constant chatter of his co-workers at his office in town. He welcomed occasional interruptions from Vita and Ishmael, since he liked to keep in touch with the things that were going on in the rest of the house. And since it was tiring to sit and write for eight hours a day, he began knocking off from work at around three in the afternoon to look after the kids and do housework, while I took some time for myself. With two hours of my own time to look forward to each day, I started to get serious about writing. Soon I began sketching this book out in my mind.

So the months passed. In the mornings, we worked on math for fifteen or twenty minutes, did some handwriting (which included more reading of poetry than writing it), wrote letters and journal entries, drew, and played piano. In the afternoons the kids went to their various classes in town, played with each other and with friends, read, and often did science experiments or read French with Bob. After supper, we played chess or scrabble—and Bob always read to the kids before they went to bed.

This is not to say that we were always quite so orderly. Often we took the day off to visit friends, to go shopping, to take a walk, or just to have a break. We weren't always as productive as I would have liked, and sometimes we went through some really miserable times together. I remember one particularly bad morning when, even before I'd washed the dishes, I began yelling at Ishmael because he couldn't figure out how many twos there were in nine. I managed to set his tears flowing— and mine too, when I sat down to comfort him. About half an hour later, Vita sat down to play the piano, and she just couldn't seem to play anything right. After my experience with Ishmael, I was prepared to be as patient as I had to be, but she wasn't, and she burst into tears. Sitting her on my lap, I suggested that perhaps it would be best if she took a break from the piano for the day. But "No!" she screamed at me, tears dropping steadily into her lap, "I want you to *make* me play!" So I did, although fortunately she agreed to drink some juice and do a few jumping-jacks to calm herself down first. Still, standing over Vita, her face red and wet from tears, I couldn't help wondering what I was doing with my life. How simple it would be, I thought fleetingly, to send Vita and Ishmael back to school.

Then too, despite the fact that Ishmael did better than ever on his standardized test that spring, I often worried that I wasn't teaching him enough. After all, the rest of the neighborhood kids spent the whole day in school, whereas I only taught Ishmael for an hour or two a day. Actually, the longer he was out of school, the more I began to notice that—regardless of how much time I actually spent teaching him—the pattern of his learning was uneven. It took the form of cycles of intense activity followed by rest. During his active periods, he tended to focus on only one or two primary interests at a time, like playing the piano and reading biographies or putting on plays and writing poetry. And, as though to recuperate from his creative outbursts, he would then spend weeks doing what I considered to be nothing—riding his bike up and down the same stretch of road, making title pages for books which he never wrote, and reading the same books over and over again. It always took an act of faith on my part to believe that he'd snap out of his doldrums. I used to wonder if I really shouldn't make him buckle down and work harder. Once, for example, I was so worried about Ishmael that I went back to his old school and spent the day as an observer in the fourth/fifth-grade classroom, just to get a sense of how much the other kids really learned each day. It was reassuring to be reminded that between roll call, snack time, lunch time, recess, and the natural confusion that takes place when you squash thirty-two kids into a classroom built for twenty-five, not a lot of formal learning takes place. The most striking thing to me, though, was the fact that even though many of the kids read quite well, they still had to read vocabulary-controlled readers and study phonics in class.

Certainly it was better for Ishmael to read Ernest Thompson Seton's *Two Little Savages* ten times over than for him to spend year after year reading colorless textbooks. And I far preferred to see him riding his bike up and down in the sun than sitting in a cramped classroom all day. I left the school knowing that, even in his doldrums, Ishmael was doing fine—at least when compared with other children his age.

Of course, I still went through periods when I felt insecure about Ishmael's education. Usually when I found myself feeling that way, though, I sat down for an hour or two and read his diaries. (Ishmael wrote "secret" before passages that he didn't want me to read.) They never failed to remind me of how much really went on at our house. I realized that, even without my teaching, the kids were learning an incredible amount. Invariably, my spirits lifted. I think it will be useful to quote from some sample entries here, since they give a marvelous account of Ishmael and Vita's lives between lessons. In fact, they are a convincing argument for doing as John Holt says—just letting children *be*, to absorb and assimilate the world around them. The diary entries I give here start during the spring of Ishmael's second year at home and continue through the summer and well into the next year—Ishmael's third at home.

> *May 2*. Me and Vita went on a walk. We saw a mouse hole. Yesterday I finished *From the Earth to the Moon*. Spring is wonderful. Me and Vita did a play. She wrote it. We had a bath and did lots of frolicking which involved the mix-up of names. I wrote a story about knights which had poetry in it. I also wrote a play called *A Debate of Parliament*. Hurray! Hurray for today! Vita's birthday cake was constructed. It will be her fifth birthday.

> *May 10*. We bought me some hiking boots and some sneakers. Then we walked up Mount Kearsarge. The path was a river bed. It was very rocky. We ate lunch on top. The view was very fine. On the way down I taught Nancy Napoleonic history as far as I knew it. We cooked supper out in the North Field and I had a quarrel with Vita over some

grapes. Then we went on a walk. There is a tremendous amount of vegetation in the forest, and not only ferns. Then we camped out and while Vita was asleep we sat by the fire and read *David Copperfield* through the night. It was very beautiful.

May 21. I had a piano lesson. Then the Garbers and all of us except Bob drove over to Jenny and Vanessa's house. They are apple pickers and pruners and live in a small house without electricity or running water. We played baseball of a sort. However Billy spoiled the game and Jenny deserted. Then several wars were waged against Billy. Then Nancy went away, Billy shouting, "I won't surrender!" The Garbers went away too. Then me and Vanessa played parcheesi and fixed supper. It was soup. After supper we made a fire and roasted apples and made popcorn. Ah, what fun to hold up a flaming torch! Then about nine o'clock we went to bed. I read *The Wizard of Oz*.

June 1. Made my bed. I wrote a poem. I also did some chopping at the woodpile. [Vita and Ishmael each had their own axes and helped to split the one-foot logs that we burned in our wood cookstove. They were allowed to split without supervision, since Bob had shown them how to use their axes properly. Their individual chopping blocks were placed at a good distance from each other so there was no danger of the kids' accidentally hitting one another with flying chips or a stray axe. Our two rules were, "Always wear heavy boots in the woodpile," and, "Don't use your axe when other children are around without adult supervision."—NW] Then we made a sponge cake. I wrote another poem called, "Robin Hood and Maid Marian." Amy, from next door, came over to play with Vita. I went on some military surveillances. Then we went to the library and Bob got a philosophy book and I got a book about the Spanish Armada and one about William the Conquerer. Then we went to *The Europeans*, a movie which is a mess of love affairs all boiling around.

June 15. Had breakfast and read *Lochinvar*. I split some wood and pretty much finished the job. I then walked on my stilts and read some of *Pogo*. I then rode my bike. We had lunch and I had a piano lesson. Then me and Bob went bike riding up Dero Road. Nancy forced me to begin *Rascal*. I had my eye on some of Shakespeare's plays, but I began it. Me, Bob, and Vita went to the cemetery and tried to fix it up. During part of the night I stayed awake wondering. If Christ saved everyone's souls, whether they were confident in it or not, I didn't have to pray for Bob and Nancy. But if he only saved people who were confident, I should, because Nancy and Bob don't believe in God and therefore wouldn't know of the peril to their souls, so how could they be confident of being saved? Nancy came in and told me that Jesus had probably died to give us a chance to go to heaven, so I might as well pray for them. I thanked her and went to sleep. [Ishmael, who was just beginning to think about religion, mistakenly assumed that because we didn't belong to a church we didn't believe in God. —NW]

July 6. After breakfast I had a piano lesson. Then I played Scrabble and War with Vita. We had lunch and then I went on a solitary walk up the Mountain Road for miles and miles. Nancy and Vita were canning peaches when I got back. Then I went on a walk with Vita to the Garber's. On the way back we saw a man driving a machine which was throwing hay in back of it to be ready for the baler in the Moul's field. We went chopping wood and then did a French lesson. Then we played Hearts and a Chess game. In the game, the board was cleared faster than Bob had ever seen in his life. One thing led to another and soon my King was alone and cornered by four big important enemies. However my King managed to keep 'em off for a terribly long time and then Bob managed to checkmate me. Then we had supper and read *Hamlet*. Last night I had had a dream about a pirate's ghost which stepped into a grave and shrieked, "It's blood!" in a blood-curdling cry. So at night, the thought of the dream got on my nerves and I managed to get the sheet partly wet from the fountains of my eyes. Nancy found me in the bathroom blowing my nose and she said I should have told her. I went to sleep.

July 25.   I wrote a story about some people who are outlawed for being demonstrators. Then Kim and Abbey Nash, our new neighbors, came over. I had a piano lesson and we picked lots of blueberries. We decided to make pies and sell them. However, when we told Nancy, she said we should just sell the berries.

We sold blueberries to the Durhams for forty cents a basket. We had let Mrs. Durham judge between the prices of twenty-five cents a basket and fifty cents for one, and she chose forty cents. She also paid for the newspaper we had given her yesterday. [Ishmael and Vita put out a regular weekly newspaper that summer, full of neighborhood news, and sometimes other children like Billy Garber and Kim and Abbey added supplements of their own.—NW]

Then we went to the Garber's to collect money for the newspaper. We saw the Edmonds, the Garber's friends from New Zealand. Next we went home and Kim went back to her house. I read some animal poems and had lunch.

After a while Kim came back and we began to do some plays. We made a play about a prince who found a princess and thought he wouldn't have to fight a dragon. But he did. We made a dragon out of the mowing machine covered with a sheet.

Then David Shendler, a friend of Bob's, came over. We quickly rehearsed the play and then performed it for Bob and David. He asked us to recite some poems so I stepped up and did "Shepherd Cor" which I had written long ago. Kim left temporarily and Bob and David Schendler talked and argued about a book in German about philosophy.

Kim came back and we did some archery. Then I read *D'ye Ken John Peel* and we made a block castle. Next we picked some peas and shelled them. After a while she went home and we had supper.

July 29.   Had breakfast. After a while we had a piano lesson. I amused myself, Vita, and the piano teacher's son with throwing apples. Then we went to the store and home. Then Nancy told Bob that she had ordered a skirt and sent it back because it didn't fit. She had bought another one and had to pay for both. We were all outraged.

Then Vita and me began a court and turned it into a debating club. Next I read a bunch of poems, especially *Horatius* to Vita, and we built with blocks. I made Rome and Vita made Jaruniculum. Then we copied the old debate, "The Water Supply." We also put down "Which Candidate Deserves to be President?" and read them to Bob and Nancy.

We had supper and Bob went away to a meeting to help some people keep their son out of school.

Sept. 2. We had pancakes for breakfast. Then I had a long piano lesson. Me and Vita put all the dolls to bed and I fixed up all the accounts. [Ishmael and Vita keep elaborate accounts of all the money they earn.—NW] Then we did a Presidential Election with the dolls and gave them lunch. Finally we warned Bob that a hen had gotten out of the chickens' yard and we did a rehearsal of a play I made called *Kingship* and also *Abdul Bulbul Ammer* and *The Burnt Cakes*.

Then I read a book to Vita and we went to the Herndon's and sold a newspaper. We also talked to them about the plays. We went home and had lunch. Me and Vita had a fight and practiced three plays. Then we decided, with Nancy's help, to make a village scene on a sheet and tack it up for the three plays. We tacked two sheets to the floor of the porch and pastelled a lot of houses and a road onto the sheets.

Then we had a French lesson. Finally we had supper and went on a walk to the Garbers. Me and Vita went ahead and sold them a newspaper.

Sept. 19. Had breakfast and I read a lot. Then I finished a letter to Benji and did French and script. I read some more, had a long piano lesson and wrote some notes on Wolfgang Amadeus Mozart. We had lunch and I did some math. We made rice pudding and did a rehearsal of *Moneybags*. Next we played on the rope swing. Me and Vita played with toy soldiers and we did some splitting. I read *Stories of Great Operas*. I did some archery and we had supper. We went on a walk and played bandits.

Oct. 11. Had breakfast. I went to work on the Mozart report and did French and geometry. We played dolls and me and Vita had a fight, did some drawing and then some math. A prisoner who'd escaped from the dolls' jail was caught and they began a Constitution.

Oct. 21.   We had breakfast. I finished the bibliography of my Mozart report and drew a picture on the cover. Finally I did some math. Meanwhile, Vita did a piano lesson. We played with dolls. It turned out that Bertha Emond, a reporter for the Eagle Times, had written an article about the Apple Hill concert we'd been to. In the article she said Vita and I had been practicing bows during the intermission. I wrote a letter to the editor saying we'd been touching our toes, not practicing bows. We played with dolls some more, did some archery, and had lunch.

Then I had a piano lesson and did math and French. Next, we began melting lead. When it was melted I tried to make an arrowhead by sticking an already sharpened arrow into it, but it wouldn't stick so we poured bits of it out on a piece of wood to make money for the dolls. Then we had an idea. We took a big piece of lead and took an arrow which had a notch which was too big. We stuck the lead in it and put some tape around to keep it in. Next we made a new notch on the other end. I tried it out but the head got loose so we had to tie it on with thread. Finally we had to wire the thing. We had supper and a walk.

October 26.   Had breakfast. We talked about how if everything is in reach, money is worthless, or something. I next had a piano lesson and me and Vita had a puppetry class. I got a book, *The Mystery of the Screaming Clock,* out of the library while Bob got some stuff copied.

We drove home and had lunch. I began playing with dolls. We had a bath and the acorns (the enemies of the dolls) were beseiged. We drove to a gas station to look at a truck but it had disappeared. Then we drove to the vet and bought some pills. Then we went to the Dartmouth Library while Bob put some books back, killed some time at the Hopkins Center, and saw a movie, *Stardust Memories,* which I couldn't understand.

Nov. 11.   Yesterday we worked on the scenery for the musical. We made it out of paper bags, which was Vita's excellent idea. We are keeping the story, the fact that it's a musical, and the scenery a secret to spring on Nancy on her birthday.

We had breakfast, did a dress rehearsal of the musical, and I had a piano lesson. Then I played dolls. The soldiers began a newspaper. I changed my pants and did some sewing on some place mats to send away for Christmas.

We had lunch and I read a book from the attic called *Makers of Music*. Then I played with dolls again. They did three plays and a ballet. We read from the scripts of the plays we'll do with puppets. I read some more, had supper, and played all my songs on the piano for Nancy.

Nov. 25.   Yesterday we made an alphabet of signals with which we can talk. We had breakfast and I did some math, script, and French. We did some archery in the snow and had a conversation with signals. I did a piano lesson and we had lunch.

After supper we drove to the Keene Fine Arts building. Our friend Tony Princiotti, who will teach Vita violin, played a Mozart violin concerto. We also heard the Beethoven Fifth Symphony. Both were perfectly perfect, but I award Beethoven the prize.

Dec. 3.   We had whole wheat Cream of Wheat for breakfast and I did handwriting, French, geometry, and math. Then I played with dolls, had a piano lesson, and lunch.

Me and Vita are working on a sort of pantomime of Loch Lomond, with Bob singing, as a surprise for Nancy. We did a little school work, played dolls, and had a French lesson. On the way home, I met Billy Garber with a friend. I walked past them and Billy shouted, "He's queer! He's queer! He's queer!" I went over to him and he aimed a kick at me. I told him that if I was queer, that wasn't any of his business, and if I was a spectacle, he had no reason to laugh. I was in a white heat of rage when, as I went off, Billy said audibly, "He's always mean."

I would have written a letter to Billy's mother only Nancy persuaded me that he acted that way because of school.

After supper we drove Chris and Denise and their son, Justin, to the school board meeting where they were going to decide if Justin could be a home-schooler. Chris and Denise have a lawyer to help them. Then me, Nancy and Vita went to the Claremont Opera House for a concert. But Nancy decided it wasn't there so we ran to the Stevens High School, but it was all dark. We met another couple in the same predicament.

Then we went back to the school board meeting. We waited a lot and read two books, one about hyperactive children and one about gifted children, both in comic strip form. They finally decided "NO!" about whether Justin should be taught at home, which was illegal according to the state regulations, because what the school board was really saying was, "We don't like home-schooling." Now they should have had a better reason than that, especially when Chris and Denise put forward millions of reasons for keeping Justin out of school.

Dec. 18.   Yesterday we visited Jenny and Vanessa. Before that I had been wondering what music I could write for my operetta *Ivan Skavinsky Skavar*. Bob suggested that I write the notes of the beginning of the song that I had gotten the story from. I was very enthusiastic, and wrote them down.

Today we had breakfast and I read a mystery of the death of Karen Silkwood, an anti-nuclear person. I strongly suspect the nearby nuclear company, Something and McGee, of killing her because it has been discovered that some of their plutonium was unaccountably missing—the very stuff that was put in her cheese!!!

I had a piano lesson and listened to the second Beethoven Symphony. We played dolls, made wonderful Christmas cookies, and did a rehearsal of our secret production we'll do for Nancy as well as *Ivan Skavinsky Skavar*. We finally drove off to a concert by some daycare, nursery school, and kindergarten kids. However, they started too late, so we could only stay and listen to three songs. Then we went to a movie, *Nine to Five*, which was terrific.

Dec. 29. We had breakfast. I did French, geometry, script, math, and wrote a submission of three poems to a certain editor who wants poems by kids. We went down to the cellar and made a clubhouse of two rooms. We were given masks to ward off the dust which made us laugh ourselves almost to death. We had a better time in the cellar than we usually do upstairs. We (except for Vita) went on a walk and I wrote a libretto for a new *Boston Charlie* operetta!

Jan 2. We had breakfast. I did math and finished the Gilbert and Sullivan report. Then I did the greater part of a piano lesson. There is so little to do. I forgot to say that yesterday I wrote a song down. I read a little bit, had lunch, and went skiing. Vita refused to go to the Nash-Graces so we skied in the woods. We had supper. I learned how to play an African recorder which I'd been playing like a flute. It is a wonderful instrument. After supper we read *Beau Geste*. It is a terribly tragic and very scary story, but that is what makes it so good.

Jan 8. We went to Jenny and Vanessa's house. We went sliding with them. We also managed to make a thunderstorm on the piano by putting down the pedal and doing loud and deep chords. It was very effective! On the way home we listened to folk music on the car radio. I forgot to say that yesterday I wrote a play called, *Othello and Desdemona or: Love's Path Is Lumpy.*

Jan. 19. I wrote my Schubert paper, did some fractions, and began writing a Tom and Mickey story. Then we had lunch. We drove off and brought Vita to her gymnastics lesson. I walked to the library. I never did this before. There was a problem at the store. I was afraid of the traffic and one car was having trouble and might have gotten started any minute. However, I got past and had a fine time at the library and had a bookbinding class with Vita and two others who were cousins, Amy and Corey. I intend to copy down my plays and operettas into the books I make.

Jan. 21. We had breakfast. We had a wonderful piano lesson with Bob Fraley. I borrowed a book about Béla

Bartok. We went to the health food store and the grocery store. Apparently Nancy heard someone make an anti-Semitic joke to his friend. We had lunch and I began writing variations on a march and we did a rehearsal. (We decided only to do the last two operettas, *Love's Path Is Lumpy* and *Rowing Down the Stream*.) Nancy practiced her part and it was all wonderful!! (We shall produce the operettas today for Chris, Denise, and Justin when they come to dinner.) They came! We had a wonderful supper. Think of that! We played cars, had cake, and did the operettas.

Chris had apparently decided that we should go with nuclear power, discover the secret of fusion, and make computers to do all our chores. Bob began arguing and I almost DIED! I *like* my chores and would HATE to have a computer programmed to do my math and I say that we might as well use wind, water, and sun power which is near at hand, dependable and safe, plus cheap.

Feb. 7. We had breakfast and fiddled around. Vita had a piano lesson and I did too. I taught myself to sing "The Battle Hymn of the Republic." It is a WONDERFUL song. I learned it to a different tune than the way it is usually sung. Then I split wood with Daddy. It's a wonderful day! We drove to the bank and then took a walk. Later we went to the Hancock Inn for dinner, but it was too expensive so we went to the Folkways Restaurant instead. There was a jazz band getting set up to play. After dinner we went to a concert. There was a trio by Haydn for cello, violin, and piano, a quartet by Bartok, and a piece by John Deak for solo string bass and string quartet about Dracula. Then there was the *Trout* quintet by Schubert.

Feb. 19. We listened to 19th century American music on "Morning Pro-Musica." It was very wonderful. We heard "Jeannie With the Light Brown Hair." We had breakfast and then worked ever so hard putting on the handle to my half-axe. I did a lot of splitting and made up a satirical song.

I pushed a cart of wood up from the elm tree and read some of the home-schooling book that Nancy is working on. We had lunch. I can't remember afternoon. Supper was had.

Feb. 23.   Sluzy, our cat, caught a mouse, who escaped. We tried to catch him so's to put him outside only he escaped us. I was almost in tears after a while. Why couldn't we have caught him in the first place? Finally I said, "I wish that mouse were DEAD!" which caused even more confusion.

Nancy had a talk with me and told me that when I got dissatisfied when I turned teenager it would hurt but we'd still be friends if we both said what we thought. So we decided to.

I did math and Nancy got mad at Vita for not wanting a piano lesson when she'd just reserved the time for one. Vita changed her mind. I had a piano lesson too and we had lunch.

We drove to town and Vita was dropped off at her gymnastics lesson. I went to the library and later Vita caught up with me at bookbinding class. The others had come early and had finished their books already. So we were given instructions so as to finish ours and we learned Japanese bookbinding. It is so hard to sew!

Supper was had.

Feb. 28.   We had breakfast and I took my book of plays and operettas to the library for an exhibition. I sang two songs out of Frank Damrosch's *Popular Method of Sight Singing*. It is a wonderful book and very handy for teaching myself with. Vita had a pretty bad piano lesson. Vita's piano lesson is getting better. (It isn't done yet.) I was going to go with Bob to get some finished (typed) Blumenberg (that's the name of the author he's translating) from the typer, Josette. The book (in English) is called, *The Legitimacy of the Modern Age*. However, because of vague orders, she left it at her office, which was locked. So I had a piano lesson and waxed my skis instead. I have waxy fingers. Lunch was had. I read *Eddie, the Dog Holder* and we went skiing in the Garber's fields. It was wonderful and we came home soaking wet. I can't remember much after that, but we did a family concert and I began a new book, *The Peasant and the Prince*.

March 2.   Home-schooling hasn't worked. I couldn't do 4 − 3 at my math lesson, though that can be blamed on Vita's awful piano lesson. I was going to run off and get to the bank and get the money from my *Mother Earth News* article, but I've decided that since the problem was Vita's bad piano lesson we shall study in different rooms. I did some more school work and had a piano lesson and read a biography of Theodore Roosevelt in the attic. It's good but the book idolizes him. T. had weak points—or at least one—like the Spanish-American War. I forgot to say that I'd written a funeral march.

We drove to town. I went to the library, Vita went to gymnastics and Nancy went to get new glasses.

Yesterday I decided to pray only when I really meant it. Otherwise, how could I be truthful?

March 8.   I'm writing this in bed. No one else is awake yet. Yesterday I had a good piano lesson and we visited Josette, Bob's typist.

It is after breakfast and I have had a good piano lesson. I wrote half of a Farce and Bob wrote the other half. He is now a full member of our Acting Company, and gets an apple pie as a prize.

After lunch I did some sledding. We went skiing and I got my feet wet. Vita played with Amy. I sledded and died of boredom.

March 13.   I did a flood of schoolwork and began Algebra! My! It is quite a strain on the imagination! I went sledding with Vita and she got me into playing house. I inveigled her into two play rehearsals while still playing house by means of a "school play." I read *Old Possum's Book of Practical Cats* to Vita and ate lunch.

I had a long nice piano lesson. I can't remember the rest of the afternoon. Bob came home and we did a Magic Show. Mine was a flop because they discovered how I did every trick except the last—which didn't work.

We went to an Apple Hill concert. They played a piano trio by Tschaikovsky, a string quartet by Borodin, and something else by Glinka.

March 26.   It is against my principles to skip two days like this, however yesterday I was too out of temper to write. John Holt, the editor of *Growing Without Schooling* and writer of educational books, shall visit!

After breakfast we collected sap from our maple trees. I went ahead to a new tree and found there was ice in the sap container. I broke the ice and Vita began screaming because I had gone ahead of her.

I brought Bob Fraley, our piano teacher, a March in 9/8 time yesterday but he said it would be hard to march in 9/8 time so I decided to call my composition *Martial Minuet* instead. We drove to a bus stop and found John Holt. I had forgotten what he looked like. We drove him home and then drove to Apple Hill for Vita's first violin lesson. I found a copy there of Monteverdi's *Orfeo* (the orchestral and vocal score). We drove home.

After a walk and supper, Nancy and John played their Vivaldi Cello Sonata (John brought his cello) and we all improvised on different instruments.

March 27. After breakfast we lazed around and rehearsed *Cabbie*. We had decided to surprise John with it as well as pancakes for breakfast. The rehearsal went very well and then we did a performance. Then I did part of a piano lesson and Vita and John improvised on the cello and violin. I practiced some Purcell with Bob, who played the recorder. The piece was called, "Pipes are Sweet on a Summer's Day." Then I improvised on John's cello and played the Purcell again with Bob. After lunch—but I'd better explain. John Holt had written down a tune to Blake's *The Divine Image*, in his own notation, consisting of each line representing a half step. We (him, me, and Nancy) spent almost the whole time deciphering and translating this tune. We used the rest of the time for going on a walk and having a snowball fight. We didn't quite get the tune down, but we got a good sketch of it. We had supper and a family concert. We named ourselves "The Bedchamber Players." The next day we brought John to the bus stop and he went off.

Chapter 5

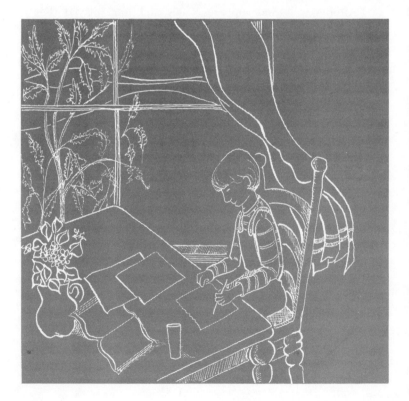

The Spring Ritual: Testing, Evaluations, Home-Schooling Applications

It was now our third spring as home-schoolers. The daffodils poked up in the flower beds, Ishmael and Vita rode their bikes through the puddles in the muddy road, and the robins pulled worms out on the lawn. Life here would have been idyllic if I hadn't begun to feel my seasonal nervousness over Ishmael's year-end evaluation and our yearly renewal application to teach him at home. And that year my nerves were more taut than ever because, in May, Vita would turn six. She would be of school age.

For a long time after we had taken Ishmael out of school, we just assumed that when the time came, we would enroll Vita in first grade, even if only as an experiment. She had always been more social than Ishmael, and although she was perfectly smart, she didn't seem as though she was going to be as driven, intellectually, as he was. And it was easy to picture her as one of those maddening little schoolgirls who always follows directions, who never gets caught whispering to neighbors, who never colors out of lines, and who gets perfect scores on handwriting papers. We never expected that school would be very stimulating for Vita; but we imagined that she'd enjoy being with the other children.

Gradually, though, as she grew older and her personality began to really take shape, our thinking changed. By the time she was four-and-a-half or five, her creative exuberance and the range and extent of her self-motivated projects began to overwhelm us. From the moment she woke up in the morning until she went to bed at night, she kept herself busily involved in one creative activity or another; and since she had never grown accustomed to having somebody else structure much of her time, she always seemed to know, for herself, exactly what she wanted to do next. She spent hours drawing pictures, and, contrary to our expectations, she had no concern for conventional color schemes. With fine-tipped felt pens, she drew people with green hair and bright yellow skin, and she put purple stars in the sky and brown and blue roses in flower gardens. We knew that within a few months of school she'd be coloring blond-haired people, yellow stars in black skies, and red roses with green stems.

Sometimes Vita would get out the scrap bag and make her own rag dolls, complete with embroidered faces and yarn hair. She sewed tiny doll clothes and beaded little necklaces for them. In the shed she built herself a desk and chair out of scrap lumber and stray nails, and once she made an almost edible meal by steaming wild bamboo shoots stuffed with herbs from her herb garden. She kept her vegetable patch weeded, and she had a little flower garden where she transplanted wild flowers from along the roadside. Mostly, they survived. During the winter months, she wrote diaries and spent long periods at her typewriter composing stories and plays (although admittedly, her spelling left a great deal to be desired!).

Then too, Vita was playing the piano for forty-five minutes to an hour a day, and she was beginning to play real music like Bach minuets and pieces by Mozart and Schumann. In addition, she had taken up the violin—after begging us to get her one for almost a year—and she took lessons with a violinist who lived almost an hour's drive away. If she went off to school from eight in the morning until four in the afternoon, she'd be too tired for her music and it would be almost impossible to get her to lessons.

It's true that she was social, and she certainly played hard and happily with her little neighborhood friends; but she also seemed to need time alone each day. She liked to play quietly with her dolls or puzzles, to look at books, or to listen to records. We knew that, in school, children were seldom—if ever —allowed periods of privacy and quiet. It was becoming obvious that school would only be an intrusion into her already highly productive little life.

Still, although we had by then become sure that home was the best place for Vita, we agreed that she had a right to try school and see for herself what she thought of it. But by the time she was five, she was already making herself quite clear: "I don't want to go to school, because if Ishmael didn't like it, I know I won't." Her decision came as a relief to us, although we never fooled ourselves into thinking that we hadn't influenced her judgment. How could we have helped it? Although we imagined that someday, in a more independent frame of mind, she might possibly want to do the normal thing and go to school, for the time being we were committed to keeping her home. As with Ishmael before her, we had to get permission from the school board.

This time the situation was somewhat different, since the state had recently adopted some permanent home-schooling regulations in place of the temporary guidelines that had been in force when we first took Ishmael out of school. Fortunately, we were in a stronger position now, too—Bob had been the "parent representative" on the committee that developed the regulations, and he knew them inside out.

So, as Vita began looking forward to a big birthday party and a chocolate cheesecake piled high with strawberries, we began getting organized. We had to renegotiate Ishmael's evaluation process to make it more in line with the new regulations: "the sensitivity and needs of the child should be duly considered . . ." We also had to write a lengthy application requesting permission to teach Vita at home.

Since we had until June to write Vita's application, we first dealt with Ishmael's evaluation. For Bob and me, Ishmael's writing, reading, piano playing, and smiling face were the things we looked at when we assessed our school at home. Actually the word "assess" is too formalistic to describe what we did, since we ordinarily took things minute by minute and day by day. With only two children to work with and observe, it was easy to know exactly what they were doing and how they were feeling about it. Our brains were constantly cataloging away little facts, consciously or unconsciously, like the words Ishmael misspelled, the new words Vita learned how to read, and the multiplication tables that Ishmael found easy or difficult. And of course, when the kids were happy, we were happy. When they were unhappy, or went through unproductive periods, we always tried to figure out why, and what could be done about it.

Although we had no personal need for a formal end-of-the-year evaluation for Ishmael, we could understand why the school (and the state) wanted to evaluate him. They didn't live with Ishmael the way we did, and from what we understood of the law, it was their responsibility to make sure that he was receiving an adequate education. What we were concerned about, though, was that if Ishmael did have to be evaluated, then the evaluation ought to be based entirely on our curriculum and on the types of things that he was learning. In the past, at *our* suggestion, the school authorities had looked over our school books and materials, had talked to Ishmael and looked over samples of his writing, artwork, and math, and they had looked at my "portfolio," which was basically a journal of our day-to-day activities. Unfortunately, as I mentioned in an earlier chapter, our school board also had written its own home-schooling regulations which had required a far lengthier evaluation. For the past two years we had allowed Ishmael to be evaluated in that elaborate manner, despite the fact that his "needs and sensitivities" were never taken into consideration. The classroom teachers had tested him on the skills *they* taught in their classrooms, not on the material we taught Ishmael, and we felt intimidated by having Ishmael's abilities and knowledge judged so harshly in terms of percentiles on the standardized test. True, all the other school children had to take the test, but their test results usually just gathered dust in their files. In Ishmael's case it was much different. School board members discussed his test scores among themselves; they compared them from one year to another while making comments like, "Look, Ishmael went from a 98% to a 94% in reading comprehension," or "He's doing better in math. Didn't he only get a 78% last year? This year he's scored in the 84th percentile." It all would have made sense if those test scores had accurately reflected Ishmael's progress or decline, but they didn't.

With the new regulations in hand, then, Bob and I decided to propose to the school authorities that our portfolio, along with two home visits a year by a school administrator (but not a teacher, since we felt the urgent need of some continuity from year to year), should be the primary methods of evaluating Ishmael. As an added extra, we decided to offer to work with the school authorities to devise a "teacher-made" test based solely on our curriculum; we would administer it to Ishmael once a year, just to please and placate them. An evaluation like that would be perfectly in line with the state regulations, since they didn't require standardized tests.

Besides having the new regulations to work with, we also had a new superintendent and assistant superintendent. Bob and I, with hopes of winning them over to our side, decided to talk all this over with them before we presented our proposal to the school board.

Our meeting with Mr. S. and Mr. L. went well. For one thing, they were quite businesslike. They said exactly what they meant, and they didn't have the "Why don't you move," mentality of the former superintendent. They knew that it was part of their job to deal with us, and they wanted to do their job as efficiently as possible. The other reason the meeting went so well was that Bob and I were now in the position of being the experts. Bob had helped to write the new regulations; we understood them better than almost anyone in the state; and we had been teaching Ishmael at home for almost three years and could speak from experience. Mr. S. and Mr. L., on the other hand, were new to the whole thing. Mr. L. quite frankly admitted, "I've been working in the public schools for twenty years now, and I've never come across this kind of education before."

Bob first went over the regulations with them, section by section. Next, he went back over the key phrases in the section on evaluation and explained how the state intended that parents and school authorities should work together to come up with mutually acceptable plans of evaluation, rather than leaving it solely to the school boards to dictate the terms of evaluation (as had happened in our case).

Then it was time to get down to the specifics of our proposal for Ishmael's evaluation. I began by explaining our objections to standardized tests and to the use of teacher-administered tests from school. The superintendent listened closely, and he even seemed to agree with much of what I said. He nodded when I explained that standardized tests only measured how good children were at taking tests, and that the score was meaningless anyway unless averaged over a number of years and then compared with the scores of other children *in similar situations*. And he seemed to understand when I explained that I couldn't discover Ishmael's real areas of strength and weakness from the test, since there were too many variables involved in the actual phrasing of the questions and the process he had to go through in order to mark the correct answers on the answer sheet.

As I was winding down, Mr. S. picked up where I left off. He explained that many teachers he'd talked with agreed with me about the tests. They mainly looked at the average test scores of whole classes so that if one class, for example, scored extremely low in math, the teacher could re-evaluate her math program and correct any areas of weakness. Despite his apparent agreement, though, he finally turned to Mr. L. and said, "But I think Ishmael should take the test anyway."

Obviously, it was time that I put forth our proposal for a different kind of evaluation procedure for Ishmael. Both Mr. S. and Mr. L. thought that it would be fine to dispense with the use of classroom teachers to evaluate Ishmael, and Mr. L. liked the idea of doing the job himself. He agreed that he'd get an excellent idea of what we were doing by visiting us, looking over my portfolio, and talking to Ishmael. But when I mentioned our proposed "homemade" test, Mr. S. was quick to point out its absurdity, and rightly so. "Why bother to give a test like that," he asked, "when you can get all the information you need by looking over Ishmael's work?" And then he said again, "I think Ishmael should take the standardized test," adding, "if only as test-taking practice. After all, Ishmael may want to go back to school some day and in that case he'll need to know how to take tests. Besides," he went on temptingly, "you could use the test-results for diagnostic purposes." So that was it—he wanted Ishmael to have a little dose of normality once a year, just for practice. Bob and I looked at each other in relief.

After that it was easy. We arranged that Ishmael would take the test once a year; I would give it to him myself at the kitchen table, without a lot of fuss or bother. Mr. S. and Mr. L. would see the results of the test, but they agreed not to use them against us (or for us, for that matter), since our evaluation would be based solely on Ishmael's day-to-day work. Finally, as an extra touch of normality, I asked that I be shown a copy of the test well before Ishmael took it, since all classroom teachers had that same privilege. Then I could prepare Ishmael in advance for what to expect. They agreed.

Bob and I left feeling really good about this arrangement. We knew, of course, that Mr. S. and Mr. L. would unofficially take an interest in Ishmael's test scores, but we didn't mind, as long as they didn't turn them into a big deal. Besides, the standardized test wouldn't be nearly so bad if Ishmael could take it at home. We had to admit, too, that our homemade test would have been quite a hassle to prepare.

Knowing that our relationship with the school board was shaky at best, Mr. S. offered to present our proposal to the board himself. He knew that it would be a bit tricky, since the board's own home-schooling regulations were in such opposition to the state's; he would have to explain, as gently as possible, that theirs were now obsolete. And, of course, our proposed plan of evaluation was quite different from the one they had formerly required.

Mr. S. did take our proposal to the board. In the middle of his presentation, however, a violent thunderstorm erupted. Between the cracks of thunder and the pounding of the rain on the roof, discussion was almost impossible. Nonetheless, Mr. S. reported to us that he *thought* the school board had agreed to let us go ahead with our plan, and so we did.

On the appointed day, Mr. L. brought the test over to our house and helped Ishmael and me get started—"as a formality, so no one can accuse us of um . . . well . . . not doing things properly." Seated at the kitchen table, we read over the instructions together. I put the clock in full view, since most of the test sections were timed, sharpened some pencils for Ishmael, and began. Mr. L. sat and watched as I read out, in a firm teacher's voice, "Open your test booklet to page one . . ." and Ishmael listened like a dutiful student.

Vocabulary was first. I read an incomplete sentence aloud and Ishmael was to mark the answer (one out of four possibilities) that best completed the sentence. He had a wonderful time since he found his choice of responses so funny, and so rich in material for thought: "A scholar is someone who has— (a) knowledge, (b) money, (c) students, (d) friends," or, "A person is an— (a) object, (b) image, (c) individual, (d) event." Ha! We were both chortling, but Mr. L. looked a bit uneasy. Was it okay to laugh in the middle of a standardized test, I could see him wondering to himself.

Soon, though, I stopped laughing and began to feel sad. With each problem I gave Ishmael, he first let his mind go, free associating, or just musing, for a second or two. "A person is an—?" Well, there was Grandpop, who always wondered if there would be a world when he was dead. Were people and things just images in his brain, he used to wonder. Was a tomato red when he wasn't there to see it? And then there was Bob, who had written a paper called, "The Concept of a Person," about the three "persons" of the Trinity—God the Father, the Son, and the Holy Ghost. They obviously weren't individuals, since they each made up an integral part of the Trinity. But if they weren't individuals, were they objects, events, or images? Thoughts like these floated happily through Ishmael's mind, but all too soon he had to snap himself out of his reverie and get down to business. "Now what answer do they want?" he thought, and he marked down "individual" on his answer sheet.

When Vocabulary was done with, Mr. L. got up to leave, satisfied that we'd manage fine on our own. I arranged to bring the completed test to his office the next day so that he could score it, and we agreed to go over it together to see if there were any big weaknesses on Ishmael's part that I should strive to correct. As I watched him walk out the door to his car, big drops of rain began falling on the path. Well, I thought, if we are going to have to waste a day on this stuff, it might as well be a rainy one.

Reading Comprehension was next. Then came Word Study Skills, Spelling, Listening, and Language. Ishmael spent until late afternoon reading dull paragraphs and pieces of stories and answering absurd and often irrelevant questions about them. He had to circle misspelled words, look at parts of words and analyze their sounds, capitalize proper nouns, put the proper punctuation in run-on sentences, and do two pages of "dictionary skills" without even using a real dictionary. I, meanwhile, fumed and paced the floor like a caged panther. The so-called skills on this test had virtually no relevance to real life outside of school. Certainly they had no relevance to our curriculum. We read whole books and stories without run-on sentences or misspellings, wrote whole words and sentences—not to mention poems, stories, and plays—and looked up real words in a real dictionary. Ishmael had grown up loving words—caressing them, really—letting their sounds roll off his tongue, delighting in their meanings, and marveling at their powers to communicate thoughts and feelings. Yet on this test he was being forced to view words as mere objects to master, or even "attack."

He was bored and droopy most of the time, but as with his chuckles over the vocabulary section, he did find more to laugh about than I did. At one point, for example, I heard him say happily to himself, "This is fun! It's the kind of thing you find on the puzzle page of the Sunday papers!" Curiously, I looked over his shoulder and saw that he was confronting a page of forty-eight problems on "Word Study Skills" that looked like this:

1. a. turn, b. re, c. de, d. N.
2. a. en, b. how, c. driv, d. N.
3. a. won, b. er, c. ish, d. N.

On his answer sheet he had to mark the syllable "a," "b," or "c" that *didn't* combine with the others to form a word, and if none of the syllables formed a word, he had to mark "N."

Furiously, I thought back to our meeting with Mr. S. and Mr. L. and how they had assured me that this test only tested "the bare minimums." To me, in my innocence, "bare minimums" had implied skills like reading soup labels and filling out forms, not skills for idling away Sunday mornings with the puzzle page of the paper. Ishmael, however, was having a grand time—so grand that he became careless. He forgot that he was supposed to mark the *wrong* answer—the syllable that didn't help to form a word—and instead he began marking the syllable that *did* form a word, like "turn" in "return." And I, playing the role of scrupulously honest tester, didn't dare to set him straight.

Around four o'clock that day, the rain stopped and I sent Ishmael out into the mud to play basketball with Vita. The next day, early, we began on the second half of the test—math. It was divided into three sections, "Concepts," "Computation," and "Applications." Ishmael, naturally enough, was dreading it. But "Applications," which means "word problems," wasn't too bad, and he found the section on concepts interesting. Although he was still dreadfully slow with his math facts, he had a greater understanding of the world of numbers than I had imagined, and he enjoyed abstract problems like:

1. $a + b = c$, therefore (a) $a = b$, (b) $c - b = a$,
   (c) $a - b = c$, (d) $c = b = a$.
2. $8 \div n = 4$ if (a) $4 + n = 8$, (b) $4 \times n = 8$,
   (c) $4 + 4 = 8$ (d) $4 - n = 8$.

The computation part was awful, though—not just because Ishmael found multiplication and division so hard, but because figuring out and then remembering how to mark the correct answer on the answer sheet was so tough. With this part of the test, I did interfere, just to keep Ishmael from total frustration. I showed him how to keep his scratch paper neat so that he could keep his problems in order, rubbed his back, and gave him a few little exercise breaks. Shortly after lunch, we finished.

After congratulating Ishmael on his valiant efforts, I drove off to take the test back to Mr. L. Unfortunately Mr. L. wasn't in, so I left the test on his desk, came back home, and joined Ishmael in the mud for some basketball.

Three or four days later, Mr. L. called and read off Ishmael's test scores to me. Ishmael really couldn't have done better. His math scores had improved dramatically, and his score for the entire test was in the ninety-ninth percentile. Mr. L. was impressed, but he nonetheless felt he ought to give me some advice. His biggest concern was the "Listening" section where Ishmael's score had fallen down a bit (to 92%). "You know," he said, "developing good listening skills in children is essential, and we have to work on them just like math or language skills. The first thing you ought to be doing is to make it clear to Ishmael that you will only be giving him directions once, from now on, so he'd better start listening closely to you . . ." I listened politely and kept my mouth shut. But perhaps I should have pointed out that Ishmael was the kind of child who could go to a concert and then come home and play the main themes he had just heard on our piano, and who could listen to Bob read a book and then come and recount every last detail to me, often word for word. Perhaps Ishmael's problem wasn't his listening skills but the fact that the paragraphs that I had had to read to him in that section of the test were so incredibly boring.

Anyway, from there Mr. L. went on a bit about "word attack skills." I'm not sure why, since Ishmael had attacked words so well on the test that he had scored in the 96th percentile. He had chopped words up, torn out their insides, and patched them together. There was no problem there, and Mr. L. knew it. Finally, though, he hit on a real problem. Ishmael's twos were terrible—they looked like eights. "You really ought to do something about that," he said. He was right, but I felt resentful. When Ishmael was three or four, I had shown him how to make a simple, old-fashioned "2," but when he entered first grade, he had been made to unlearn it and start making ornate "2's" that had a nasty habit of looking like eights when written quickly by little boys.

Aside from those gripes, mentioned more out of duty than anything else, Mr. L. didn't have much to report. Although I'm sure that he would have let me go over the test results in more detail if I had asked him to, I didn't. Frankly, I didn't care about the test. I knew that Ishmael read and enjoyed books, wrote stories and plays, and generally loved learning new things, and that was all I did care about.

With Ishmael's test over with, we now had to turn our attention to getting permission to teach Vita at home. Intellectually, I knew we had nothing to worry about. In the first place, we were now experienced home-schoolers, and Ishmael was obviously thriving; secondly, not only was Bob an acknowledged "expert" on the interpretation of the term "manifest educational hardship," but he had gained the respect of several top bureaucrats at the State Department of Education, who we were pretty sure would stand behind us (as much as they could without jeopardizing their jobs, of course). The only possible snag we could think of was a statement in the *old* school board regulations which read: "All students to be eligible for consideration for a Home Tutorial Program shall have attended school for at least 30 days." We knew that Mr. S., however, had already explained to the school board that the new state regulations superseded the old ones, and we assumed that there wouldn't be a problem.

But while I could give myself all kinds of reasons why we'd have no problem keeping Vita out of school, emotionally, I could already feel her being pulled away from me by the State, the School Board, and the Superintendent. While most people were passively turning their six-year-olds over to the schools for most of each day, I had the feeling that Vita was being wrenched out of my arms. Once again, the old anxieties from Ishmael's school days returned. Sometimes I sat and just watched as Vita played. She was tiny—she couldn't have weighed more than thirty pounds, and she had the skinniest legs I'd ever seen on a well-fed child. Her cheeks were rosy, though; her eyes sparkled, and when she was happy she bounced around as though gravity couldn't hold her down. I couldn't imagine her in school. Meanwhile, Bob kept repeating, as though to convince himself, too, "There's nothing to worry about. We'll write the longest, most thorough application they've ever seen, and they'll have no choice but to give us permission." And that's just what we did, although we found out later that for a while, anyway, the school board had thought that it did have a choice in the matter.

Once we got started, it really didn't take us too long to write the application, despite the fact that we wrote far more than was required. The most important part of the regulations was the section on "manifest educational hardship," since it was the presence of a supposed hardship which would be the key to getting permission to teach Vita at home. We had the choice of either claiming that Vita had some kind of physical or mental problem that prevented her from attending school *or* that the educational benefits she would receive at home were great enough so that she would suffer *hardship* if she were denied those benefits by being forced to attend school instead. Naturally, we chose to address this second type of hardship. The regulations stated that, "In demonstrating the special benefits to be derived by the child in the proposed home-education program, one or more of the following quality indicators may be considered." There followed descriptions of nine possible indicators that made some pretty dense reading for any ordinary person innocent of educator's jargon. Words and phrases like, "stated learning objectives," "interaction with peers and adults," "developmental characteristics," and "specific competencies," dotted this section. Despite our dislike of this lingo, though, we decided to play it extra-safe and claim that our school had all nine of the "qualities" listed, although only "one or more" were actually required or meant to be considered.

While taking care to express our educational philosophy in a form that we hoped even the school board could stomach, we systematically tried to be as long-winded as we possibly could be. "Never say in one word what you can say in two" was our motto, since we knew that most people are impressed by length. Even more importantly, without in any way being dishonest, we made Vita look like an exceptional child in an exceptional family. We did this by mentioning *everything* that might look impressive. Most people are so unobservant that they just don't notice all the terrific things that they and their children do; we, on the contrary, by being detailed, made ourselves look great. Finally, we never mentioned our college degrees. This was partly because my *lack* of a college degree would then become obvious, but mainly because we knew that even with Bob's two Master's degrees, the school people wouldn't consider him qualified—he would need a degree in Early Childhood and Elementary Education before he'd ever be up to their mark. Instead, we tried to make it clear that we felt that the qualifications for home-teachers had nothing to do with degrees but instead involved a love of children and learning, and a multitude of different life experiences and skills. And actually, thanks to my perfect typing job (which was painful) and the appearance I always gave of having complete confidence in my educational philosophy (at least when talking before the school board), I got the feeling that everyone not only assumed that I had gone to college, but suspected that it had been one of those Eastern "snob" schools like Radcliffe or Sarah Lawrence.

Altogether, our application was seventeen pages long, but unfortunately we still had more paper work to do. We had to write Ishmael's year-end evaluation and home-study renewal application. By that time, though, we had become so fluent in application writing that we whipped off eight pages in one evening. The next day we dropped everything off at the superintendent's office (packaged in a large book bag, no less), and then took a much needed vacation.

About a week later a close friend and neighbor dropped a few casual words which threw us into complete turmoil. She was the town reporter for the local paper, and a few days previously she had been at a school board meeting where we had been discussed. Mr. L. had apparently mentioned that he had received a "well-written application from the Wallaces" to teach Vita at home and one of the board members had piped up, with reference to their old home-schooling regulations, "I thought Vita had to go to school for thirty days before the Wallaces could apply for permission to keep her home." Well, there was our snag, and, according to our neighbor, Mr. L. had done nothing to set the board member straight. In fact, our neighbor said, the board had instructed Mr. L. to call and inform us that Vita would have to start school in September. Obviously he was taking his time about performing such a distasteful duty.

The next day Bob called the New Hampshire Civil Liberties

Union lawyer who had been on the Home-Education Committee with him, and also called Charles Marston at the State Department of Education. Both of them reaffirmed what Bob and I already felt pretty sure of—that our school board's regulation's were obsolete and that our application for Vita could only be considered under the new state regulations. They also reassured us by hinting that our school board was being ridiculous, if not outright cruel. Next, Bob called Mr. L., who mumbled something about being sorry he hadn't called us and explained that he had been waiting until he could get his hands on a copy of the school board's old regulations to see for himself what they said. After some discussion, Bob suggested that he call Charlie Marston and talk the situation over with him. Mr. L. agreed.

On re-reading my diary, I see that for the next three weeks, while waiting for the school board meeting where everything would be resolved for better or for worse, I was a bundle of nerves. There are few things worse than waiting around for a group of completely unsympathetic people to make a decision about your own child. Throughout the day I would make up sample scenarios for the meeting, and I made myself practice answering the most difficult questions I could think of. "Why is it that you can't seem to 'let go' of Vita like all normal mothers?" "What provision have you made for teaching her how to play with other children?" "Why haven't you been more specific about your goals and objectives for Vita? And why don't you keep weekly lesson plans?"

The worst part about those three weeks of waiting, though, was the loneliness. When we had taken Ishmael out of school, most of our friends and neighbors had been sympathetic since he had been so obviously miserable. Experimenting with home-schooling had seemed to them like a reasonable short-term solution. But we were past the experimental stage now, and Vita was neither miserable nor (what they would have considered) exceptionally bright. Nobody seemed to have any doubt that she'd fit in perfectly at school. Hence, the casual way our reporter friend had mentioned that the school board wanted to insist that Vita go to school for thirty days. Since she was not particularly sympathetic with the idea of home-schooling, it had just never occurred to her that it would be misery for us to be forced to send Vita to school—even for such a short period of time. Also, I noticed that many of my other friends seemed to be anxious to avoid talking about our plans to teach Vita at home, even though they knew the subject was foremost in my mind. And for me, of course, it was painful to be able to talk about only cabbage seedlings and manure with them when I was so worried about Vita.

On the third of June, the day before the school board meeting, I was surprised to get a call from Mrs. H., the chairman of the board. "I thought you might be feeling nervous about the meeting tomorrow night," she said, "and so I just called to reassure you." She went on to say that Mr. L. had called her to explain that Charlie Marston at the State Department of Education had told him that the board could not demand that Vita go to school for thirty days, and that, overall, the new state regulations superseded the board's old ones. Mr. L. had then asked Mrs. H. to convey the information to the rest of the board so that no one would make a fool of himself at the meeting by trying to insist upon something that had no legal standing. Mrs. H. had just called each board member and she told me their reactions. Two were very pleased at the news and had been planning on asking the board to waive its thirty-day requirement in Vita's case anyway since, as one of them said, "I couldn't honestly deny the fact that Vita will receive a better education at home." Another member had said resignedly, "Well, I guess we can't fight it," and the last had simply growled in disgust. Tallying up the votes, it was obvious that with Mrs. H's apparent support we had nothing to worry about.

But somehow, I couldn't get myself to feel the elation I had expected to experience. Walking into the meeting knowing that we had a majority on our side was a lot better than not knowing what to expect, but I guess I really wanted more than that. I wanted the whole board to admit that we were doing a *terrific* job with our kids and to be interested in our approach to education. After all, there was a lot that the public schools could have learned from us. What disturbed me the most was that not only were two of the board members completely uninterested in what we were doing but they seemed to want the kids to go to school no matter what. When I wrote about this to John Holt, he responded with some very insightful remarks that I'll never forget. "One of the saddest things I've learned in my life," he said, "one of the things I least wanted to believe and resisted believing for as long as I could, was that people in chains don't want to get them off, but want to get them *on* everyone else. 'Where are your chains?' they want to know. 'How come you're not wearing chains? Do you think you are too good to wear them? What makes you think you're so special?'"

Not having been able to find a babysitter, we took the kids to the school board meeting the next evening and left them in an empty science classroom to watch fish swimming around in aquariums while we went into the library where the meeting was to be held. First on the agenda was a discussion of the school's fire extinguishing system with the town's fire chief. It turned out that the school's system was not only inadequate but that, in the kitchen, it could have *caused* a fire. The school board was obviously a bit taken aback when the fire chief explained that it would cost about $1,000 to bring the system up to standard, and it soon became clear that the board preferred to take its chances rather than to spend that kind of money. As one board member put it, "Look, there are all kinds of people making requests for money—the reading program wants an extra $1,000, special education needs money, and the art teacher is ready to quit unless her allowance for art materials is increased. We are constantly having to play 'bad guys' as we scrimp and save to please the taxpayers, so we'll just have to look at this expense like all the others and see which programs or building improvements most deserve the money." With unanimous nods, the board members decided to delay any decision about the fire extinguishing system. As he was getting up to leave, the fire chief said, "This building is already a fire trap and if you decide not to improve the fire extinguishing system you may never have to worry about the reading program or special education again, because you may end up with no school and no students, just a charred ruin."

With that, it was our turn. Mr. L. opened his folder on us, held up all our nicely typed paper work, and explained that we were requesting permission to teach Ishmael at home for another year and had also submitted a request to teach Vita at home. Dead silence. Finally, one of the sympathetic board members began asking Mr. L. questions, more as a formality than anything else. Had Mr. L. evaluated us, and by what means? Was Ishmael keeping up with his grade level? Was Mr. L. satisfied with his progress? Mr. L. answered briefly, but favorably, and then the board member moved that our request to teach Ishmael at home be approved. There was a second to the motion and then everyone, looking uncomfortable but resigned, voted in our favor. Then it was time to discuss Vita. Mr. L. flipped through our seventeen pages a few times and said that it was his opinion that we were offering Vita a quality education and that according to the state regulations we should be given permission to teach her at home. Once again the same board member made the motion to approve our application; but this time, rather than voting unanimously, two of the board members sourly abstained.

It was all over before we knew it. We were free for another year and Vita was now a bona-fide home-schooler! Vita, who had had perfect confidence all along in our ability to keep her out of school, was more interested in the fish than hearing about the meeting; but Ishmael, who had experienced school, was jubilant—for himself as well as for Vita. I felt less tired and bitter watching his joy. He was right, of course. I had to forget about the school people and make the most of our freedom. And with Vita and Ishmael bouncing around, I knew it wouldn't be too hard.

Chapter 6

More School
at Home

During our third week of school, when Vita was in "first grade" and Ishmael in "fifth," I wrote to John Holt:

September is here and with it comes "school." The other day a friend asked me whether I would still do schoolwork with Vita and Ishmael if I didn't have the public school people looking over my shoulder. Often I try to tell myself that I believe in "organic learning"—that given the freedom, the kids will learn all they need to know on their own—and that the only reason we do organized school work is because I worry about what the school people would think of us if we didn't. But the real truth is that "school" adds some important structure to our lives, since it gives me, and Bob too, the excuse to stop our own work and spend a few hours each day with all our attention focused on the kids. We are such busy people ourselves—Bob is desperately trying to finish his book, get in the wood, and paint the house, while I have the garden to harvest, the housework to do, and my music and writing— that we could very easily lose track of Vita and Ishmael in the rush of our everyday lives. School gives us the opportunity to relax and enjoy the kids while they are young. And it is so exciting to watch them learn!

For a while, particularly during August when the garden was smothered in weeds and we had a constant stream of house guests, I wondered how I would ever fit school into my already overflowing schedule. Would I have to give up my writing and piano? I dreaded the thought. Then too, I was a bit worried about Vita. She was so obstinately independent that I feared that she'd never be willing to sit down and learn to spell, write neatly, or use a dictionary. Ishmael had learned all those things with a minimum of help, but he was so much more intellectual than Vita. And Vita's dancing, music, and art were not talents that the school people particularly valued. How would she do on the standardized test? I couldn't help wondering.

Having Vita in "school" was definitely eye-opening, but it was not the struggle I had feared it would be. While she was certainly strong-willed, she had never even spent a day in school and she had never learned how to be bored or how to dislike everything connected with school-type subjects. Instead, her mind was like a vacuum cleaner, intent on sucking up as much information as it would hold. She insisted on learning things in her own special way, though, and I was constantly startled by the inventive ways she took the lessons I gave her and twisted them around to suit herself.

Take the calendar I asked her to make during our first week of school, for example. I was concerned because she was still writing her numbers backwards. Having her make a calendar at the beginning of each month seemed like a fun way for her to practice writing them correctly, but Vita didn't see it that way at all. She had no interest in making numbers correctly, and I didn't have the heart to insist that she fill in the calendar my way. Instead, I watched in amazement as she drew elaborate pictures in each calendar square with her new felt pens and pastels. Her September calendar was without a doubt one of the most beautiful I'd ever seen. But beyond that, it had sparked her interest in time and time-keeping. She asked questions about the days of the week, weekdays, weekends, and holidays, and she began keeping track of when her dancing, gymnastics, and music lessons were. She wanted to know why each month didn't begin on a Sunday, and she became so interested in the history of time-keeping that Bob read her parts of a book on the history of calendars. She continued to write her numbers backwards, but the experience greatly diminished my anxieties about the standardized test. Why should I worry about whether Vita was learning certain specialized (and relatively unimportant) skills at age six when she was so eager to learn far more important things, like how we measure time? Watching her, I was reminded of a lecture in which Carol Bigler, a Suzuki piano teacher, said, "I tell parents, 'Your children are perfect, only you can make mistakes.'" It seemed like kind of a far-out statement at the time, but now it began to make sense. Vita knew what she wanted and needed to learn far better than I did, and I had to trust her.

I loved being part of the learning that went on at the kitchen table. When Ishmael recited his multiplication tables, "$8 \times 2 = 16$, $8 \times 3 = 24$, $8 \times 4 = 32$," Vita mimicked him, only backwards: "$2 \times 8 = 16$, $3 \times 8 = 24$, $4 \times 8 = 32$." Once, hoping to improve his descriptive and observational skills, I asked Ishmael to describe a tomato. He delighted me by writing, "This unearthly tomato is made of three gigantic bulges and reminds me of a bureaucrat, except that it doesn't have a tie."

As much as I enjoyed the kids, I didn't have a lot of time to just sit around the kitchen table with them indulging myself. If I was ever going to fit music and writing into my day, I had to get the family running on a tight schedule and stick to it— which is what I did. At six-thirty every morning I would begin nudging Bob. By twenty of seven, I had tumbled him out of bed and was clattering around getting breakfast in the kitchen and making enough noise to wake up the kids. By eight at the latest, we had eaten and done the chores, and I had piled the school books on the table. "School" was ready to begin. While I helped Ishmael with his multiplication, Vita wrote stories or lists of rhyming words, or drew pictures in her "something-to-do" notebook, a small sketch pad I had given her at the beginning of the year. In it I had made up easy crossword puzzles, anagrams, and codes for her to crack; but mostly I had left the pages blank for her to fill with drawings and short stories. While she worked on her abacus, Ishmael painted or did his handwriting. And while both kids collected leaves for collages or wrote letters, I squeezed in some time at the piano.

Around nine or nine-thirty, when I felt that they were really wide awake and the house was toasty-warm, it was time to get to work on the piano and violin. By then we had two pianos, so both kids often played at the same time while I ran back and forth helping them with any difficult spots. Ishmael, who was really playing a lot by that time, was working on a Mozart concerto and an easy Beethoven sonata. It was heavenly to listen to him. And Vita was playing some lovely little pieces by Mozart and Schumann and a sonatina by Beethoven. Afterwards, Vita and I would have a violin lesson together. I was now teaching her myself, since her former teacher had become too busy concertizing. Every day she played the Suzuki literature that she had already learned on the piano, and in the evenings I studied a book on how to teach Suzuki violin to young children. More fun than playing Suzuki pieces was the improvising we did together with me playing the piano or my old viola from my school days.

After music, the most formal part of our "school" was over with for the day. But the learning didn't stop by any means. Vita would flop down on the dining room rug with books, or type on Bob's old typewriter. Sometimes Ishmael spent hours reading books on chess and replaying famous games by the masters. He also wrote plays, and he would often come to me for criticism. Almost every day both kids played with their doll game in their bedroom. They helped the doll populace to write up laws, incarcerate prisoners of war, and keep the doll economy from falling into the clutches of inflation. Often Vita drew, sewed, and painted, and both she and Ishmael rode bikes and shot their homemade bows and arrows.

Going to town was also educational. Ishmael liked to hang around in the library while I did my shopping. He especially enjoyed walking there himself from Main Street. At home we didn't have any challenging roads he could cross, since we lived so far out in the country, but town offered some terrific challenges—particularly since cars hardly ever stopped for pedestrians in crosswalks. Although I was always nervous about letting him cross the street alone, I knew he had to learn sometime, and so I reluctantly let him go off feeling grown-up and free.

Vita, meanwhile, stayed with me while I shopped. Shopping was usually a perfect occasion for a math lesson. One day, for example, we went to the shoe store. I bought a twenty-five dollar pair of shoes and handed the salesperson two twenty-dollar bills. When I asked Vita if she could tell me how much money the two twenties made together, she thought hard for a second or two; then she divided one of the twenties into two tens and counted, "20 (the first twenty), 30, 40. Twenty and twenty is forty!" Then I asked her how much change she thought I ought to get back. First she divided 25 into 20 + 5 and figured out that the five would have to come from my second twenty-dollar bill. Then, counting by fives, she discovered that there were four fives in twenty and reasoned that, if the saleswoman had a right to one of the fives, then I should get the remaining three back. By counting out, "5, 10, 15" on her fingers, she was then able to figure out my change. "Fifteen!" she said triumphantly.

Just going outside was educational, too. Once, for example, when Vita and Ishmael helped me harvest the squash and pumpkins, they found a beautiful green monarch butterfly chrysalis hanging from the underside of a squash leaf. We put it outside the front door and watched day by day as the outer skin appeared to thin and become transparent. Finally, we could see the orange and black markings of the butterfly curled up inside, and the next day it broke free and unfurled its wings to dry in the sun. Then, after a few agonizing hours (for me anyway, who always seems to want to play the role of meddling midwife), it flew away.

We had far too many squashes, so the kids decided to haul a cartful up to the main road and try to sell them. They were eager to earn some money, since they were saving up to buy a guitar. Soon they had made a small fortune in the squash business. Ordinarily, they kept very strict accounts, but this time they collected nickels and dimes so fast that they had a terrible time straightening out what they called "the finances." They both started yelling and screaming at each other. So, to calm them down, I showed them how to use a calculator to count out their money. Thanks to the squash business, they also met a lot of interesting people at their roadside stand and learned how to handle themselves in business dealings with customers.

At three o'clock each afternoon I went into my room and closed the door. Having finished most of my work at the piano by then, I spent the next two hours reading and writing. No one dared to interrupt me, and it was now Bob's turn to look after the kids. On the days when they had classes in town, Bob drove them in and picked them up. Sometimes he read French with Ishmael or listened while Vita read aloud to him, but usually he just made himself available—out in the woodpile or in his study—in case they needed him. The time he had set aside to have "school" with them didn't come until after supper, when he and the kids did science and history together.

Actually, these two subjects—as "formal" subjects—were the ones that we felt most uncomfortable with. True, I had spent a delightful six months studying Indians with Ishmael when he was in second grade. Despite our fun, though, and despite the fact that Ishmael learned an incredible amount, I had begun to see (almost from the beginning) that what I had planned on doing was either crazy or at least practically impossible. Although he enjoyed reading with me in the afternoons, his mind leapt so far ahead of mine and went off on so many tangents as he made connections between remote historical events, that all my careful planning had gone down the drain. We never managed to cover even half of the material on my prepared curriculum; and yet, through his own reading, Ishmael had learned more than most schoolchildren do in history classes over the course of three or four years. In the end, rather than acting as a "teacher," I had mostly just helped Ishmael to find the books and articles he needed and had answered as many of his questions as I could. During the next two years we had carried on like that—writing vague curriculums to please the school board, but basically letting Ishmael's mind range over all the material that interested him while giving him whatever encouragement he needed.

Our experience with science had been somewhat different. Once a week Ishmael and Vita had had a nature lesson with Jenny Wright. Although Vita just loved the lessons, Ishmael had usually seemed indifferent—well, indifferent to the actual lessons, although not to Jenny, whom he really seemed to like. I knew that he was picking up the names of a few trees and flowers, and I knew that he was developing a close relationship with Jenny; but I couldn't exactly claim that it was very successful as a science class. Although I noticed, when I watched and listened carefully, that the kids learned all kinds of science just through their everyday experience and reading, it was easy for me to go blind with guilt as I imagined fancy science classrooms filled with test tubes, fish tanks, and colorful science textbooks. Bob tried to ease my guilt by doing science experiments with the kids. They enjoyed them, but I doubt that they learned very much. Often Bob felt as if all he was really doing was providing them with a little entertainment, much like a magician performing magic tricks. That was nice of course, but he would have preferred to have taken them hiking or to have gone to a concert with them. After a few weeks, the experiments gradually ceased.

So, we bumbled along. Sometimes we felt more sure of ourselves than at other times, and during our "unsure" periods we often attempted to play teacher. I assigned Ishmael history reports to research and write, I read biographies and history books to Vita, and Bob, as I said, did science experiments. Then, when we had regained our self-confidence, or rather our confidence in the kids' abilities to learn on their own, we would go back to pretty much letting them be.

But then, with my blessings, Bob decided to be more organized—not by planning a curriculum in advance or by acting as an entertainer, but by making himself available for an additional half hour or hour each evening to read books and magazines to Vita and Ishmael on scientific and historical subjects. The kids liked the idea and were eager to spend their evening time with him that way, so it has developed into a regular, ongoing, family ritual.

Bob soon discovered through these evening reading sessions that the sharp distinction that schools make between science and social studies robs both "subjects" of a lot of their potential for exciting children. As he wrote in our school journal:

> After all, what is more fascinating than the *history* of science, including the people who contribute to it, make use of it, resist it, and so on? The idea of the solar system, for example, becomes far more interesting when one realizes how late a discovery it was, what intellectual and imaginative barriers had to be overcome to make it possible, and what social and political upheavals accompanied its introduction. The idea of inertia stands out in sharp relief when one has an idea of the Greek physics—the Greek "world-view"—within which it was unthinkable. Geology and paleontology come alive in the story of Darwin, and so on.
>
> The reverse is also true—within history or anthropology, the history of ideas (including "sciences") and the study of "world-views" are just as exciting as the political and social aspects. That was the way my interest in science was rekindled, after years of being turned off to science and immersed in the "humanities"—especially in philosophy and social theory. But finally I began to realize that to understand philosophy one had to understand its history, and to understand *that* one had to understand its interaction with science. And then I discovered the fascination of the history of science in its own right, in figures like Aristotle, Copernicus, Galileo, Newton, and so on, all of whom, after all, were philosophers as well as scientists!
>
> But until recently I had never thought to explore the possibility that my own kind of interest in science might be one that Vita and Ishmael could get excited about.

So now, with both kids together, he began reading books that combined natural history, social and intellectual history, and geography. For example, *Minn of the Mississippi,* by Holling Clancy Holling, is about a snapping turtle who is born near the headwaters of the Mississippi River and winds up exploring the entire length of the river in the course of her long life. From this book the kids learned about the river's formation, the geology of its basin, the Indians and explorers who used the river, plantation society, and the contemporary residents—birds, animals, and people—who lived along its banks. Other books they read were *The Tree on the Trail,* also by Holling (about the history and geography of the Santa Fe Trail and the Southwest), and Thor Heyerdahl's *Voyages of the Ra* (about how he built a reed boat and sailed it across the Atlantic, as Egyptian or Phoenician sailors might have done).

Usually at around seven-thirty, I read a story to Vita and put her to bed while Bob read more sophisticated books to Ishmael. Once again in our school journal he described one of his more exciting evenings with Ishmael:

Ishmael and I read half of chapter one of T. Goldstein's *The Dawn of Science,* about Pietro Toscanelli, in Florence in 1492, writing to Alfonso V of Portugal (he sent a copy to Columbus) about how it should be possible to sail west to the Indies. Goldstein goes on to sketch the scene in Florence: Lorenzo the Magnificent, his painter friends, and the subsequent debacle with Savonarola. Ishmael knows about Savonarola from his own reading. But he didn't really realize that Leonardo, who was mentioned as the artist/scientist who culminates these developments in Florence, was a painter —he thought of him as an inventor. So we pulled down our art books—the *Louvre* book in particular—found Leonardo's Mona Lisa and Annunciation, and other Italian paintings, and talked about the development of perspective, Mona Lisa's smile, etc. Ishmael doesn't know many dates—he was surprised that Shakespeare and the English "renaissance" came a hundred years later. He wanted to lay out the development of music, parallel to art—he figured that baroque music had begun to develop in the twelfth century when people began to go beyond Gregorian chants. I couldn't help. All in good time, I suppose. But what an exciting session. Nothing is alien—Ishmael said early on, "Is this book about *science*?" His attitude is one of unqualified enthusiasm, which is not what most of our efforts at science usually evoke—polite boredom has been more the rule. Everything we read about is grist for the mill, so why separate things when connections are at least half the fun? I forgot to mention Ishmael's greatest pleasure: pulling out our old book of *Children's Costume from the Old Masters*, which he had already studied and I had never really looked at.

Of course it was inevitable that many of our days were far less orderly than the kind I've just described. If we went to a concert at night, for example, the kids missed their evening of science and social studies; and, since they had stayed up past their bedtimes, I let them sleep late the next morning and didn't bother with schoolwork or much formalized music practice. Then there were the nice days when we dropped everything and took walks or skiing trips. Such interruptions to my routine were welcome, even if I missed my two full hours of peace and quiet in the afternoon. Other times, what we really needed was to be apart for a whole day—since when we are together day in and day out for too long, we tend to feel smothered by each other. One day during that fall, for example, when the kids had been bickering more than usual, Bob took Ishmael with him to the library and Vita and I stayed home together. We had a lovely time playing duets, cooking, and working in the woodpile. I really began to feel as if she were a woman friend spending the day with me. Bob said he enjoyed talking to Ishmael without being interrupted by Vita (who just can't keep quiet when he is around) and that Ishmael had fun learning his way around the library. He got bored towards the end of the day, but then he wandered outside and found a soccer game to watch.

What I hated, though, was having my day interrupted by the

telephone, or by friends who just "dropped in." It was then that I realized how vulnerable I was without a classroom set off from the world where I couldn't be reached. Because I didn't get paid, it was hard to get friends and neighbors to understand that what I did was "work." Sometimes I offended people by telling them I was too busy to chat, but just as often I endured them. It was at times like these that many of my worries about the quality of our teaching arose. Once, after a particularly bad day, I woke up in the middle of the night and began berating Bob for not teaching enough geography—which happened to be a part of our written curriculum for that year. The poor man was groggy and very hard to wake up. I'm sure that for as long as he could he hoped that he was just having a bad dream, but when he finally realized what was going on, he was far more patient than I deserved. He calmed me down in minutes by listing everything he had read to the kids during the past month or two: *National Geographic, Cobblestone* (a history magazine for children), *The Origins of Modern Science,* by Herbert Butterfield, *Benjamin Franklin's Autobiography,* and much more. Although he had read nothing with them that could have strictly been considered straight geography, his list was so impressive that I settled right down and slept late the next morning! Other times I worried that I wasn't keeping up with the chores around the house. The grass would glare up at me and beg to be cut, I felt guilty because I hardly ever made bread or cakes, and the pile of wood I needed to haul onto the back porch would appear to grow day by day (although in reality it was shrinking at a respectable rate).

My greatest worry, however, was not about our teaching or my endless chores; it was about what I perceived as the kids' increasing isolation. It wasn't that they didn't see other children—there were plenty in the neighborhood who often hung about our house—but there were no children that Vita and Ishmael saw regularly with whom they could share the things that really mattered to them. This fact became more and more apparent as their talents and interests formed and grew.

Fortunately, our adult friends helped to fill in the gap. When John Holt came to visit with his cello, for example, the kids immediately brightened up in a way that I seldom saw. Often, I felt sad as I watched them raucously playing trios together: after all, John was only an infrequent visitor to our house, and I wanted to see that same glow on the kids' faces far more often. Then too, when he had the chance, Ishmael used to enjoy talking to our friends about the books he was reading; but he never had an opportunity to experience that rapid "back and forth" that happens when two friends discover that they have both read and loved the same book. Likewise, Vita (who, as I have mentioned, loves to draw and paint) took art classes in town —but the teacher manipulated (or should I say "taught") the classes in a way that encouraged very little real creative expression, and she discouraged the children from talking during class. Perhaps Vita's happiest time painting had been the afternoon she and Bob's sister had spent together messing around with watercolors and talking quietly. But since Bob's sister lived three thousand miles away, we obviously couldn't count on her to enrich Vita's life in that way very often.

For the first couple of years that we had taught Ishmael at home, I hadn't been aware of any emptiness in the kids' lives. School had been so awful for Ishmael, and continued to be such a fresh and painful memory, that we all felt that *anything* was better. In any case, Ishmael had still been experiencing the exhilaration that had come with the sudden freedom to really learn. Then too, he had had Dilly, and, to a certain extent, Vanessa, to play with and talk to. But Dilly had decided to go back to school. Even if he hadn't, I doubt that he and Ishmael would have remained close friends. Although they had a great respect for each other, their interests had diverged. While Dilly spent his time designing solar rockets, Ishmael now busied himself composing operettas and producing them in his little theater.

Vita, meanwhile, had been so little that she had played happily with almost anyone. But that, too, was changing as her interests developed.

Although Bob and I talked a lot about this problem of isolation, the one thing we seemed to be clear about was that school was not the solution. The very nature of its *structure* precluded the kind of social interactions we felt the kids needed. (I say "*we* felt," because neither Vita nor Ishmael ever openly expressed any feelings of loneliness, and I'm sure that they seldom, if ever, felt either lonely or isolated. After all, their lives were very full and busy. In any case, how could they have missed what they had never really experienced?) It's true that we lived in an impoverished working-class community with few, if any, children who could have been considered Ishmael's intellectual peers; but even if the school had been full of them, we knew that the formal school environment would not have been good for him. He didn't need to compete against his classmates for grades, and he didn't need the "stimulation" of assigned projects to work on with other students. Instead, he, and Vita too, needed to *make music* with other children, to play spontaneously with friends as quick and as adventurous as they were, and to get to know children who cared about books and art the way they did. The artificially controlled environment of a school wouldn't have provided them with those kinds of opportunities. Only the real world could do that. But our problem, and the one we pondered often, was just *where* in the real world should we look?

I mention these worries—some obviously more rational than others—because they were a part of our everyday lives. Fortunately, though, they weren't great enough to obscure or dampen our generally cheerful outlook, and, really, we had a lot to be thankful for. Vita and Ishmael were rosy and healthy, they both had a burning desire for knowledge and the self-confidence to feel that the world was waiting for them to explore. Just as importantly, Bob and I had the satisfaction of having the daily opportunity to be a part of our children's lives and to share our lives with them.

Chapter 7

Reading
and Writing

In our house, we have four desks (not including the kitchen table, which is often heaped with papers), two pencil sharpeners, and three typewriters. Hundreds of books sit in five floor-to-ceiling bookshelves and several smaller ones. What we don't have is a television. Is it any wonder, then, that our kids are always reading and writing? Of course not. And quite frankly, there isn't much else to do around here on long winter days or on hot, humid summer ones when you've had your fill of swimming or splitting wood at the woodpile.

It always puts me on edge when people talk about Ishmael as being "gifted." I get even more uptight when they politely inquire whether Vita is "the same" as her brother. No, Vita isn't the same. Her personality is quite different and so are her interests and ways of learning. But most important, neither child is an aberration—a creature born from a normal set of parents but with an extra set of wrinkles on its brain.

True, even I am struck when I see Vita, who is five, happily typing away at a story on the living room floor, or hear Ishmael, at age nine, alluding to Hamlet or Macbeth; but at the same time I know that Bob and I had a lot to do with the way the kids are—they weren't born that way. (I must also thank the former owners of our house, who left boxes of books in the attic, and

Bob's mother, who bought children's books like a maniac when he and his sister were little, and who has, over the years, shipped most of them to us.)

Now if Ishmael had become a math whiz while growing up in this house, which was almost barren of numbers before we took him out of school, I'd seriously begin thinking about "gifted-ness" or brain wrinkles, but that never happened. Instead, we are raising two normal kids who happen to enjoy reading and writing—so much so, that I don't have to worry much about teaching them those subjects. They learn mostly through their own enthusiasm.

Neither Ishmael nor Vita slept through the night until they were about three or four years old. Not only did they liven up at around midnight, but they always insisted on company. Poor Bob and I, exhausted and cranky, would refuse to play and then roll over and attempt to doze. But sleep was impossible with a child bouncing around in our room and on our bed.

Finally, we managed to hit upon a fairly satisfactory compro-mise. Ishmael first, and later Vita, would sit in bed and listen as Bob and I took turns reading to them. We read thick books with few pictures in the hopes of boring them to sleep. When Ishmael was a year old, we started him on *Winnie the Pooh*. By the time he was two, he had graduated to Robert McCloskey's wonderful *Homer Price*. When he was three, we read him *The Wind in the Willows*. The big trouble, though, was that the kids didn't bore easily. Often we had to read for hours at a stretch —but at least Bob and I insisted on reading the books that we liked. The only books that the kids refused to listen to were "scary" ones like *The Hobbit, The Lord of the Rings*, and the "Narnia" books by C. S. Lewis. But we had a wide variety of children's books to choose from, and our nights were more tol-erable than they could have been.

When Ishmael was almost three, I became pregnant with Vita. Numerous complications arose, and I had to spend most of the nine months in bed or curled up on the couch. Bob took

Ishmael to work once or twice a week, but Ishmael mostly stayed with me and I read to him for hours and hours each day. That winter we read all the Laura Ingalls Wilder books, beginning with *Little House in the Big Woods* and *Little House on the Prairie*. When we had finished them, Ishmael insisted on starting all over again.

With books like these, which are quite difficult to understand, he memorized whole passages and repeated them to himself over and over again during the day until a glimmer of meaning shone through the haze of words. He committed so much of the Laura Ingalls Wilder books to memory that I often wondered whether he thought he was living here or out in the blizzards of South Dakota.

During our "Long Winter," I showed Ishmael how to write his capital letters. Although I don't really remember how, he must have grasped the idea that all letters have sounds associated with them and almost instinctively figured out the sounds of all the consonants. Occasionally, when he was interested, we would play rhyming games with sets of words like pat, sat, hat or bee, see, tree. Sometimes I'd just spell a word like "pat" and Ishmael would haltingly spell out "hat" and "sat" and any other rhyming words he could think of. Other times I'd make up a sentence with blanks like "The cat sat on the —— wearing a brand new ——," and see if he could spell out the logical rhyming words to fit the spaces. Actually, Ishmael had more fun inventing new words like "tat" or "lat" and pondering their meanings or laughing over silly sentences like, "The cat sat on the bat wearing a brand new drat."

Meanwhile, he was spending a good deal of time drawing and painting. By the time he was three and a half or four, most of his "pictures" involved large, shakily drawn letters or words, sometimes expressing a thought about the picture itself, but more often just worked into abstract designs on the paper. When he was about four and a half, his pictures were relegated to the status of mere illustrations and he was now busily writing stories—most often in rainbow colors and spelled with a rather freestyle phonetics. "Kaity went to the mieusiem, Wut ded you do thar?"

For a long time Ishmael showed no apparent interest in reading. His friends were busy reading "STOP" and "Shop Rite" and "SLOW" from the back seats of their mother's cars, but he wasn't very observant and didn't often notice road signs. He did seem to be intently concentrating on the pages of the books we read to him each night before bed, but I didn't pay much attention to that.

For his fifth birthday, Ishmael's grandmother gave him a copy of *Little Bear,* an "I can read" book by Else Holmelund Minarik, with illustrations by Maurice Sendak. It's a delightful book—any book that I can read two hundred times and not get sick of has got to be good.

The first chapter is titled, "What Will Little Bear Wear?" and it begins, "It is cold. See the snow. See the snow come down. Little Bear said, 'Mother Bear, I am cold. See the snow. I want something to put on.'" Lots of repetition and short sentences —on first glance it seemed as though Ishmael could learn to read the book without too much trouble. Since he liked it as much as I did, he was delighted when I offered to teach him how to read it.

For the next week or so, we spent a few minutes every afternoon struggling with the book. We couldn't spend much longer than that since Ishmael became exhausted in no time, it was such tough going. The first word was "What"—an awful word, really. I later learned that in school it is called a "key word"—a word you just have to memorize, with no apologies given. But I apologized to Ishmael. It was embarrassing to have to try to explain just why the word "what" didn't sound like "waahat." "Will" went a little better, and I hastily told Ishmael to forget about the silent "e" in "little" since I didn't know what it was doing there. "Bear" didn't make any sense, but once he accepted that b-e-a-r really did spell "Bear," he managed to read

"Wear" on his own. It was frustrating and exhausting work. I was shocked to discover just how many crazy words there are in the English language that are essential, those everyday words that we read without even thinking. In the first chapter of *Little Bear* alone, there were plenty—"said," "head," "out," "oh," "again," and so on.

Ishmael was great at memorizing, though. After we had read the book to him four or five times, he managed to memorize it word for word. After that, I didn't think it made much sense to try and have him "read" it and I felt so discouraged that I figured it didn't make much sense anyway. Ishmael was too young, I thought, to start messing with such a confusing language. "What am I bothering with this for?" I asked myself. "Why not just leave it up to Ishmael's first grade teacher? After all, it's her job to teach him how to read anyway."

I really had given up, but somehow we still managed to accumulate quite a few "easy-to-read" books: Dr. Seuss's *ABC* and others, more *Little Bear* books, and a wonderful little book, *Mouse Tales*, by Arnold Lobel. Sometimes we read them to Ishmael, and occasionally he picked them up himself and looked through them. Mostly, though, he preferred "reading" his favorite read-aloud books—*Make Way for Ducklings, Mike Mulligan and His Steamshovel*, and many others.

Then one day, when Ishmael was almost five and a half, we drove up to the nearest bookstore (about forty-five minutes away) to make one of our semi-annual book hauls. We let Ishmael and Vita each pick out a book. Ishmael chose *Mr. Brown Can Moo! Can You?* by Dr. Seuss. All the way home, he sat in the back seat, slowly picking out the words. I helped him with a few of the harder ones like "wonderful" and "whisper," but mostly, he was reading—all on his own! "Oh the wonderful things Mr. Brown can do! He can go like a cow. He can go MOO MOO. Mr. Brown can do it. How about you?" Bob and I were dumbstruck. Here was Ishmael reading away, and we had been without any idea that he was even *near* being able to. I don't think Ishmael had known he could read either. After a while we just couldn't suppress our excitement and all of us, even Vita, burst out laughing. Ishmael could read!

By the next month, he had reached the point where he could read almost anything. His only problem was stamina, since reading, for him, was pretty hard work. After he exhausted himself with a book, he sought a little relaxation by traveling around the house testing his newly found skill on package labels, book titles, and newspaper headlines. He delighted in reading all the hard words he could find—like "dictionary," "pasteurized," "iodized," and "crisis."

Looking back now, after having watched other children, and particularly Vita, learn how to read, I realize that Ishmael didn't just suddenly begin reading out of the blue. He had been preparing himself gradually for years. He spent his first years falling in love with books—perhaps his most important step towards learning how to read. After all, why bother to learn if you aren't motivated? And Ishmael certainly was. He had become acquainted with the idea of the printed page by constantly looking at the books while we read to him. Because he had memorized so many books, he was able to pore over them and quite unconsciously to match the words he had retained in his memory with the words he saw on the printed page. Gradually, his brain mapped out the letter combinations and patterns used to create the various sounds we hear in words until suddenly he was able, with very little difficulty, to read new words.

Ishmael has a tendency to focus himself solely on one interest at a time, to the exclusion of almost everything else. When he was three and a half, for example, he spent a whole summer trying to build an airplane. This was a nightmare for me, since he was determined to build an airplane that really flew, and he would burst into tears when his plane refused to perform. He spent hours planing the wooden wings until their shape was right—the top surface thicker and more rounded than the bottom—to give his airplane lift. He experimented with the tilt of the wings and the weight of the body. Hoping to find the secret of his plane's failure to fly, he asked Bob questions about aerodynamics—but he refused to listen when we gently tried to explain to him exactly why his airplane would never be able to leave the ground on its own.

Anyway, as with the airplane, Ishmael was now totally focused on words. This meant, though, that when other children his age were learning how to tie their shoes and zip their jackets, Ishmael remained pretty helpless in those respects. When his friends were learning how to ride bikes and skip, Ishmael was still bumbling around clumsily. And I think, too, that being so entirely directed towards language probably slowed him up with numbers. He had no interest in addition and subtraction, not to mention money or telling time. But he was now carrying home armloads of books from the library, and he was nice enough to read to Vita before her afternoon nap.

That summer, about the time Ishmael turned six, we spent three days in Chicago while Bob was at a training session for community organizers. While he went to seminars, we explored the zoo, which was right across the street from our hotel. Although Ishmael was interested in all the animals, his great delight was to read off the Latin names on their cages. I still remember how some of the zoo keepers stood and stared open-mouthed as Ishmael happily trotted from cage to cage in the monkey house reading out names like, *Seimiri sciureus* or *Macaca silenus*.

With a feeling of rivalry, I too began trying to read off the Latin names, but more often than not, Ishmael read them more quickly and fluently than I did. Resting on a bench while the kids ate a gooey zoo snack and feeling a bit miffed, I began to analyze just how I approached those foreign words and I was soon embarrassed to discover how sloppy I was being. I would look at the beginning of a word; if it didn't lead me quickly through the whole thing, my eyes would nervously leap over to the end in hopes of finding a clue there. It was only if I was really stuck that I would go back and read the word phonetically, syllable by syllable. What a waste of time! Meanwhile, in his calm, collected way, Ishmael read straight through the words, not looking for any short-cuts at all, and usually managed to be quicker than I was.

Vita's initial approach to reading was much more drawn out than Ishmael's. I think that being the youngest member of the family created problems for her that he never had to contend with. For one thing, even from toddlerhood, she felt that she *ought* to be able to read, since the rest of us could, and so she pushed herself (with our encouragement) before she was really ready. She began recognizing large numbers of words when she was about three and a half, reading them off whenever she got a chance—words like "No Hunting," "off," "on," "hot," "cold," and "STOP." By four she was expressing interest in actually learning to read books, and once again we turned to *Little Bear*. She didn't stamp her feet and demand "Why?" as Ishmael had when I told her what "W-h-a-t" spelled; instead, she memorized it easily. We got through the first pages quickly, but she always refused to "sound out" new words. Once she had been told a word, though, she seldom forgot it. If she did, she flipped back to the place where she had originally seen it, read the word in context to help her remember what it was, and then flipped back again to her new page and continued reading. As she learned these new words, she almost always learned how to spell them, too. So her written vocabulary increased at the same time.

Over the months, Vita learned how to recognize hundreds of words, and she was able to read all kinds of simple books. Out of insecurity, though, she was still afraid to risk sounding out new words and continued to rely on Bob, Ishmael, or me to help her.

Much of her insecurity was due to the fact that, like the little girl, Lisa, in John Holt's book, *How Children Learn*, Vita had never realized that the rest of us, just like herself, had had to *learn* how to read—we hadn't been born with that ability. Lisa had solved her problem by going to kindergarten, where she immediately discovered thirty other kids who were in the same boat she was. As John writes (page 92), "She must have decided that, since older people could read, they must have learned, and if they learned, so could she." And she did, of course.

Since by this time we weren't planning on sending Vita to school, and since it would have been ridiculous to squeeze thirty five-year-olds into our house just to prove to her that not everyone knew how to read, we had to think of other solutions. Finally we hit upon the idea of letting her read to herself in bed at night, like Ishmael did. That way we figured she'd be forced to be more self-sufficient. Maybe, in the privacy of her room, she'd have the courage to experiment with sounding out words.

She liked the idea and decided to read to her rag doll. They cuddled up together in bed, and I gave Vita a stack of books. Our plan didn't work perfectly, though. Vita was so used to asking us for help that she continually shouted to Bob (who was attempting to read to Ishmael) "What does s-o-u-p spell? What does e-a-r-t-h spell?" Bob and Ishmael were nearly driven to distraction. In desperation Bob made her promise to try sounding out new words first and then ask for help only if she really needed it. That worked a whole lot better. In fact, after a few weeks I found myself beginning to tell friends with a certain confidence that Vita was reading.

Soon, though, I realized that I had been hasty. The weather broke quickly that spring, the sun shone, the mud dried, and Vita forgot about books as she threw herself into the outdoors. All her little neighborhood friends started hanging around again, and they played from morning 'til night in the hot sun. We still continued to read to Vita each night, and on cold or rainy days she lay on the floor and looked at books; but I remember asking myself on numerous occasions, "When can a child safely be said to be reading?" With Ishmael it had happened so fast that the question had never crossed my mind, but Vita had been on the verge for so long . . .

One day towards fall I found her reading a Dr. Seuss book to herself, "Up past the North Pole, where the frozen winds squeal, I'll go and I'll hunt in my Skeegle-mobile . . ." That was a real breakthrough, since in order to really be able to read Dr. Seuss you have to know your phonetics backwards and forwards. I could see that Vita really was sounding out words. "Ah-ha," I said to myself hopefully, but still, not much seemed to happen.

I began to feel a bit nervous. She was about to become a first-grader. Would she ever learn to read? I wondered. And if she didn't, would the school board revoke our home-schooling permission? That fall, we decided to have reading lessons every day before our evening reading-aloud ritual. Many times, though, we forgot, or were just too rushed. Often, I felt guilty, but just as often I didn't—since the reading lessons didn't seem to be doing much good. Vita still came out with her habitual "What's that?" every time she met a new word and the last thing she wanted was for me to say, "Sound it out."

About that time she started insisting on going to the library by herself and checking out her own books, so I acquiesced by dropping her and Ishmael off while I went to the grocery store. Each week she brought home four or five skinny books, most of which we didn't have time to read to her since we were usually in the middle of a much fatter book from our family library. At first, she used to return most of the books to the library unread. As the temperature outside began to drop, though, I noticed that instead of just looking at the books, she had begun whispering the words to herself as she ran her finger under them. Soon, her finger had so much trouble keeping pace with her whispered words that she left it at the edge of the page.

With a mixture of happiness and sadness, I realized that I had found the answer to my question. A child can be safely said to be reading when he goes up to his mother and says, "I just read the most wonderful book!" and the mother feels unexpectedly sad, because she realizes that never again will she be able to share all her child's books with him because he just doesn't have the patience any more to sit around waiting for her to find the time to read to him.

So how did Vita ultimately learn to read? I really don't know. Like Ishmael, the process she went through remains a mystery, but one important thing I learned after the fact, was that, in the end, she just had to wait until she was good and ready. Fortunately for my nerves, she started reading when she was six—just the right age for the school people—but it could have happened much later, say when she was eight or nine, and would have been just as easy.

As I mentioned before, Ishmael's first attempts at writing were very freely spelled. The more books he read, though, and the more he wrote, the better his spelling became. Now he rarely misspells a word. By the time he reached first grade, he had been keeping a daily diary for about six months and had put out four or five issues of a neighborhood newspaper called "Ishmael's Weekly Times." The paper was a great success both financially and in other ways. Since Bob had access to a spirit duplicator, Ishmael was able to make lots of copies and sold them for a nickel each to friends, neighbors, and relatives. He stuck a little pad and a pencil in his pocket and walked from house to house collecting news and copying it down almost verbatim from the lips of our neighbors. He wrote items like, "An old friend from elementary school came to visit Mrs. Durham Sonday," or "David and Tina grageuated from eighth grade. Congratulations." The neighbors all loved the paper, particularly since Ishmael broke some pretty hot stories. I guess the most exciting one from that summer was, "Becky Moul is going to get married to Peter Trudelle June 18." But there were many others, too. Ishmael even went to an evening meeting in a neighboring town, took notes, and wrote an informative story about it.

> We went to a resiceling meeting Monday night. It was in Lempster. Vita and I were the only kids there. Someone said

he had a dump in his backyard. People toced about resicaling glass, payper and tin cans an they thout they cood make money.

About this time too, Ishmael became interested in bookmaking. At first he sat at his desk and patiently copied out his favorite picture books in fairly messy printing. Later, he wrote his own stories. He drew illustrations for them, and I helped him sew the pages together. We used construction paper for the covers. In fact, one of his first original books included an essay entitled "How to Make a Book."

> Start with twenty pieces of paper, then fold them and take a sheet of construction paper and fold it and open it up and put the folded paper inside it and sew it down the back—over, under, over, under. And write in it. And there is your book!

I wish it were that easy!

Ishmael's first stories were about his everyday life—a party we went to and a trip we took, for example—but he always wrote about himself in the third person, and his style was already quite literary.

> Once upon a time a little boy was sleeping. When he woche up he remembered that his mother had told him that today he would go to the city.

Gradually, as the fall progressed, he turned to fiction.

> One day dockter mole came into his ofice late. Instently miss mouse called and her babys had colds so he grabed his medicen and ran to the house. After he got to the house he said, "I can't do anything about it. The only thing I can tell you is to wait." So they waited and waited and waited and won day they told ther mother that they felt better and went to play in the garden. Wen miss mouse saw them in the garden she said they must be well. And she called docter mole.

He was delited. And from that day to this they have nevir caught a cold. The End.

Ishmael's next discovery was the Thornton Burgess books. He was entranced with all the animals that lived in the Green Meadows, the Green Forest, the Smiling Pool, and the Laughing Brook. Quite frankly, these books were too soppy for me. I was grateful that he could now read, so he could indulge himself without my help. Soon he began to write charming stories of his own, highly influenced by *The Adventures of Peter Cottontail*, *The Adventures of Johnny Chuck*, and the others (there are at least a dozen volumes). He wrote one about our cats, Homer and Alice, one about a rabbit named Ishmael, and a wonderful tale about Billy Chuck.

When Billy Chuck got out of school he ran away. After a while he found a little hollow and began digging a hole. Then he put some chairs, two of them, in the back, and a table in front, and that was his home. Billy liked to travel and so one morning he set off to find a wife. Almost instantly someone said, "I'll be your wife." Billy Chuck spun around with surprise and looked around and saw a young chuck sitting on a stump and he said, "Really?" And the young chuck said, "Yes, really, of course." "Oh wonderful," said Billy Chuck. He loved her. He asked her what her name was. It was Nancy Chuck. Billy led her home. And that is the story of how Billy Chuck got a wife.

Ishmael never showed his stories to his teacher. I think he was afraid she'd say something disparaging about his handwriting. When he won a prize in the *Cricket Magazine* story contest, though, I begged him to tell her. I'm not sure what kind of a reaction I expected from her, but I was awfully disappointed when she showed no apparent interest in his news. Ishmael just took it for granted—he didn't expect her to be interested in the things he did at home. Bob and I, though, were extremely proud of Ishmael. He had written:

One day Ishmael and Vita and Bob and Nancy (their father and mother) went camping in Hawaii. Ishmael and Vita got mad at Bob and Nancy and wanted to run away. So the second day Ishmael and Vita woke up at four o'clock in the morning and made a boat for themselves. Then off they went in search of a hollow tree for a house. After a while Ishmael and Vita found an island. And they stopped for a rest. And after exploring they found the banks of a big lake. Then they walked to the ocean. They got the boat ready. Ishmael pushed off, and sat in front. Just then a huge wave came running towards the boat! What should they do now? Ishmael and Vita snatched up their paddles and sweat ran down their cheeks. The wave just then collapsed over the boat. Everything they packed was washed away. The wave made them go so fast that they shot across the ocean like a thunderbolt all the way to the redwood forest. Then they stopped and climbed onto the beach and there was a hollow tree. They made furniture out of stones. And a bed of leaves. What a snug house! And that is the story of how Vita and Ishmael went on a quest for a house of their own.

Ishmael continued to write voluminously for a while. Then he stopped quite suddenly, almost as soon as we had taken him out of school the next year. He was as surprised and disconcerted as we were, and I think he also felt guilty. He wanted to write, to please us, but he just couldn't! I couldn't help wondering to myself if Ishmael wasn't like those neurotic artists we are always reading about, whose creative efforts are produced as an outlet for deep-rooted miseries and psychological disturbances. Once he was out of school and happy, perhaps he didn't need that creative outlet. (Of course this was sheer nonsense. What had happened was that he began devoting all his time to history, and with his usual monomania he had temporarily pushed writing aside. But it took me many more months to understand this.)

Naturally, I was glad that Ishmael was happy, but it would have been convenient if he'd continued his romance with writing, too. (After all, we needed to impress the school people at the end of the year!) Fortunately, I was able to get him to do enough writing to make an impressive showing. Since they do almost no writing in school, even the small amount that Ishmael produced had the desired effect.

Sometime during the next fall, when Ishmael was eight, Bob read him *Oliver Twist* and *Kidnapped*. Ishmael also read *Robinson Crusoe* and *Tom Sawyer* by himself. Each of the four books totally captured his imagination, his everyday speech took on a distinctly Victorian character, and he began writing again—this time under the influence of Dickens, Stevenson, Twain, and Defoe.

The beginning of Ishmael's first story during this period was quite reminiscent of *Kidnapped*.

> The priest came around the corner. He was carrying my bag. He quickly told me not to start believing in any of the heresies, gave me a recipe for lily-of-the-valley wine, and bid me fervently good-bye. He gave me my bag and went away, weeping loudly. As I walked down the path, I thought my troubles were over. My father had died mysteriously (no one could guess what killed him), I couldn't remember my mother, and I was ordered to go to live with some friends of my father. I slung my bag over my shoulders and ran down the path so that no one would see me cry.

In the middle section of the story, our hero is shipwrecked on a tropical island (straight out of *Robinson Crusoe*). At the end, once again reminiscent of *Kidnapped*, everybody's identities come to light, our hero discovers that he is the relative of a wealthy man, and, naturally, he lives happily ever after.

Ishmael's next three stories, "Two Little Runaways," "The Voyage of the Vasa," and "The Forest Path," were about an unusually extended family. I could never get all the relationships straightened out, but the main characters were Tom, Mickey, Cabbie, Mary, and Lucy, the Mayor's daughter. These stories have love scenes between the "roguish" Tom and the pure and good Lucy, similar to those in *Tom Sawyer*. They also have scenes on desert islands as in *Robinson Crusoe* and pathetic slum scenes like those in *Oliver Twist*.

"The Voyage of the Vasa" begins,

> "Hurrah! Hurrah! Tomorrow it will be my birthday! Hurrah! Hurrah!" Thus sang a little boy named Christopher Cabot, commonly known as Cabbie. His friends crowded about him, from old alleys where they had been stoning cats, from mansions in which they had been exploring, and all of them were ragged. "Are you really going to have a birthday?" "Of course he will." "No he won't." A fight broke out. The little boy ran away quickly. No one noticed him. Suddenly, down swept the police. "Their glorious helms hath conquered many realms." Quickly they struck. The children melted away, and if you had paused to look, you would have seen the police haughtily turning their backs on the corpse of a dead boy.

Ishmael sent this story to a well-known author of children's books who lived in a neighboring town. The author replied:

> I have certainly enjoyed reading your story. You ask me to tell you what is wrong with it. There is nothing wrong with it at all for an eight-year-old boy to write, quite remarkable, I'd say. Of course adults look at things more critically, and you will find things in it when you are grown up that will strike you right off as improvable. . . . But to get more specific and down to brass tacks, as people say, my first advice to you would be to write about something you know well in your experience. I imagine you have not had any real experience with ships and pirates. Write about what you see around your home and about the people and kids you know well, the woods and the animals and many things like that. Then the stories, or non-fiction essays, will be much more plausible.
>
> A story has to have plausibility first of all, that is, the reader will really believe it happened. On page two, you have the police "haughtily turning their backs on the corpse of a dead boy." This sounds improbable to me . . .

At the end of the letter he added some encouragement, "So keep on writing." Then he wrote a postscript that said, "I forgot to say that, in regard to punctuation, each character's speech should be a separate paragraph."

Poor Ishmael. His "reality" was largely based on books and his main contact with the police had been through *Oliver Twist*. We waited curiously to see how this letter would affect his writing. At first, he didn't seem to pay any attention, but went on writing exotic adventure stories as before. About two weeks later, though, he came to me rather meekly and asked me to teach him about paragraphing and quotation marks. I knew the letter was in the back of his mind. Over the next month, Ishmael's story writing gradually died out (whether because of the letter or not, I don't know), and his diary began to take precedence. Although I was unhappy about this at first, I have found the diary to make delightful reading. Since Ishmael claims that he writes it to accommodate his future biographer, he doesn't mind if we read it—in fact, he likes to hear our comments.

That spring, we went out to California to visit relatives. Ishmael recorded almost every detail of the trip, beginning with our plane ride.

We woke up at five o'clock. Then we (after a lot of bustle) drove to Lebanon in forty-five minutes. We stayed for a while and had our belongings checked and then we flew on an airplane to Boston. It was a beautiful trip. We saw lots of lakes and lots of woods. As we got into Massachusetts it became more and more civilized. We waited at Boston Airport and boarded a TWA airplane. We have just begun flying toward California. We are in Massachusetts. We are in St. Louis, Missouri and it is about twelve o'clock local time. It is snowing. We made the acquaintance of a woman who lives in Wichita, Kansas. One of her grandchildren who lives in New Hampshire had his upper chest paralyzed and can't swallow anything, so the doctors feed him through a tube and into his stomach. We are now crossing the Rocky Mountains. We are

seeing lots of canyons. We are seeing part of the North Colo-
rado River also. We are seeing deserts of red earth broken
with buttes and mesas. We are in Utah. I cannot see one
town. I see a plateau or mesa or mountain with a snow covered top. Hurray for the wilderness! Clouds are wisping
along far below us. Now there are so many clouds that it is
impossible to see ground. Now we are in California around
Mono Lake. We can see the jagged mountains of Yosemite
Park. Bob can see Mount Clark. (He once attempted to climb
it.) I see a waterfall. In a while we will be over Yosemite Valley. (The waterfall was named Bridalvale.) It is getting civilized now. We are almost across the Central Valley now. We
saw two astronomical observatories. It has stopped snowing
long before. We are seeing a big city. We are over the San
Francisco Bay. We see salt pans and a hill of salt. We are
heading to the airport. We've landed! 2:45 P.M. Then we flew
to Monterey across a bay. The airplane was only big enough
to carry six people in it. At Monterey Airport we met Bardy
and Grandpop!

Since then, Ishmael went through a period during which, except for the detailed diary, he wrote nothing but poetry. Poetry
after all is allowed to be fanciful! Recently, he combined his interests in writing and music and has begun to write songs and
"operettas." I have no idea where his writing will eventually
lead him. Probably he'll go through stages where he writes
nothing at all. An adult friend of ours who corresponds with
Ishmael swears that, if his letters are any indication, he will become a music or literary critic when he grows up. But who
knows? What I know from experience, though, is that Ishmael
can't be pushed, or told what to write. If he's going through a
poetry-writing stage, there's no way I can get him to write a
story. If he's having one of his barren periods, so be it.

And what about Vita? She is not one to be pushed around either. Her very first words were spoken quite late, and they
burst out in the form of a sentence. "I do it!" she screamed as
Ishmael tried to zip her sleeper. She has lived by that creed

ever since. I can't often get her to write "thank you" notes to her grandmother, but she does write quite a bit on her own terms. She types letters to friends, writes entries in her diaries in an ornate script which is almost, but not quite, illegible, and she writes stories and books. She has recently started to write a book about her life and she continually wanders around the house complaining, "This book is going to take me years to write!"

Unlike Ishmael, she has always been visually oriented. She notices and remembers the minutest details of the landscapes and people she encounters (although the makeup of individual words still seems to escape her most of the time!), and these are incorporated into her drawings. Being so absorbed with color and line seems to have made her less concerned with words than Ishmael was at her age. Only in the last year has she begun to write in earnest. Whereas Ishmael's first written words were free of vowels altogether and his later writings evolved into a unique style of phonetics, Vita, from the beginning, insisted on spelling all her words correctly. At first, she always asked us to write out her stories for her as she told them to us and then copied them painstakingly in her neat little letters. Then came a period during which, independently and full of confidence, she'd get paper and a pencil and begin to write on her own. But in a matter of minutes, regular as clockwork, she'd start calling frantically, "Nancy, how do you spell 'bear'?" or "Bob, how do you spell 'come'?" Although that was a rather tiresome process, we always helped her. After a while, she found that kind of dependence just as tiresome as we did. So she took to hunting through her "easy-to-read" books for the words she needed to spell. It was entertaining to peek at her, writing away intently—with a stack of *Little Bear* books, which she used like dictionaries, at her side.

Most of Vita's stories have been domestically oriented, with titles like "Mother and Father," "No Lunch," and "No Wine." "Mother and Father," written a few months before she was five, was one of her first. She wrote it on tiny pages, each one care-

fully illustrated and stapled into a book with a red cover. It
goes:

> I am sick. You are sick. Why not stay in bed. Now Daddy
> is coming home. Oh, Daddy is coming home. Good, Daddy
> is coming. Hi, Daddy. We were waiting for you all that time.
> Oh yes, I have been away for a long time. Yes you have been
> away for a long time. Let's sit down and eat. So they did. She
> sung and swallowed.

During that period, many of her stories had abrupt endings.

> Once there was a little boy and he went out the window
> and tiptoed along the path. Suddenly he came to a creek . . .
> His shoes were untied and they slipped into the water.

Another one went:

> On the day that Annie left for school, she saw that the goat
> pasture was quiet. If anything was wrong with the goats she
> would tell her father. If there wasn't, she wouldn't. School
> was very hard that day. She was thinking about how her fa-
> ther would feel if the goats were not o.k.

Like Ishmael, Vita also put out, sporadically and in warm
weather, a weekly newspaper called, *Weekly Newspaper*. Her
news was mostly about ourselves: "Vita Wallace had a gymnas-
tic class," or "Bob built a bookcase for the Wallaces." She also
indulged in quite a bit of editorializing: "I love the Durhams."
She typed and illustrated the paper herself, and Ishmael helped
her go around the neighborhood peddling it. Everyone thought
it was a great buy at three cents, especially since it gave so
many intimate details about what went on in the Wallace
household. None of our neighbors would have missed it!

Lately, as Vita has really begun to read, she has seemed
much more confident in herself and about her writing. She has
begun allowing herself the liberty of spelling out words phonetically, at the risk of making numerous spelling mistakes. I am
pleased at this turn of events, despite the fact that her spelling

is atrocious. She can now say the things on paper that she wants to much more quickly than before; through her own method of trial and error, she is beginning to recognize, unconsciously, the letter patterns that form the sounds that she wants to write; and, slowly, her spelling is improving. For example, until recently she used a "k" for the hard "c" sound at the beginning of words like calf (only she'd also omit the "l"), carrot, and cart. But now, almost imperceptibly, she has switched over to using the "c." For past tenses, she at first just added "t"s to the ends of words. Later she started using "d"s, and now she most often uses the correct "ed."

Several people to whom I've shown her writing have smiled (because it is cute) and have asked if I ever plan to give her spelling lessons. I am very much against that idea, though. For one thing, I'm afraid that I would cramp her writing style by encouraging her to worry again about spelling. But also, I think that deep down she has a great desire to spell the way we do. Since she gets great personal satisfaction each time she figures out how to spell a word correctly, I think I can rely on that ultimate feeling of satisfaction to be her teacher. Meanwhile, we are all enjoying Vita's inventive spelling.

With her own money, Vita often buys herself tiny pads. When Bob and I are feeling generous, we get her blank books with flowery covers, fancy paper, and colored pens. Since nice paper seems to spark her creativity, she's lucky that she doesn't have to go to a school where the kids are usually given only newsprint to write on. She would probably develop a serious case of writer's cramp!

Speaking of school, it is often hard for me to believe that schools put so much emphasis on reading and writing and yet get such meager results. Probably half, maybe even three-quarters of the students who graduate from high school will be able to write only with difficulty. They will seldom read for pleasure, will rarely enter a library voluntarily, and would rather spend their money on a long-distance telephone call than write a letter. I won't hazard a guess as to how many of those graduates can't be counted on to write a grammatical sentence with the proper punctuation, are lousy spellers, or can't use a telephone book. But the percentage is probably disconcertingly high.

When I volunteered in the fourth/fifth-grade classroom at Ishmael's school, the only kids I encountered who seemed to me to be functionally literate were the children of middle-class, literate parents. It seemed that kids learned how to read and write effectively only if there were books and paper in their homes.

Why does school seem to make so little difference? And how can this happen when, from first grade on, teachers stress reading and writing skills so heavily? How can so many children fail with such heavy doses of suffixes and prefixes, phonetics, "advanced phonetics" (the phonetic instruction that takes place after a child is reading), alphabetizing, syllabication, parts of speech, handwriting, punctuation, reading comprehension, dictionary skills, and so on? From my experience, I would have to say that it is precisely *because* the kids are taught those reading and writing skills—to the exclusion of almost anything else—that many of them will end up not reading and writing. Does this seem paradoxical? It isn't, really, when you take a closer look at how most schools function.

In Ishmael's school, for example, the first graders were introduced to reading and writing as a set of complex skills that they would have to master. No one showed them with conviction that reading is fun or that writing is a satisfying way to express your thoughts. No one showed them how wonderful the insides of a book could be. And only seldom did anyone read to them.

In the classrooms, textbooks were kept on shelves away from the reach of the children. When the books were passed out, children were taught to treat them as precious objects that were to be looked upon and treated with awe. It was a tragedy if a book was lost or a page was stained or torn. The children loved the books they were given. I often saw books petted and fondled. But I rarely saw books opened in a relaxed and happy manner.

The library was off limits except once a week during "library period." Kids weren't allowed to read on the playground, and they weren't allowed time in class to read for pleasure. Nor were they given much of a chance to write. When they used their pencils, it was usually to fill in blanks or to circle answers. When they were given the very occasional opportunity to really write something, they were assigned topics and their writing was returned covered with the teacher's red ink.

Who would enjoy reading and writing under those circumstances? I certainly wouldn't, and for the most part didn't. I grew up in a house full of books, so school didn't entirely squelch my literary habits; but still, I seldom read a book for pleasure during my school days.

It wasn't until the fall after I had graduated from high school that I really discovered how delightful books could be. I had been hired to teach weaving at a tiny private school up in the coastal mountains of California, and I rented a shack about a half a mile up a dusty dirt road from the school. All alone and quite lonely, I took to walking down to the school at night to ransack the library. There I discovered Thomas Hardy, Jane Austen, Virginia Woolf, Tolstoy, and shelves and boxes full of other books. I was very fortunate. Under different circumstances, I could have ended up spending my evenings watching TV—and never known what I was missing.

That will never happen to Ishmael and Vita. It's possible that they will go through a phase of TV-watching, but I can't imagine that they would ever just stop reading and writing. Books give them far too much pleasure for that, and writing is as natural a form of communication for them as speaking.

As for formally "teaching" the kids their reading and writing skills, they themselves have taught me that that isn't necessary. Through our mutual frustrations, they have shown me that they learn best when they are really ready. Only they know when that time has come. We can offer them help, but their own efforts are their best teacher and pleasure is their real reward.

Chapter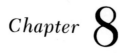

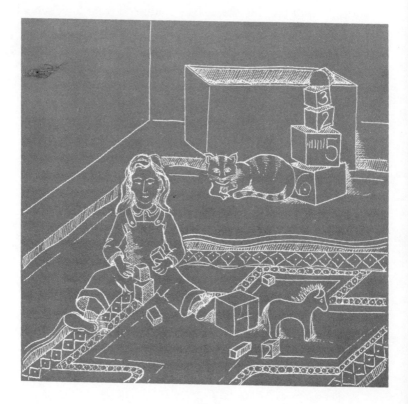

Math

Most of us, at one time or another, have been in the position of teaching math to our children. Most of us also remember those times as being particularly unpleasant. Perhaps our child has come home from school with a lousy grade in math, or perhaps fractions or long division have just stumped him, and miserably he has begged us for help. In any case, as we sit down to work with him, the situation is pretty awful. Our child has already experienced failure, he is feeling badly about himself, and his face is wearing a bleak expression.

He finds a paper and pencil, opens his book, and we begin to work. Unfortunately, we are a bit fuzzy in math ourselves. It's been *ages* since we've had to find a common denominator, and the book is one of those wordy modern math texts where it takes forever to figure out what they're driving at. Almost without thinking, we grab the pencil and start explaining common denominators *our* way—the old-fashioned way we learned in school, where you just do things and don't get all mixed up trying to understand why. In five minutes, our child has flown into hysterics.

We sigh (or groan) and try to be loving, comforting, and understanding, but not for too long. After all, we don't have much time. The teacher is going to be introducing a new unit on geometry next week, and the test on fractions is this Friday. Once again, our child settles down and opens his book. This time, though, it takes only three minutes before he has slammed it shut and stomped off to his room.

After experiences like this, it is no wonder that one of the first questions people ask me when I tell them that we are educating Ishmael and Vita at home is, "How do you ever teach them math?" In fact, when I first told my father about our home-schooling plans for Ishmael, he treated me as if I were a heroine. Did he have visions of my spending day after day, year after year, desperately trying not to throttle my kids as they wept and screamed over their multiplication tables? Most likely he did, and I don't blame him, considering his experiences with me.

I can't deny that during the first couple of years after we had taken Ishmael out of school he occasionally shed tears over an open math book. But this had nothing to do with what most people assume to be the traumas that occur when a parent sets out to teach his own child. In fact, I soon discovered that, thanks to Ishmael's miserable math experiences in school, for me to play the role of teacher at all was absurd. What he needed was "rehabilitation," not teaching. The school had left me with a child who felt so miserably about his ability to work with numbers that it was only with great difficulty that he could add a simple sum like $3 + 2$. Just the thought of opening a math book was painful to him. School had obviously turned Ishmael into an invalid with respect to math, and the healing process at home, we realized, was going to take a long time.

Ishmael's teachers had used what I call the "layer" approach to teaching math. Not having the time to divide the class into math groups and to teach those with greater or lesser mathematical experience at different levels and speeds, they began by gearing their lessons toward the quickest kids in the class (the top layer). They reassured the confused majority by telling them that there would be plenty of time for review later on. When the top kids had grasped the given concepts, the teachers would start all over again, re-teaching the previous lessons. This time they geared the lessons to the second layer of kids and justified the boredom of the top layer by telling themselves that review was essential. This process would be repeated (and it might take years) until almost everyone in the class, hopefully, had caught on.

What really happened, of course, was that as the quicker children grew progressively more bored and learned to think of math as a dull subject, the slower ones were made to feel stupid. Whatever ability they had for math in the first place was lost to their feelings of insecurity and frustration.

Ishmael was one of the kids who didn't "get it" the first time, and his confusion during math class made him extremely anxious. To make matters worse, his teacher couldn't understand how he could be so good at reading and writing and yet so slow with numbers. She wasn't very understanding about his repeated failures. The more he failed, the worse he felt; and the worse he felt, the more he failed. The teacher's solution was *drill*. Ishmael agonized over his "math facts," and the frequent timed math tests he was given gave him headaches.

In the months after we had taken Ishmael out of school, I was acutely conscious of the fact that all the other kids in Ishmael's class had to do at least an hour a day of math. But with Ishmael, that method seemed to do more harm than good. So, although we were faced with a standardized test at the end of the year, I tried my best not to be daunted by it and began experimenting with ways to help Ishmael.

One of our problems was that the math workbook the school had given us was awful. It was full of flashy colored pictures, but even they couldn't disguise the fact that all it really consisted of was page after page of boring "math facts." Both Ishmael and I found this humiliating, and I was disgusted because the book never adequately explained mathematical procedures like borrowing and carrying.

Friends suggested that we use Cuisenaire rods (colored wooden rods whose various lengths are in multiples of one centimeter) to help Ishmael get a concrete grasp of addition and subtraction (and later, multiplication, division, and fractions). He enjoyed building castles and towers out of the rods, but he was uninterested in putting them to any mathematical use. When I say "uninterested," what I mean is that although Ishmael almost always did what I asked him to do, it was hard to bear his grimacing or frowning as he worked. After all, we had taken him out of school so that he could enjoy learning.

Doing math problems with Cuisenaire rods wasn't the only thing that Ishmael didn't like. If I gave him a page of easy problems to do, for example, he would yawn, go sharpen his pencil, scratch all the imaginary lice on his head, and actually seem to forget to do them. Sometimes when I reminded him of that page lying on the table waiting for him, he'd burst into tears. In desperation, I made a graph to plot out the number of problems Ishmael completed against the time it took him to do them. I hoped that graph would encourage him to work, with a little speed if possible, and I figured he'd learn something about graphs at the same time. But try as he might, Ishmael just couldn't seem to get going. Many a time, I ended up plotting "all day" by ten problems. Besides, he wasn't interested in graphs.

After about a week of this I tore up the graph and decreased the actual number of problems I gave Ishmael to about five a day. When it was time to do them, I sat right down with him, put my arm around his shoulder, and nudged him lovingly to do his problems. It was then that I noticed his "method." He would sit looking at a problem and wait indefinitely for the answer to appear, magically, out of thin air. No wonder he yawned so much!

It became apparent that the school's emphasis on drill had caused him to separate, in his mind, math problems on paper from the everyday casual math that he did all the time. If there were two oranges in the fruit basket, for example, Ishmael knew that he would have to grab two extra bananas or apples so that the four of us could have fruit for lunch. Yet problems like

$2 + 2 = x$ or $4 - 2 = x$ were difficult for him. Hoping to help him bridge the gap in his mind between math problems and real life, I reminded him of how to count on his fingers and gave him easy word-problems to do orally that were based on his everyday experience. Slowly, he began to regain some of his competence with numbers. If we spent even five minutes a day doing formal math this way, with no yawns, I felt good.

One thing that Ishmael did enjoy was playing "21," or blackjack. That he often had trouble adding up his own scores didn't seem to interfere with his pleasure. In fact, many of the games we played—Scrabble and cribbage, for example—required difficult addition.

"Math games," made up specifically to help children with their math facts, didn't appeal to Ishmael, however. Mostly they just weren't much fun. He preferred doing straightforward black-and-white problems to ones ineptly disguised as a game. During those first months, I didn't feel very happy about math. I did feel that we were coping, though, and we decreased the number of tears considerably.

Surprisingly, Ishmael did all right on the standardized test that June. That is, he got an average score. As soon as it was over, we stacked the math materials in a box and carried them up to the attic to gather dust over the summer. We figured we'd just forget about math until the next September.

Doing "nothing" was the best thing we ever did, since it gave Ishmael a chance to relax over the summer. We actually did do a lot with numbers, but it wasn't "formalized" math. Ishmael and Vita helped out with the jam-making by weighing strawberries and blueberries, measuring honey and sugar, and checking the candy thermometer. We observed the difference between the boiling point of water and the boiling point of grape jelly. Ishmael became familiar with quarts, pints, and bushels.

It was that summer, too, that Bob helped Ishmael build a raft. They figured out how big the raft would have to be in order to float with Bob on it. They calculated that Bob's weight was equal to that of two or three children, which meant that

Ishmael wouldn't have to be a solitary "rafter." They spent hours together (with Vita, too) measuring, sawing, and hammering. What's more, the raft really did float! Later, they added a small sail, and what fun Ishmael and Vita had paddling around our little swimming hole with hopes of catching a good wind!

That summer I acquired two new math books. The first was *Lennes Essentials of Arithmetic,* an old-fashioned, black-and-white workbook. Half of it contains word problems and the other half is straight math facts. All the answers to the problems are included in back. Along the side of each page of problems, the book offers advice and examples of how to do the new kinds of problems being introduced. It also has a detailed index that made it easy for us to hop around and concentrate on various types of problems. Although it definitely was not exciting, I felt that it allowed children the integrity of learning basic math on their own, with no crazy gimmicks.

Of course, the book also has its drawbacks. It relies entirely on the old-fashioned method of "Just do what we tell you to do and you'll get the answers right." When explaining how to do a difficult division problem for the first time, for example, the book says, "Divide 48 by 2. Think $2\overline{)4}$. Write 2. Think $2\overline{)8}$. Write 4. To prove, multiply 24 by 2. The product should be 48." This is all very well, of course. But *why*, for God's sake?

That's where the second book I discovered came in handy. It is called *Patterns in Mathematics* and is part of a "modern math" series called the *Understanding Mathematics Program.* I know that modern math has a bad name, and that many people find it hopelessly confusing, but Ishmael ended up loving this book. It helped, modestly, to change his outlook on math by allowing him to understand what he was doing.

In September, the day after Labor Day, we began our math lessons again—once more for about five minutes a day. We had considered continuing to do "nothing" since that was working quite well, but we had the school people looking over our shoulders. Besides, doing five minutes a day was really quite painless, and it would give us a daily opportunity to allow a math lesson to blossom into a more in-depth experience if Ishmael ever got inspired.

Thanks to the summer break, when we opened our math books again he wasn't nearly as jittery as he had been the year before. In *Patterns*, we plowed through sections on equivalent and non-equivalent sets, unions of sets, numerals vs. numbers, etc., in a matter of days. Finally we reached a section entitled "Open and Closed Sentences." The book started out by comparing the sentence, "Bob is a third grade pupil," to the number sentence, "3 + 4 = 7." Because it is possible to tell whether these sentences are true or false, the book explained, they are called "closed sentences." And because you can't tell whether the sentences, "He is a third grade pupil," or the number sentence; "x + 2 = 5" are true or false, they are called "open sentences." This simple little concept intrigued Ishmael, primarily because of the way the book compared number sentences to English sentences. It began to dawn on him that math was just another form of expression, almost like another language. On the next page the book showed him how to translate a word problem into a number sentence in order to solve it and he burst with excitement. It was fun to learn this new language! And it was actually useful. That day our lesson lasted for about an hour.

As it happened, those overly long words like "commutative" and "associative" that the modern math people seem to revel in so systematically really appealed to Ishmael. He is always up for learning new words. By retaining those words and their meanings in his memory, he was able to mull them over in his head until he understood the concepts they represented.

I'll never forget the day he learned that addition and subtraction were "inverse operations." In school, Ishmael had always had a terrible time with problems like x + 5 = 9. How was he supposed to do it, he'd wonder, especially since he had become accustomed to neglecting his fingers. But now the book showed him, with the aid of a number line, that since subtracting 5 "undoes" adding 5 and vice-versa, you can say that addition and subtraction "undo" each other or are "inverse operations." Ishmael loved the word "inverse" and learned right away how to translate $x + 5 = 9$ into $9 - 5 = x$, putting the unknown on the other side of the equals sign so that he could more easily solve the problem. That day Ishmael exclaimed, "This is neat!"

Another thing this book helped him with was the idea that $14 - 6 = x$, for example, can be translated into the problem $(14 - 4) - 2 = x$, which is much easier to solve. I thought that this concept would give Ishmael some trouble, but he actually laughed when I explained it to him. No more freaking out, trying to draw the answer out of his memory.

As I write this, we have started working on long division —this time with the fourth-grade versions of the same books. Where *Lennes* gives a ridiculously quick, "divide, multiply, subtract, compare, bring down, divide" explanation, *Exploring in Mathematics* (the fourth-grade version of *Patterns*) spends twenty or thirty pages preparing kids by teaching them how to round off numbers, make estimates, do simple division, and "distribute division over addition." It shows them that $42 \div 3$ can be written $(30 + 12) \div 3$ or $3\overline{)30 + 12}$. And once it actually gets going with long division it tends to further bog down with endless examples like:

	Thinking steps
1342	
7)9394	$7 \times 1000 < 9394$ and $7 \times 2000 > 9394$
7000	$7 \times 1000 = 7000$
2394	$7 \times 300 < 2394$ and $7 \times 400 > 2394$
2100	$7 \times 300 = 2100$
294	$7 \times 40 < 294$ and $7 \times 50 > 294$
280	$7 \times 40 = 280$
14	$7 \times \square = 14$
14	$7 \times 2 = 14$
0	

When we get sick of "understanding," we just skip over to *Lennes* for a little practice work. So far, picking and choosing from both books seems to work.

These days I don't usually have to cuddle with Ishmael as he does his math, but I do like to be close by in case he needs help. Since we have a piano right next to the kitchen table where he works, I usually play scales and work on Czerny exercises while he does a few lines of multiplication or division. After ten or fifteen minutes, we are both ready to quit and go on to something else.

Despite the incredible progress that Ishmael has made, he still bears scars left over from his school days. He just can't seem to memorize his multiplication tables, for example, even though he has an enviable natural memory. He can play a simple piece on the piano two or three times and memorize it without even realizing that he has done so. He can hear the name of an obscure Russian tenor on the radio and keep the name permanently in his memory. If you ask him an innocent question like, "Who was Amerigo Vespucci?" he will bombard you with facts—the date and place of his birth, all his ocean voyages, including when and where they occurred, the date of his death, and so on. And then if, in amazement, you ask Ishmael when he last read up on Vespucci, he'll probably answer casually, "Oh, about a year ago."

With a memory like that, you'd think he would have memorized his multiplication tables in no time. After all, even people with the dullest of memories manage to retain those tables in their heads indefinitely. But somehow, they just won't stick in Ishmael's mind. Of course, this problem of his isn't the end of the world. He understands enough about numbers to be able to figure out the answer to, say, 6×8 by multiplying 6×10 and then subtracting twelve, or by adding 24 $(8 \times 3) +$ 24. But this slows him down considerably and adds to his confusion, especially when he is doing immense problems like 348×26. His scratch paper gets so messy that he loses track of what he's doing, and more often than not he gets the wrong answer.

Though this situation is frustrating for both of us, it is worse for me. I end up feeling incredibly bitter. Ishmael obviously has a mental block against "math facts," and I know I didn't give it to him. School was responsible for that, and now both of us are stuck with the consequences. Like a person who has suffered a stroke and may take years to regain the use of certain parts of his body, Ishmael is likely to spend many years recovering from the damage that was done to him. Judging from the progress he has already made, though, I am now confident that he will recover. Meanwhile, we have to be patient.

I wrote about our experiences with math to John Holt and Donna Richoux at *Growing Without Schooling* and attributed the success that we have had in part to the math books we are using. Donna wrote back to ask the names of the books. She said that if they were really so terrific, then she could spread the word to all sorts of hungering families who were searching desperately for the perfect books.

Unfortunately, I couldn't in good conscience recommend either of the books to other families without reservations. While Ishmael loves words like "associative" and "commutative," I imagined those terms would be enough to turn many kids off to math for a long time. And whereas Ishmael prefers doing problems in plain old black-and-white, maybe other kids would prefer those gimmicky workbooks in living color. Besides, there is sometimes an ideal situation, in which the child doesn't need a math book at all. Most likely he or she is being raised in a family that is heavily involved in mathematics, occupationally or for pleasure, and just absorbs mathematical knowledge from the environment.

Vita, who is five as I write this, does use math workbooks. She uses them partly because she likes to play "school," but also because our house still is not as oriented toward numbers as we would like. Nonetheless, since the age of three, she has had the almost daily opportunity to hang around and listen to Ishmael's math lessons. She has pored through his math workbooks, she has always played cards and other games involving numbers with us, and she has spent endless hours doing carpentry work with Bob. It's no wonder, then, that she feels comfortable around numbers and is eager 'to discover what they can do for her.

Recently, Vita has been working with large numbers. I had suggested that she practice writing the numerals from one to twenty in her handwriting notebook since she often writes many of them backwards. On her own, she just took off. I was in another room when she yelled, "How do I make a thirty?" and I called back absently, "3, 0." Before long Vita asked how to write "40," and then there was a long silence. When I finally got around to seeing what she was up to, I found her working on her eighties. True, many of the individual numerals were written backwards, but she had discovered the pattern on her own and she made it easily to 99. I helped her with 100. The next day, after I showed her the correct way to write 100–110, she picked up the pattern again and managed to find her way up to 199. I guess it won't be long before I have to buy her a new notebook!

Another recent interest of Vita's is our calculator. Ishmael's grandparents gave it to him for his ninth birthday, but he showed little interest in it. Bob was pleased to have it since he figured it could save us some time with our taxes, but I found it positively distasteful. My life is centered around the (highly unlikely) possibility that I'll be shipwrecked on a desert island, so I try not to let myself get overly fond of or dependent upon amenities that I'd lack out there on the hot sands beneath the coconut trees. I try to avoid relying on machines of all kinds (with the exception of cars, which I'm sure I would find unpractical on a desert island anyway). Understandably, I kept my distance from the calculator.

Vita, however, doesn't share my prejudice, and she has been toying with the thing ever since we got it. More than anything, it has acquainted her with some of the crazy types of numbers that lie in dusty corners of the mathematical universe. When she is feeling somewhat serious, she likes me to "give" her hard problems to do, like $150 + 27 = ?$ or $189 - 54 = ?$ As well as reinforcing her ability to write large numbers, this process seems to encourage her mathematical common sense. She is constantly making mistakes like pressing the wrong buttons or getting her digits mixed up, and she is often able to catch the absurdity of the answers that the calculator gives her. This seems to me to be a very important skill. Because Vita knows, for example, that the answer to $189 - 54 = ?$ ought to be less than 189, she becomes surprised and indignant when the calculator blinks 243. She likes to come to me so I can help her figure out her mistake (she apparently has blind faith in the machine, unlike me), and we usually laugh when we are able to figure out what silly thing Vita did. "Looks like you added when you should have subtracted, ha, ha!"

When we drive places in the car, Vita often begs "Give me some math problems," and so we pass the time. I struggle to make up interesting word problems and Vita happily solves them. There is one problem I made up, though, that she refused to get right. It went, "If there are three little girls, and they divide a chocolate cake into six pieces, how many pieces does each girl get?"

"That's an easy one," Vita answered casually. "They each get one piece." No matter how many times I went over the problem she always answered, "one." Finally, when I was totally exasperated, Vita explained that almost certainly, considering that the cake was chocolate and the pieces were so large, the girls' mother would never have let them eat seconds. Oh, Vita, you're always so rational, I thought. But something else passed through my mind as well. In school, Ishmael had had to do an awful lot of problems involving candy and cookies, and I wondered how many of them he had gotten wrong by following the same logic.

Besides addition and subtraction, Vita understands simple fractions, multiplication, and division. And so do most children her age who aren't already hung up. She uses these operations in everyday life, when she's cutting up cakes and pies, figuring out how much toast to make at breakfast time, playing half notes and quarter notes on the piano, pulling up carrots and figuring out how long it's going to take her to finish the row, and so on.

She also works with these mathematical processes in a workbook put out by the Key Curriculum Project. What I like about this book is that it is focused on individual numbers and the various numerical ways that we can express those numbers— rather than on addition and subtraction as totally separate processes. In other words, rather than concentrating on addition for three months and then introducing subtraction, as is often done in conventional first-grade classes, this book introduces addition, subtraction, multiplication, and division all at once. By encouraging kids to look at different ways of expressing the number ten, for example, it leads them to discover answers as various as $5 + 5$, $12 - 2$, 2×5 and $\frac{1}{2} \times 20$. By being introduced formally to multiplication and division early, Vita will never look upon them as "that hard stuff you learn in third or fourth grade." They will be as natural to her as cutting up her own birthday cake (which, I admit, does occasionally get a bit messy).

The other workbook we have for her is called *Arithmetic Readiness*. It is put out by the same people who publish the *Lennes Essentials of Arithmetic* series that Ishmael uses. I like this book mainly because on every other page there are four or five word-problems in the form of nursery rhymes and Mother Goose tales. They not only seem interesting mathematically, but Vita is also eager to *read* them, just for the story content. On the opposite sides of each page there are about twenty simple "math facts," nicely laid out, which Vita also seems to enjoy doing.

About ten pages into the book, though, I began to notice that Vita was getting a startling number of her answers wrong. It looked as though she was just putting any old number into the answer space. Watching her closely, I discovered that was exactly what she was doing. I think that the more she worked abstractly with numbers on the page, the less she related them to possible real-life situations and the less she expected them to make sense. Eventually, they had become meaningless problems for her that she allowed herself to answer with real abandon. It was frightening to see how quickly she had separated the math in the workbook from ordinary life—and frightening, too, to think what would have happened to her in school. After a few weeks of receiving bad marks on her math papers, she would have just assumed that she was stupid. Then, like Ishmael, she would have become "stupid."

Now that I have seen the harm that a workbook like that can do, I don't encourage Vita to use it. Sometimes she does get it out, though, to do a page or two for fun. That is fine—she actually reinforces her knowledge of math facts as long as she has plenty of practical, concrete math experience in between workbook sessions.

Vita and Ishmael are obviously two different individuals, and I am doing my best to meet each of their needs. I am also reminded quite often, though, that I am dealing with kids outside of a classroom, and that what works for even the best classroom teachers does not necessarily work for us. A few days ago, for example, I was re-reading John Holt's *How Children Fail* and was particularly interested in all the work he did using Cuisenaire rods with his classes. Frankly, I was also a bit jealous. Why were the rods such a success with those kids, I had to ask myself, but not with Ishmael or even with Vita, who also shows little interest in them?

I think the answer lies with the fact that John was working with children in a classroom. Those kids had complete faith that whatever John gave them to do would be useful and educational. He was the teacher with the awesome responsibility of directing their educations, and probably none of those kids even considered taking over part of that responsibility. If John suggested working with Cuisenaire rods, they were delighted. The rods were more fun than most things they did in school, and it went without saying that the rods must serve some educational purpose.

Ishmael, on the other hand, knew he was behind in math and he felt pressure, from inside, to do something about it. Math as he knew it from school meant solving "problems." To him, Cuisenaire rods seemed like a waste of time, since they didn't appear to have anything to do with that. He couldn't trust me when I suggested that the rods might eventually increase his understanding of mathematics.

As for Vita, her use of numbers is only incidentally on paper, and constantly involves concrete objects, from oranges to firewood. She has no need of a *special* set of concrete objects, such as Cuisenaire rods, to create this relationship. The kids John was dealing with, on the other hand, had been trained by years of school, as Ishmael was, to experience math as a school subject, entirely separate from reality. Cuisenaire rods played a vital role in helping to bridge this split in their minds.

Sometimes people, particularly those who know about my limited background in math, ask me questions about the future. They want to know how long I feel I can continue to act as a math teacher for the kids. Some people even hint that I may end up limiting them, mathematically. I can't blame them, either. Even I occasionally ask myself what I am doing teaching fractions to Ishmael when I can barely do them myself.

School fouled me up in math about as badly as it did Ishmael. Unlike him, though, I had to put up with nine or ten years of it.

When I was in third grade, my family spent a year in Europe. While I learned all kinds of things—how to speak fluent German, for example—math wasn't one of them. When I returned home I discovered, to my dismay, that everyone had been taught long division in my absence. Nobody bothered to teach it to me, and so I struggled with it on my own. Just as I was finally getting the hang of it, we were suddenly introduced to a "new" kind of long division by the modern math people. I had to start all over again from scratch and I must have just fallen apart, because in all the years to come, I never did catch up with everybody else. As for my teachers, they avoided my problem. It was far easier to give me an "A" or a "B" than to take the trouble to figure out where I went wrong and help me.

My other trouble is that I have never been able to retain facts in my head unless I understand what they mean. I did badly in physics, for example, because we were given a bunch of "laws" to memorize, which were important since they were the foundation of the physics we were supposed to be learning. But since the teacher would never explain why the laws were *true*, they didn't make any sense to me. They floated past me at an embarrassingly fast rate of speed. Math was taught to us in the same manner—except for a brief interlude when modern math was in vogue. Then, although we were *swamped* with explanations, the teachers were so confused that their explanations made no sense. As soon as the principal allowed them to, they went back to their standard approach. Once again, we were expected to take all mathematical procedures on faith.

Despite my troubles with math, I think, and Bob agrees, that I am more than adequate as a math teacher for the time being. Even though I am only able to stay about five minutes ahead of Ishmael, I am very conscious of what I just went through myself to learn whatever concept it is that we are working on. This makes me patient, and it also makes me enthusiastic. Here I am, over thirty years old, and finally I am able to begin making sense of fractions! Yay! My enthusiasm is at least somewhat catching, too, judging by Ishmael's response.

Besides using me as a teacher, Ishmael works quite a bit on his own—especially with geometry, where I seem to be able to work up very little interest. Ishmael has been using a workbook called *Key to Geometry* that is geared toward having children work on their own. Also, being aware of Ishmael's interest, Bob is good about helping him to find books at least partly based on geometry. They've enjoyed reading together about surveying, astronomy, and cosmology.

As the kids get older, and particularly if my interest should wane, I am confident that they will be able to pick up the math they want to learn on their own, from books. But if one of the kids (and this is quite possible, particularly with Vita) begins to take a real interest in abstract mathematics, I think we'd hire a tutor—not a professional tutor, but either a college student or a retired person with a genuine interest in math. Bob and I agree that it is important for the kids to be able to share their enthusiasms with likeminded people. A tutor could act primarily as a colleague, happy to impart his or her thoughts and ideas about whatever it is that the kids want to explore. We also imagine that it must be possible for a teenager who is really interested in math to find apprenticeships or volunteer-type positions in laboratories, with surveyors, or whatever, where real math is used.

So I am optimistic about the future. I look forward to staying five minutes ahead of Ishmael for the next few years anyway. I want at least to learn algebra, and then we'll see what happens from there.

Chapter 9

The Doll Game

Margery, the Victorian doll mother, is harvesting potatoes in the garden. Gently, taking care not to intrude, Ishmael helps. The potatoes are blue and green marbles which they pile into little china pots. At the edge of the garden, feeding on pink paper flowers, are the barnyard animals—a red plastic sheep, a glass pig, and a white metal horse. The animals are no more than a half an inch high, whereas Margery must be a towering six inches. Ishmael doesn't seem to mind this incongruity and, of course, neither does Margery. The rest of the members of the Victorian doll family are idling away their time in the second story of their block house, which is in the middle of the rug on the bedroom floor. Thomas, the father, is staring at the grandfather clock; Auntie-Governess is standing over a wounded toy soldier who is lying on a bed of paper towels, and the Victorian children are sitting at a table covered with a flowery tablecloth made by Vita.

Across the blue-velvet-ribbon river, things are more lively. Vita is helping her family of wooden Fisher-Price "Little People" to have a picnic. Outside their modest block house, they are standing around a table, complete with a red checkered tablecloth, and they are drinking from a little green bottle of champagne and a slightly larger mug of frothy beer. For food they have a large plastic roast beef.

Suddenly, all eyes turn on the mother. "Look, I've had a baby!" Vita helps her to exclaim. Sure enough, lying on the floor right next to Mother is a tiny pink baby. Vita helps everyone crowd around in admiration, and then she takes the father away to find a cradle and a bottle for the baby. When it is comfortably settled, the Little People continue with their picnic.

"Brr," says one of the picnickers. As if brought back to reality, Vita calls across the river and through the wooden evergreen forest to Ishmael, "What season are they having?" "Fall," he answers. "Fall?" she complains. "But we haven't even had winter yet and I thought fall came after winter. And anyway, if Margery is digging potatoes it must be summer, because Nancy harvested our potatoes in the summer." Patiently, Ishmael explains, all the while working with Margery in the potato patch. "No Vita, fall comes between summer and winter. You know, it's when the leaves turn color and we have frosts. I know Nancy harvested the potatoes in the summer, but that was because we had an early frost. Sometimes there are frosts around here in the summertime. Most people, though, harvest their gardens in the fall. That's why they have jack-o'-lanterns at Halloween and big dinners at Thanksgiving. After that comes Christmas, but then there's lots of snow and it's winter." "Oh," says Vita thoughtfully as she feeds the baby and helps Mother put a rug over it to keep off the chill, "well, let's have Halloween then."

Ishmael hesitates. "I suppose that's okay. But it will have to be tomorrow, because Margery has to finish getting all the vegetables put away for the winter first." "Alright," says Vita, "but why don't the Victorian children come see our new baby while Margery works?" Ishmael leaves Margery in the garden and moves over to the house. Father is drilling the children in multiplication. "6 × 3 is how much?" "Um—er—18!" gasps the boy. "Good," says Father. "Now how much is 8 × 4?" "25," he blunders. "Dunce! Fool!" taunts his sister. "Don't call each other names," says Father sternly. "Now why don't you go and visit the family across the river? And take a soldier with you for protection in case you meet any robbers in the forest." Ishmael helps the children and the soldier walk through the woods and across the block bridge over the ribbon river. They greet the gay picknickers. "Hi," says the Fisher-Price father. "We just had a baby a couple of minutes ago." "What a calamity," says the Victorian girl, rudely. The Little People try to ignore the remark. "Come see the baby," they say. "It's sleeping in its new cradle." The children walk over and peer into the cradle. "What an ugly baby," says the Victorian boy. This time, the children's rudeness is just too much. "Don't you dare!" shout all the Little People. The girl tries to make amends to the mother by saying, "Well, ah, er, it does have your complexion." But it's no use. The Little People yell and scream and drive the children back across the river with their bodyguard, the toy soldier. They arrive at home a bit abashed, avoid Margery in the garden, and go up to Father, who pays the soldier for looking after the children with a hunk of cheese fresh from the dairy.

Back at the potato patch, Ishmael helps Margery load the last of the potatoes into pots and put them into the storehouse next to the Noah's Ark barn. "Well," he says to Vita doubtfully, "I guess if they only eat a potato a day they'll get through the winter." "Hey, I know, Ishmael," says Vita, "if you trade us some wool from your sheep we'll give you our pig." "Well, okay. But is your pig dead or alive?" "It's dead," she answers. "We just butchered it yesterday." "That's good. We'll smoke the meat and it'll last for a couple of months anyway, and come spring, the glass pig will have piglets again and we won't have to worry about meat."

While one of the Little People takes his brown-spotted pig over to the Victorian family and exchanges it for yarn, two of the Little People's children have decided to be naughty. "I want to build a fire," whispers a little boy to his sister, "but I don't know how. Will you help?" "Sure," she agrees, pretending to be an experienced firebuilder. Vita helps them collect wood, paper, and make-believe matches, and she helps the little girl strike a "match." Almost before the imaginary fire is lit, it has burst out of control and the Little People begin shouting, "Fire! Fire! Fire! The house is burning down!" Vita, working as fast as she can, helps them to find cups and bowls, and they rush to the river for water. Quickly and efficiently, they smother the fire. But it is too late. The house is in ashes. With a casual kick, Vita fells the block walls. After building a new house, the family take a nap and then eat supper.

Still a little worried about the winter's food supply, Ishmael looks over and asks Vita where the Little People get all their food. "They traded for a bowl which happened to be full of roast beef," she answers. "And they still have a pile of Easter eggs left." At Vita's place, food is apparently not the problem it is over at the Victorian family's farm.

After a good night's sleep, which seems to last only a few minutes, the families begin stirring in their beds. It is Halloween morning! Thomas, the Victorian father, climbs down the ladder to the storeroom to get the daily potato. While Margery cooks it on the wood range, he wakes up the children. Auntie-Governess, who has nothing to do, stands around admiring the new pearl necklace that Ishmael has casually thrown over her shoulders. Meanwhile, Father calls the children for the third time. "We're coming. We're just getting dressed," they complain.

While both families are eating breakfast, Vita suddenly gets worried. "Oh, no. We don't have any candy for the trick-or-treaters." "Well, my family is just going to give away potatoes," says Ishmael. Vita looks disgusted, but then brightens up with an idea. "Why don't we use beads for candy?" "Okay, but my family is going to make its own treats." Vita gets her box of beads, puts a few into a bowl, and sets it on the Little People's table. "Ishmael," she says, "see my candy. I have three of one kind and three of another." Ishmael, who is preoccupied with the farm animals, says, without looking up, "Yes, you have very nice candy." A bit perturbed, Vita responds, "If people don't want candy for treats, they don't have to have anything. *Or* they could have a vegetable."

Ishmael doesn't answer. He is looking after Margery and Thomas, who are talking near the barn. "Alright, let's water the animals." "Should we let them out?" "Yes, it's not winter yet, but we'll put them back in the barn if it should start to snow." "The air does feel awfully chilly. We'll have to remember to close the kitchen door when we go back to the house." "Okay, but it always makes me feel sad to close up the house for the winter." "I know." "Well, we'd better go feed the horses."

Before long, dusk falls and everybody hurries to get ready for the Halloween celebrations. Ishmael brings in a quince from outside and carves it into a jack-o'-lantern with his Swiss army knife. Vita has all the troll clothes out and she is dressing both families up in outrageous, ill-fitting costumes—a Santa Claus suit, a wedding dress, jewelry, feathered hats, and sequined capes. "Okay, time for trick-or-treating," she says. "Not yet," Ishmael reminds her. "We forgot to get little bags for the candy." "Well, we don't have any bags, so why don't we use bowls instead?" "Alright," Ishmael agrees.

"Have your family come to my house first, okay, Ishmael?" Ishmael helps the two Victorian children and their father walk over to the Little Peoples' house. "Trick-or-treat, trick-or-treat, give us something good to eat!" The children greedily grab at the bowlful of candy offered to them. "No! No! Don't take so much. Only take four pieces, okay? Two for each of you." "Well, that's not enough," say the rude children. To keep the Victorian children quiet, Vita hastily gets a bowl full of tiny, multicolored beads from her windowsill bead box and she gives each child a scoopful. Over at the Victorian family manse, the marble potatoes have miraculously turned into large hunks of candy and the Little People help themselves contentedly. Only Vita complains, "It's so troublesome changing everyone's costumes and rationing the candy. I think Thanksgiving will be easier." Ishmael, who is watching the reserve of potato-candy diminish at a frightening rate, is too preoccupied to respond. Instead he says musingly, "Let's pretend that pigs *do* have babies in the winter." Vita nods as the Little People continue their chant, "Trick-or-treat, trick-or-treat, give us something good to eat!"

This is the "doll game." Every day, during the cold months anyway, Vita and Ishmael play it, in one form or another. And despite the fact that Bob and I have little to do with it, except as interested observers, it is a key aspect of the kids' learning at home. Although it is only a "game," they use the dolls to replay, sort out, and transform events in their everyday lives. Through their fantasies they act out and experiment with the adult roles that they may later fill. For me, the game is a constant reminder that when they are given the time, the space, and the encouragement, children can find imaginative ways to teach themselves the primary skills they need to acquire in order to enter the adult world.

Of course, children's fantasy play is nothing new. It has been around, and parents have encouraged it, ever since the beginning of time. When our little girls, for example, play with baby dolls—nurse them and change their diapers—we think that the way they are imitating us is charming and we know that, through their games, they are unconsciously preparing for their own motherhood. Like mother cats, who encourage their kittens to pounce on balls of string in preparation for mousing, we trust our daughters' early play and see it as a crucial aspect of their growth. The same holds true, of course, for our sons' play, though some of us may have doubts about their guns and toy soldiers.

But ordinarily, when our children reach school age, our attitude changes. Now the world of school—schoolwork and homework, organized recess play, and "socialization"—begins to take precedence. We no longer trust our children to learn without adult interference the important things they need to know. We begin to view fantasy play as merely childish, as an "escape from reality." We forget or suppress our early recognition that it not only made our children happy but offered them a chance to get acquainted with adult roles in one of the only ways open to them, namely, through their play.

I never thought much about the conflict between fantasy play and school until I began watching Vita and Ishmael playing with their dolls during school hours. What never failed to amaze me was the way that they always seemed to weave the threads of our everyday lives into their games. Take the game I just described, for example. It really did take place during the fall—only three weeks before Halloween, in fact. I had harvested the garden, and boxes of pumpkins, squash, and potatoes filled the pantry and overflowed into the kitchen. But despite the abundance of our harvest, I kept wondering aloud whether it would get us through the winter. Ishmael, who dislikes grocery stores almost as much as I do, was obviously a bit worried about whether we'd have enough to eat come spring. Then too, on a walk the week before, we had seen two happy pigs rooting in the remnants of a farmer's vegetable garden, and we naturally got to talking about the future prospects of those pigs as Christmas hams and bacon. And for a couple of weeks previous to that particular game, Bob and I had been painfully discussing whether or not to slaughter our friendly three-year-old chickens. The kids didn't like the idea, but like us, they were trying to get themselves into a farmer's frame of mind. (Actually, we never succeeded. Instead, we decided to let the hens enjoy a well-earned retirement.)

Unlike the Victorian father, Bob doesn't drill the kids on their multiplication tables. But it is interesting that whenever the dolls do have schoolwork to do, it is always at home—either loosely structured and pleasant, or more like the real school Ishmael experienced, with drill work and children teasing each other.

And as for Vita's desire to have proper Halloween candy for the dolls and her odd statement about how if people didn't want candy they could always have vegetables, I'm afraid I am to blame for that. Halloween is my least favorite holiday, partly because I hate to sew and I always find myself coerced into making costumes, but also because the thought of so many children gorging themselves on chocolate bars, lollipops, and other disgusting, multicolored candies always makes me ill. Hence, I usually put off buying Halloween treats for the neighborhood children until the last minute. That year, though, in fun, I had told Vita that I thought we should hand out celery and carrots instead. She had apparently taken me seriously, and she had decided to try the idea out on her dolls. I was relieved to find that in the end, the dolls were able to indulge themselves with all the candy they could hold.

Aside from the fact that it is marvelous to see the ways in which they use material from real life in their games, I am always delighted to see that Vita and Ishmael can, with the help of the dolls, really act out and involve themselves in all the parameters of daily living—eating, sleeping, learning, socializing, working, and playing—with the feeling of control that adults have over their lives. And I can see that, through the medium of fantasy, the kids are ultimately (though unconsciously) trying to achieve for themselves what the schools are trying to help kids in general to achieve, namely, to grow up and become productive adults.

Of course, when I tell people about the doll game, it naturally brings questions to their minds. "Even if Vita and Ishmael's fantasies do help to prepare them for adult life," they ask, "won't they be oddballs? After all, how can you ever expect them to 'fit in' if you allow them to play with dolls, while the rest of the children their age are in school?" These are difficult questions, and it would be dishonest for me to claim to know all the answers. But there are things I do know that shed some light on these questions.

First, and of the greatest importance, the kids are happy when they play. As far as I can tell, they feel no anxieties or tensions, except during their occasional, and very normal, squabbles. And it seems to me, from the people I've known, that happy, secure children grow up to be happier, more secure adults. Secondly, the kids' games are so rich in content—with the dolls' complicated family lives, their governments (complete with written laws and rulers), their monetary systems, their complicated economic transactions, their political discussions, their ballets and circuses, and their battles and revolutions—that I just can't see this kind of play as evidence of "isolation." If anything, it is just the opposite. Their play is proof that they are very much interested and in touch with the real world. Just as important as all of the educational benefits that the kids derive from the "doll game," they find it fun and relaxing, and it has given them more hours of pleasure than anything else I can think of.

I can't really remember when the game got started. In a way, it is fair to say that it has been growing and evolving since Ishmael was two, when he was given a set of blocks for his birthday. Before that, he had always shunned toys. He preferred to play with our telephone, to climb up onto Bob's desk and destroy his typewriter ribbon whenever he had the chance, and to pull all of my pots and pans out of the kitchen cupboards and bang them on the floor. But the small set of colored wooden blocks delighted him. He built tall towers oh-so-carefully, adding block after block until the entire structure would begin to tilt precariously and finally crash to the ground. Within three months, he had become so expert at balancing blocks that he could easily beat Bob and me in tower building competitions. By the time he was three-and-a-half and Vita was born, he had acquired a set of large, plain-colored Childcraft blocks, a set of plastic cowboys, and perhaps a dozen Fisher-Price "Little People." Vita grew up in the midst of these toys. At first she was content to lie on her back and watch Ishmael "build." When she was six months old, she rolled over for the first time and almost knocked over one of his buildings. At a year, she was making buildings of her own—not towers, like Ishmael, but low enclosures. She put some Little People inside, and Ishmael was fascinated. I guess he realized for the first time that he could use blocks to build forts for his cowboys. Soon, the cowboys, which were plastic and really quite unsympathetic creatures, were placed outside the forts and relegated to the role of exposed invaders. The Little People huddled within the safety of the block walls and hurled marbles at them.

Meanwhile, Vita was accumulating all sorts of marvelous dolls, large and small tea sets, a miniature cast iron stove, and even some dollhouse furniture—all from adoring relatives. All she needed was a dollhouse, which Bob indulgently built. When it was finished, it was lovely, with a painted tile roof, and blue walls, which Bob let the kids paint themselves. Vita crammed her dolls and pieces of furniture into it and went back to the blocks and cowboys, while I excitedly asked my mother to send all the dollhouse furniture I had made when I was younger, as well as my two trolls with all of their clothes.

When I was five or six years old, I went to a neighbor's house and was overwhelmed with her real dollhouse filled with miniature furniture. I must have realized that it had cost a fortune, because I never asked my parents to buy me one. Instead, I spent the next six years meticulously making my own. I used cupboard shelves for the actual dollhouse, and I wove rugs, sewed quilts, wrote real, miniature books, modeled a toilet, sink, and bathtub out of clay, and built dressers out of matchboxes. My father made me a wooden sink with a real drain, and my mother made me a stovepipe out of black construction paper. For a dining room table, I used a piece of mahogany that had once been a wood sample in a furniture store. It stood on Lincoln Log legs.

I seldom actually played with my dollhouse, although it did have little animal inhabitants, because I was always too busy building furniture. Later, I got plastic trolls with long exotically colored hair to live in the house. And although I didn't play with them either, I made piles of elaborate clothing for them —dresses with lace collars, cut glass buttons and velvet ties, silk underwear, sandals, hats, necklaces and earrings, and even fur coats and bathing suits.

All these things my mother sent to Vita. I expected her to love them, to place the furniture carefully into her dollhouse and to keep the trolls' clothes neatly folded when they weren't being worn. Naturally, she did nothing of the sort. She jammed the furniture into the house helter-skelter and then actually *played* with her dolls in it. She put the big ones in right alongside the little ones. She not only kept the troll clothes jumbled in their box, but she went so far as to dress her other dolls in the clothes.

Ishmael also liked to play with the dollhouse, perhaps even more than Vita. Since it was too small for both of them to play with side by side, they began moving the furniture onto the floor and playing there. When Bob's sister, Miggles, heard about the kids' games, she sent them her old dollhouse furniture, more trolls and clothes, and a beautiful old doll in a paisley box. This doll wore petticoats, a pink dress, and a red coat with a white fur muff. When Ishmael saw her, he exclaimed, "We'll make her the queen of the dolls!" That was the beginning of the doll country of Skirmishia (although it didn't get its name for another month or two).

Ishmael described the first Queen's ascent to the throne, and her reign, in his brief "History of the Old Civilization of Skirmishia—from divers old records." It was an essay inspired by the books that the Bronte children wrote about their toy soldiers.

The oldest record we have in our hands shows that there was a kind of democracy in Skirmishia before the first Queen arrived. However, when a person lost an election, he would fight the winner, so people were quite relieved when a queen appeared and took the throne. The first Queen was given to a genie by a genie called Miggles. The genie put her into Skirmishia. She had yellow hair and several changes of clothes. She married a piano player who was henceforth called Prince Concert. Her greatest service to the country was to set up a new economy, based on a newcomer, the Little Farmer, which was not dependent upon Skirmishia's neighbors, the acorns and chessmen. Her reign was one of intermittent warfare with them.

With the advent of Skirmishia, the doll game took on an entirely new character. Each doll family—the Queen and her new husband, the Little Farmer and his barnyard, the Little People, the toy soldiers, and even the acorns and chessmen—had separate dwellings, placed in various corners of the kids' room. The main action of the game took place on their braided rug, but at night everyone was put to bed in their own homes. Morning, noon, and night, the whole crew had to be fed and taken care of. If we went out for the day, the kids left the Skirmishians snacks, and if I wanted to vacuum the kids' room, I didn't dare misplace one doll. Sometimes, when I wanted to do a thorough cleaning, the Skirmishians all took a holiday; but that involved giving quite a bit of advance warning, so that they could have time to plan their trip and pack their bags.

The Skirmishian economy centered around the Little Farmer, a one-inch-high wooden man who had a few cows and pigs of about his size who all fit into a tiny Ark. He also had an apple orchard. With the apples and the milk and cheese from his dairy, he fed most of Skirmishia. The Little People bought half of his food with two pennies. One of these pennies the farmer paid to the Queen as a tax, and the other he paid to Sambo, a minstrel doll who was about twenty times his size. In return, Sambo gave him piano lessons. With her penny, the Queen paid the Little People to work in her blueberry fields. She had all kinds of dependents—soldiers, ancestors, indigent friends, and the guards who looked after Skirmishia's dragon.

People didn't work all the time in Skirmishia, though. There were circuses, concerts, and plays to attend. One of the most successful plays they put on was *Beau Geste—A Fascinating Story!* Many of Skirmishia's leading citizens—like Sir Charles, the Honored Prussian Hussar, and the Honored Commander —were actors in the drama. During periods of leisure, when there were no staged entertainments on hand, Skirmishians liked to go to their library, where one of the Little People's grandmothers volunteered as librarian.

Unfortunately, Skirmishia was not on friendly terms with its neighbors, the acorns and chessmen. All the citizens were on constant war alert. Ishmael, who acted as a consultant to the toy soldiers, was a great fan of Wellington, so he usually got them to agree to re-enact battles from the Napoleonic wars. Fortunately, this style of warfare always seemed agreeable to the enemy as well, despite the fact that it was seldom able to beat the Skirmishians. Later on they sometimes experimented with revolutionary war battles; but still, the Skirmishians usually came out victorious.

According to Ishmael's "History," after the Queen had ruled for a few months, "she chose as her successor a person called, 'The Queen's Friend.'" The "friend" had come to Skirmishia in this way: a genie named Sherry gave her to a genie named Vita, who put her into the country. On assuming power, this queen tried to take as prisoners all who wanted to have the first queen back. She grew up to be so unpopular that finally she was deposed and the first queen nominated a new queen from an African tribe.

This Queen had a very short reign, during which, for the first time, there were no wars. She read stories to her subjects. This was the main characteristic of her reign.

There were three or four new queens during the next few months, and then

a genie made a queen out of a toilet paper roll. She was a great legislator and diplomatist. The chronicler is not quite sure that the laws were all that great, but they were efficacious. She had a few wars and was defeated twice, having successful rebellions fix her up again. She had the longest reign ever. (She abdicated once and then had to return to fix up the economy.)

It was during this queen's reign that the Skirmishians wrote a constitution. They had a Constitutional Convention which every member of the citizenry attended—including all the children, since Skirmishians believed in "children's rights." Each of the proposed laws was debated hotly before it was voted upon, and while many were rejected outright, others were revised or amended. The final document read:

Law I. No one shall declare war on any nation or country without permission from the Royal Family.

Law II. Prisoners can't get out of jail unless given permission.

Law III. People can have feudal rights, but if they get too uppity they must be deprived of their feudal rights.

Law IV. People must all be told if prisoners escape or if the jail ladder is left up.

Law V. The army must be paid after work.

Law VI. Everyone should go to a meeting if there is one, unless the person has something else in mind.

Law VII. We should remember that Pinnie needs a bed.

Later some amendments were made to the Constitution.

Amend. I. We should clean the country.

Amend. II. The Royal Family should go to every trial.

Amend. III. We should be sure the dragon is fed.

Amend. IV. We should make sure the Farmer has piano lessons.

Unfortunately, the Constitution was unable to bring order to Skirmishia. Some shiny new soldiers, complete with a brass cannon, arrived on the scene. And since they were constantly picking fights with the acorns, Skirmishia was plunged into a state of almost continuous war. Vita soon tired of the battles and longed to play with some of her dolls by herself; but she wasn't free to, since all her dolls were Skirmishians who disliked having their daily routines disturbed. Consequently, it wasn't only the soldiers and acorns who did the fighting—Vita and Ishmael began having battles of their own. The kids' arguments drove me crazy, especially since I wasn't sure how to handle them. Once I went so far as to insist that they stay away from Skirmishia for three whole days. We had three days of peace, and then they went back to their battles.

Soon after, we went to see an Australian movie called *Breaker Morant*, which was about the moral complexities involved in the Boer War. It focused on the British army's confusion—not to mention desperation and frustration—fighting the Boer guerillas, who were, after all, just members of the Boer populace. The British fought viciously because they couldn't "see" their enemy. They killed prisoners of war and rounded up Boer women and children and put them into camps in which many died of hunger and disease. Fortunately, the movie wasn't too overtly bloody. It was quite powerful, though, and Ishmael couldn't stop thinking about it. He had always thought of battles or warfare as orderly and almost intellectual endeavors. In Skirmishia, the two opposing generals would arise at dawn, survey the battlefield, and then arrange their men strategically among the evergreen trees and the block hills, and along the banks of the ribbon river. The side with the weakest formation lost by retreating back to its own borders. There were never any fatalities in these battles. When soldiers were occasionally wounded, the Little People carried them off to a pleasant hospital where they rested on flowered sheets and were surrounded by doting nurses.

But now Ishmael realized that wars weren't always fought so cleanly. They were bloody, dirty, ill-planned, and cruel, and he was disturbed. The day after we saw the film, we spent hours discussing World War II (I'm not sure why Ishmael didn't ask about Vietnam). We talked about why the war had begun in the first place and how it was fought. Ishmael thought that maybe that war, and others, could have been avoided if countries were smaller, "like Liechtenstein." Just to get Ishmael to think even harder, Bob said that perhaps a world government, with true economic interdependence, would have been even more effective. During all the hours of our discussion, we could find no easy solution to the world's problems. Finally Ishmael said, "Well at least the world should disarm, say, to the point of Cromwell's day. Then at least there wouldn't be too many people killed." Bob and I let the discussion go at that. Ishmael obviously needed to get back to the certainties he held before the movie, and he wanted to be able to go back to his toy soldier games again and enjoy them. That was fine by us, as long as he and Vita stopped bickering.

Their room was ominously quiet when I peeked in a few days later. Where Skirmishia had once stood I was surprised to find the kids building block houses for some newly organized doll families—self-sufficient folk living in a peaceful land with no war, no economy, and no ruler. Ishmael had apparently lost interest in his soldiers, and he and Vita were playing happily again. When I asked Ishmael how the dolls felt about the dissolution of Skirmishia and their changes in occupation and character, he said somewhat defensively, "Well, they are just dolls, aren't they? And if they do come alive at night, like dolls in books, they have their own lives anyway, and don't much care what we do with them in the daytime."

I admit that I had to swallow hard when I heard him talk like that. Was he suddenly growing up, I wondered anxiously. But I shouldn't have worried so soon. Although Skirmishia was gone, the doll game continued as intensely as ever.

As I write this, a "New Skirmishia" has emerged. Ishmael explained that a drought had befallen the old Skirmishia and the residents had all been forced to flee and seek their fortunes in far corners of the world. But lately, the land of Skirmishia has had plenty of rainfall and it has turned lush and green again. Now the Skirmishians are returning.

This time, Skirmishia has been divided into two counties which can only be crossed, as Vita explains, "by boat, train, or car." The transportation industry has become one of the biggest employers in Skirmishia. Its scale is approached in magnitude only by the Little Farmer, who employs the soldiers to work in his marble cabbage field with plastic rakes, shovels, and hoes from a game of Pick-Up-Sticks. The farmer pays the Little People to transport his vegetables by boat, train, and car, and the Little People use their money to buy the Little Farmer's food. With no more war, New Skirmishia hasn't been plagued by inflation and everybody seems happy.

That is the game as it stands today. Tomorrow it is sure to be different, and I look forward to seeing how it changes. Mostly though, I look forward to seeing the kids' happy faces as they play.

A few months ago, a reporter came over to talk about and gather material for an article he was writing about home education. He was generally sympathetic with our unorthodox ideas about education, but when he saw the kids playing with their dolls and discovered that they had no battery-operated or computer-type toys, or even a television, he asked us how we thought they would fare when they grew up into a world full of computers and space travel. Shouldn't we concern ourselves with preparing them for the world of the future, he asked.

When I think of the world of the future, I usually think of no world at all, just a bunch of craters left by nuclear bombs. That is why I think about the future as little as possible. A world run by machines, a world where flying around in space is more challenging than figuring out how to feed hungry people, is also a world I hate to think about. We try to provide our children with a secure, loving, and culturally rich environment. We expect that even in the world of the future (if there still is a world, of course) there will at least be corners of it where people who care about art, music, books, and honest, loving relations with one another will survive. And the kids, too, with their world of Skirmishia, are evidently putting their faith in a future of real people, strong families, and wholesome work.

Chapter 10

Music

When I think of all the fun we have with music and how close our family has grown through playing music together, it scares me to remember that we blundered into music, and the piano in particular, almost by sheer luck. Would we have started taking piano lessons if there hadn't been an immense old upright in the kitchen when we moved into our house? I always wonder.

The piano was painted a hideous tan with gold gilding highlighting the scroll work on the legs. I painted the whole thing a dull green, had it tuned, and bought myself some John Thompson books as soon as I had a chance. I figured that I could teach myself to play. For a while I was so enthusiastic that, losing myself in the music, I often burned supper or forgot to make it at all. But soon I became frustrated. I kept making mistakes, and I grew sick of John Thompson. With working on the house (which was in need of a drastic overhaul), looking after baby Vita, and driving Ishmael back and forth to nursery school, I just gradually stopped playing.

I never thought of either of the kids as being particularly musical, perhaps because they showed so little interest in the piano. Other children who came to visit always seemed to make a beeline for the piano and would plunk away happily for as long as their parents could stand the noise. But Vita and Ishmael seldom touched it.

When Ishmael was in first grade, though, a music teacher visited his class for forty-five minutes every week. Ishmael hated to be sick on those days. One of the most traumatic experiences he ever had in school was when he had to miss music because he hadn't finished underlining the suffixes and prefixes on a worksheet the teacher had given him. When he was in second grade, he began making his own crooked lines for a grand staff and a squiggly treble clef and trying to write tunes. Nonetheless, it wasn't until the grueling school board meeting at which our request to teach Ishmael at home was considered that we really began to think about the lack of musical experiences in Ishmael's life.

The school officials had offered an "in-school" proposal as an alternative to our home-schooling proposal. It was entitled, "Considerations for curriculum with respect to Ishmael Wallace—second grade student with advanced capabilities in Reading/English." The document included a bunch of curriculum enrichment suggestions in various subject areas. Under "Music and Art" was written, "While there has been no indication of advanced talents in these areas, it is proposed that both the Music and Art teacher become aware of the boy's abilities and be on the look-out for such indications." My God, I thought, what is an "indication of an advanced talent?" And what could the teachers do even if they discovered that he had one, in a noisy, crowded classroom with one forty-five-minute class a week? This was the first time it had dawned on us, though, that by deciding to keep Ishmael at home, we would be denying him that weekly music class that he appeared to love. Obviously, we would have to fill in for ourselves.

We did some singing together after dinner during the next few months. I also thought vaguely about finding a piano teacher for Ishmael, but by then I was so skeptical of teachers and teaching as such that I didn't make much progress in that direction. Then one day a friend told me about Bob Fraley, who had recently arrived in the area from New York City. He was now teaching piano in his own studio and encouraged families to learn together. "Families?" I asked. "What does that mean?" She didn't really know, but I was intrigued.

Ishmael seemed open to the idea of taking piano lessons, so that evening I called Fraley and made an appointment for the following week to talk. Since Ishmael and Vita—and Bob, too—were all so interested to see what he was like, we drove over to his house together.

After welcoming us into his studio, Bob Fraley began our talk by explaining that he taught children according to the Suzuki method, which involved having them listen intensively to the music they were going to be playing so that they could then learn their pieces by ear. This method would free them from the initial burden of having to read notes and would allow them to concentrate entirely on the music itself. Since listening is so important, he went on, and since he would only see the kids for a short period of time each week, it would have to be my job to be the "home-teacher," as he put it, during the rest of the week. And it would be the job of all of us to create as rich a musical environment as possible. Obviously, this was what my friend had meant by "families learning together."

I was immediately enthusiastic. Ishmael felt the same way, and so did Vita. Although she was barely four, she kept nudging me and whispering, "I want lessons, too!" I had always wanted to play the piano myself, and I also felt that I would be able to help the kids more at home if I could actually play the music they were going to be learning. So, in the end, all three of us decided to take lessons.

The first thing Fraley did was to give us a tape recording of Suzuki Piano Book One. It included almost twenty pieces, many of them common folk songs, that we would initially be learning how to play. We were to play the tape as often as possible so that the pieces would become ingrained in our memories, and this would be the best possible preparation for playing them.

Fraley wanted to start lessons with me first, since that would give me a head start and I'd be better prepared to help with the kids. So we arranged to start with half an hour a week and to add more time as the kids' involvement grew.

Vita and Ishmael brought books, paper, and crayons to the first lesson. They were good about occupying themselves while I worked at the piano, but as soon as we stepped out the door, Vita burst into tears and Ishmael cried out, "We wanted to take lessons too!" So the next week we extended our lesson to an hour, and that is when our musical experience really began.

Because of my past acquaintance with the piano through John Thompson (and earlier experience with the viola), I learned the first pieces quickly. Ishmael and Vita, on the other hand, really needed to get the feel of the piano first. Fraley helped them to explore the keyboard, to discover its range and its ups and downs, and to distinguish note patterns and rhythms by ear. Everything he did was focused on developing their ability to listen to music.

The first song we learned was "Twinkle, Twinkle Little Star," played in four different rhythms called "The Twinkle Variations." As Carole L. Bigler and Valery Lloyd-Watts write in their book about Suzuki piano, *More Than Music*, these variations "contain most of the elements of technique required for Baroque and Classical repertoire. The 'Twinkle Variations' are pure technique disguised as a piece. While children are learning these variations, they are, without realizing it, developing and practicing their first technical assignments at the piano."

Ishmael enjoyed playing them and, although he had some minor coordination problems, he made rapid progress. Vita, however, balked. She definitely did not want to be taught. And anyway, as she told my grandmother, "I already know how to play the piano. All you do is just hit the keys." I was pretty upset, since I was paying for lessons, and I was ready to stop them entirely and wait until she was older. But Bob Fraley reassured me. "Just play the tape recording often," he said. "Let her watch you and Ishmael play, and encourage her to explore the piano playfully. Give her time and she'll catch on." I was skeptical, but he was right. Gradually she began to work out "Twinkle" by herself, with a little help from Ishmael. When she finally had it, she was delighted and played it over and over again.

She still wouldn't accept any help with the four variations, though. This whole period, which lasted for about two months, really tried my patience. I readily admit that I often lost my temper. But just as with the original "Twinkle," by listening to the variations so often and tinkering away on the piano, she began to pick them up.

I, too, was not only learning how to really listen to music, but also how to transfer what I heard to the piano. The first songs I learned were fairly easy, but before long I was working desperately to "play by ear." To help myself learn the longer pieces, I had to sort out the phrases in the melody and discover repeated phrases and simple variations. Often, as Fraley suggested, I would label the phrase patterns A, B, or C and the variations A_1 or B_1 and chart them out on paper. The tape recorder sat on our washing machine near the only electrical outlet in the kitchen, and the piano, unfortunately, was on the other side of the room. This meant that I had to stand at the tape recorder and play a phrase over and over again until I could hum it. Then, humming steadily, I would dash across the kitchen— only to lose it as soon as I sat down at the piano. Then I'd swear disgustedly and repeat the whole process again. Sometimes, in desperation, I got Bob to stand at the tape recorder and play the phrase as I agonized at the piano. Another problem I had was learning how to distinguish the left-hand harmonies from the right-hand melody and hear the chord changes and variations. I soon learned, though, that these early pieces rely almost entirely on broken chord patterns in the left hand. With the help of Bob Fraley, I was able to learn how to listen for and identify C chords, G and G^7 chords, F chords, and D chords.

Ishmael, meanwhile, was having an easier time of it. Since his finger coordination wasn't as good as mine at this early stage, he took longer to learn each piece; but that was actually an advantage. It meant that he spent more time listening to his pieces on tape before he ever sat down to play them, which made it easier for him to keep the tunes in his head. Then too, he didn't seem to mind my help, unlike Vita. With "Twinkle" and his next piece, "Lightly Row," I told him what notes to play and what fingers to use. He needed this kind of help because, although he could sing the songs, he was still so unfamiliar with the piano that he had no idea how even to begin to play them on his own. As he picked out the notes on the keyboard, I sang along: "First finger on C, repeat, fourth finger on G, repeat, fifth finger on A, repeat," and so on. By the third piece, "Honeybee," he was beginning to hear and remember the sounds of the intervals on the piano. With only a bit of help, he learned it by himself.

These first pieces were arranged so that both hands play the same melody. The fourth piece, "Cuckoo," however, calls for a left-hand harmony which consists mostly of broken C and G chords. As Ishmael approached this piece, I felt much the same as when he had first approached potty training or reading. How is he ever going to manage this, I kept worrying. But once he had learned "Cuckoo" "hands separately," he was eager to play it hands together. So I sat down with him and we cautiously set to work. The first measures were tough. We inched along note by note. But soon Ishmael realized that the left-hand chords merely tap out the basic 1-2-3 beat and that the notes just fell into place if he kept his right-hand melody even. Before long, he was working the song out on his own. It was such an incredible relief to watch him that I could have kicked myself. Toilet training and reading, as I had learned after the fact, had been quite natural "humps" to get over, and so was this. Ishmael laughed and laughed when he was done.

All was not easy going, however. Bob Fraley had told Ishmael that music is a matter of individual expression and that to play music is to interpret it. I'm not sure how literally he expected Ishmael to take this, but I do know that he wasn't at all prepared when, as he was pointing out the correct phrasing of a piece, Ishmael lost his temper and burst out, "I'll play it the way I want to!"

Vita, meanwhile, was stubbornly working on her own. She loved to play the pieces that she already knew—the "Twinkles" and by now "Lightly Row." But she so resisted learning new pieces that Suzuki's cheerful advice to "practice for three minutes, ten times a day with joy" was a constant irritation to me. If Vita practiced, it was on her own terms, and I couldn't exactly rave about her progress. She certainly wasn't one of the four-year-olds playing Beethoven sonatas that I had read about in the Suzuki literature.

Finally, Bob Fraley gave me two pieces of shocking advice. First, he suggested that I use snacks as rewards for practicing. Second, he said that it was time I encouraged Vita to view her daily practice time as compulsory, just like brushing her teeth —something that had to get done whether she liked it or not. As I say, I was shocked. In the first place, I have never believed in bribes, and anyway I thought piano playing was supposed to be fun, a reward in itself. Besides, I had vivid memories of the stage Vita went through when it took both Bob and me to hold her down while we brushed her teeth. The analogy between teeth brushing and piano playing certainly wasn't very appealing.

In time, though, I did become desperate enough to break down and try the "snack method." To my amazement, it worked. Once a week, in the grocery store after our piano lesson, I let Vita pick out a healthy snack, such as grapes or yogurt or whole wheat crackers. If Ishmael saw something that looked good to him, he too could get it. I didn't want to make a big deal out of "Vita's snack." At home, she'd put her grapes on the piano, and every time she played a piece she could eat a few. It didn't matter whether she played the song badly or well; I wasn't really rewarding her, I was only offering her sustenance—a chance to rejuvenate herself after the hard work of playing. Afterwards, she'd offer some of her grapes to Ishmael, since she didn't feel they were her property exclusively. Certainly, this snack business was a game, and I did feel rather uncomfortable playing it; but I was amazed at the results. Not only did Vita begin to play a lot, but with a cracker on hand, she seemed to enjoy playing and playing well.

As she began to play regularly and to enjoy her playing, she gradually began to forget about her snacks. After perhaps four or five months, she only used them if she was feeling particularly grumpy. Best of all, she also began using me as a resource, and I soon found that we could work well together for about half an hour or forty-five minutes a day. I had to be very careful, though, not to push her too far. It was better to let her work through as much as she wanted to on her own, even though it was occasionally frustrating for me to wait when I could show her how to play a difficult passage much faster than she could figure it out by herself. I found, too, that it generally seemed best to stop a practice session too soon, before she became tired and while she was still eager to play. Then she looked forward to the next day's practicing much more, and she also spent more time improvising and playing old pieces for pleasure on her own at the piano.

Ishmael, too, was playing a lot—often for as much as two hours a day—and he sounded like it. Sometimes his music was too beautiful for words. People who heard the kids play often asked me how I ever got them to practice. I usually explained, sheepishly, about Vita's grapes and crackers, but in truth I had stopped thinking in terms of "getting the kids to practice." In fact, I now seldom think or talk in terms of "practice" at all (although I've used the word in this chapter to distinguish between the work we do at the piano and the playing we do for fun) since it always draws up bleak visions from my past. I see myself playing a piece on my viola alone in my bedroom after school—knowing that I am hopelessly out of tune and getting the rhythm wrong, and yet finding myself unable to figure out how to fix it. Or, I see a little friend of mine sitting at what appears to be a monstrous black piano and watching her timer while struggling along until her thirty minutes are up so she can resume her game with me. What lonely images, and yet they are so typical of what many children experience with music. It was John Holt who wrote, in his clear-sighted way, in an issue of *Growing Without Schooling*, "Why talk about 'practice?' Why not just talk about playing?"

So why do the kids play as much as they do? First, and most importantly, they do it because they have the time. Whereas most children have to dash off to school after breakfast, stay late for Little League or basketball practice, come home with a pile of homework, and then have to choose between going out to play for half an hour before supper or "practicing," our kids have virtually all day to play music. Watching them so happy with it and so accomplished at it, I always feel a deep resentment towards school, which snatches so much precious time away from children.

Then, too, thanks to Suzuki, who made us aware of how important it is for our whole family to share our kids' musical experience, Vita and Ishmael never have to think of their "practice" times as being lonely. I am almost always right there to help and encourage them and to enjoy their music. And since we have our pianos in rooms that are natural gathering places for ourselves and our friends, there is usually someone else in the room when they stop by to play for a few minutes or when they sit down for their more serious work. Far from distracting them, having an informal audience around seems to bolster their playing.

Finally, thanks to Suzuki's emphasis on listening to music— and not just to the Suzuki recordings, but to the whole range of baroque, classical, romantic, and modern music—Vita and Ishmael have learned to listen and to appreciate music in a way that I have seldom seen in anyone, child or adult. For them, the musical world is a natural extension of their world. They think of all the music they hear as theirs—out there waiting for them to play some day. They listen most regularly, though, to the Suzuki pieces that they are later going to play. As a matter of course, they long to play them—particularly since even the earliest pieces are real music, from traditional folk songs like "Twinkle" to easy compositions by Mozart, Bach, Schumann, and Beethoven. Since they are so eager to play the pieces, they actually find it pleasurable to learn them. They know exactly what the pieces sound like before they ever try to play them, so they don't have to go through the struggle of painfully counting out rhythms and they avoid working in mistakes that they would later have to correct.

Take Vita with her first Bach minuet, for example. She had been listening to it almost every day for a year—either on tape or when Ishmael and I played it—before she sat down with me, full of eagerness, to learn it. Mostly, she picked out the notes herself, although I was there the whole time to show her the proper fingering and to help her find the more difficult notes before she became frustrated. With less than half an hour of concentrated effort, she was able to play the right-hand melody all by herself. When we played it together, with me filling in with the left-hand melody, she was so excited that she ran to Bob and dragged him away from his work to listen to us. She had a bit more trouble learning the more difficult left-hand melody, and it took her a few weeks before she could play both melodies "hands together." But because she could feel the beauty of the music, she was always eager to work on it.

Just this past week, as another example, Vita memorized two-thirds of the second movement of a Beethoven sonatina. Actually, all that Bob Fraley had asked her to do was to "read it through" a few times, more as a means of helping her with her music reading than anything else. As if by accident, she just *happened* to memorize it, shakily, to be sure, in the process. The remarkable thing, though, was that more than just playing the correct notes, she played all the staccato and legato notes as marked and added crescendos and decrescendos where they were appropriate. After hearing Vita play, Fraley turned to me and said, "You are a good teacher, Nancy." But actually, I had hardly helped her at all. She had played the sonatina that way because she loved the piece and she wanted to play it the way she had heard it on her tape. And there was no need for her to intellectualize anything abstractly, because her ear had told her how to play.

She didn't always play so beautifully, though. Often, I used to be horrified as she banged out pieces, and I used to watch in amazement as Bob Fraley would smile calmly and perhaps only make a mild suggestion or two as she massacred a piece at a lesson. At such times, I was always very conscious of the story Fraley used to tell about Suzuki, who would turn to his students at lessons and say, "Good, now that you know the notes we can get to work on the music." The notes in music, I was well aware, provide only its framework. The rest has to be filled in with phrasing, dynamics, a beautiful tone, and musical feeling. But I was just as aware that there was no way I could get Vita to work on the musical subtleties in her pieces, since she had no sense of delayed gratification. When she played, it was solely for the immediate pleasure her music gave her. Once she learned the notes, she was convinced that she had mastered the piece. But she didn't master it and discard it, she played it over and over again for fun, from week to week and even month to month. And the more she listened to her Suzuki tape, the more her playing began to match what she heard. What a relief! It really was like the process of learning language—where a baby utters his first words and sentences in order to communicate, but only gradually speaks clearly and grammatically, as he quite unconsciously strives to match his utterances more precisely with those he hears around him. To this day, Vita continues to occasionally bang out pieces, but now I don't worry so much. I just play our Suzuki tape all the more often and try to be patient.

Ishmael, because the music he is working on now is so technically demanding, spends much more time actually going over difficult passages and polishing up pieces. He also does advance work before he formally starts to learn a piece. He stands at the kitchen piano for at least an hour a day picking out and then improvising around the more advanced pieces that he hears me play or hears on our tape. A few months ago, for example, I began working on a little Mozart Rondo in C. Before long Ishmael was playing it in a rather haphazard fashion in G, with parts of the left hand played correctly and parts made up. In a few days, the piece had developed into a totally different one, but many of the more difficult passages remained intact. By the time he got around to playing the piece correctly, he found it relatively easy, since his fingers had already prepared for it. Some people might fear that by constantly messing around with real pieces, Ishmael will lose or never develop the ability to play coreectly. From experience, however, I know that just the opposite is true. While improvising, he is exploring the depths of the music he will later play.

Many people complain because the Suzuki concept doesn't emphasize or even deal with the problem of teaching students to read music. Suzuki actually does think that the ability to read music is quite important, but he leaves the method of how reading is going to be taught up to the individual teacher dealing with the individual child. He simply reminds us that just as it is absurd to try to teach a child to read before he can speak, so it is senseless to try to teach a child to read music before he can speak and feel the language of music.

After Ishmael had been playing the piano for almost a year, Bob Fraley did begin to teach him to read music. He did it, however, by showing Ishmael how to recognize the intervals between notes rather than by stressing individual note names. Within a few weeks, Ishmael began to spend hours with the Suzuki sheet music I had piled on the piano. He was happily matching the notes he saw on the music page with the notes he heard in his ear. This reminded me of the way he had taken picture books that he had memorized and had taught himself how to read by matching the words he knew with the printed words he saw on the page.

Once he was able to read music with a minimum of fluency, he felt like a whole new world had been opened up to him and he scoured the house looking for sheet music to read. One of his greatest finds was a series of antique "Music Readers" that I imagine were meant for girls in late nineteenth-century finishing schools who were preparing for genteel lives as parlor hostesses. With the aid of the piano, Ishmael practiced the solfeggios and triads at the beginning of the books, and he worked hard on the songs without even realizing that he was working. Despite his pleasure, he taught himself to recognize chord patterns and sequences with a good deal of speed, to sing *and* accompany himself, and to sight-sing by systematically training himself to sing away from the piano. He now has what is called "perfect pitch," but I am convinced that it wasn't entirely a gift from God—he worked hard to realize the potential for it that was in him.

Since he developed his ear through reading music, he can now look at notes (not to mention four- or five-note chords) and hear them in his mind before he ever plays them. Then, since he also knows how the piano keys should sound *before* he strikes them, his ears carry that anticipated sound from the printed page to his fingertips, which then seem to fly, almost automatically, to the proper keys on the piano. People who watch Ishmael are very impressed with his sight-reading ability, although actually his playing isn't as perfect as I have made it seem. He often has rhythmic problems, and he occasionally plays in the wrong octave. But that is because those skills have nothing to do with his ear, and he is, after all, still a child who has a lot more to learn about how to create music from black notes on a printed page.

Vita, too, is learning to read music, although her progress has understandably been more gradual. Watching Ishmael's initial experimentation with the Suzuki sheet music, though, gave me an idea for using it with her as well. She learns all her pieces "hands separately" at first, whether it be a Bach minuet or her Beethoven Sonatina. Since she learns these pieces primarily by ear, she needs to be able to hum both parts before she actually begins to learn how to play them. Often, though, the harmonic line (the left hand) is difficult to remember. It is usually less melodic and is made up of numerous two- or three-note chords. To help her get started, I often put the sheet music in front of her and follow the harmonic line with my finger as she plays. By watching the flow of the music on the staff, she is more able to keep the sound of the harmony in her mind and she can pick it out more easily on the piano. At the same time, of course, she is becoming comfortable with the printed page and is almost unconsciously learning about intervals, note values, and accidentals.

One evening, while listening to a small chamber group, Vita, who was then about five and a half, pointed to a violin and said in her most determined manner, "I want to play *that*." She never stopped talking about the violin, and Bob and I knew that she meant business. Unfortunately, the nearest Suzuki violin teacher lived almost two hours away; but Vita was so desperate to play that we decided to buy her a little violin anyway. I figured that since I had played the viola when I was in grade school, we could get by with the help of an instruction guide for Suzuki teachers until we found her a teacher.

Where were we going to find a violin small enough to fit her? Once again, John Holt, who played the cello, was there when we needed him—this time, though, under happier circumstances. He told us about a stringed instrument shop in Boston that deals in a wide variety of violins. He felt sure they'd have an instrument small enough for Vita to handle.

I'll never forget that shop. We went in through a side door, climbed three flights of dingy stairs, and walked down a long dark hallway before we found the brightly lighted doorway welcoming us. Inside, we found a room cluttered with violins— new, used, rare, some of them broken—plus big double basses, a harp, and three or four cellos lying on their sides. Two men behind the counter were bent over a violin and were examining it inch by inch. They put it aside as we walked in, and we described to them what we needed.

Vita was trembling with excitement as they measured her little arm, searched through the clutter, and, finally, placed a 1/10 size violin under her chin. Both men wore broad smiles as they set her up to play for her first time. One of them rosined a miniature bow, and the other showed her how to pull it across the strings. The violin was practically a toy, but the tone was better than I had imagined it could be. We were all delighted, especially Vita. She proudly helped to pack up the violin, carried it out to the car, and, fondling the case on her lap, refused to give it up.

Once at home again, though, Vita quickly discovered that actually playing the violin felt very awkward. It required the use of all kinds of rarely used muscles and some pretty tricky coordination. In order to play anything at all, not to mention a tune, she had to press the violin firmly between her chin and shoulder to hold it up, thereby freeing her left arm from doing that entire job and letting it be at least somewhat relaxed. This would give her fingers and wrist the freedom to move around as she pressed down on the strings to make note changes. Then there was the tricky business of trying to play in tune—putting her fingers where she wanted them, on the right string and in the proper position. Add to all of that the difficulties of bowing, and you can understand why Vita was a little taken aback by the reality of what she had gotten herself into. Often, after spending a few minutes with her violin, she headed straight to the piano for some much needed relief.

At first, I left her pretty much alone with her violin—partly because I was afraid that I would teach her something wrong, but also because I loved to watch her explore the instrument on her own. A few weeks after she had gotten it, for example, she managed to put her left-hand fingers down in order on her highest string. "Every time I put a finger down the sound gets higher!" she exclaimed. Gradually, as my confidence grew, I cautiously began helping her to improve her bow hold and her violin position and helping her move her bow straight across the strings. When I thought she was ready, I showed her the fingering for "Twinkle." She caught on fast and, before I knew it, she had taught herself "Lightly Row" and "Go Tell Aunt Rhody." If she started with her fingers in the proper position, she could stay pretty much in tune for the whole song.

After about six months, she began to make so much progress and seemed to be so seriously interested in the violin that we felt it was time that she should begin studying with a real teacher. We found a young man who had recently graduated from Julliard. Unfortunately, Tony lived over an hour's drive away, and he had no experience teaching children as young as Vita. He played the violin beautifully, though, and I thought it was important that Vita should have a real musician for a teacher. Since he had initially learned how to play the violin by ear himself, he was willing to use aspects of the Suzuki method (namely, intensive listening to music) with Vita. He also felt, however, that she should begin learning to read music as soon as possible, and he was unclear about the desirability of having me participate in the lessons. So I stayed as much in the background as possible.

Tony spent a great deal of time during the first lessons showing Vita how to get into proper playing position. First she had to put her feet together, then spread them apart comfortably with her toes pointing out. Then she had to place her left leg slightly forward with her knee bent. Finally, she had to turn her head so that her nose was in line with her left foot, to be ready when he placed her violin under her chin, where it was to be supported entirely by her shoulder. Next, she had to work on her bow hold and do a series of bow exercises. In no time, her half hour was up and it was time to make the hour's drive home. Poor Vita's interest in her violin began to flag—after all, she wanted to play, not learn how to stand.

Actually, Tony hadn't made up the standing routine or the bow exercises. That was pure Suzuki pedagogy. He, too, realized that Vita was losing interest, but he wasn't sure what to do about it. Like me, he felt that it was important for Vita to learn how to handle her instrument properly. During the next few lessons, though, he decided to experiment a bit to see if he could revive Vita's former enthusiasm. He brought out his violin and harmonized while she played the pieces she knew. Her whole body seemed to glow as she played. It was so exciting to make music with someone else! Unfortunately, Tony soon felt the responsibility to act like a teacher again, and he went back to showing Vita more exercises.

John Holt, who was now a frequent visitor at our house, came with us to one of Vita's lessons. He also was disturbed by Vita's joyless expression—particularly since when he and Vita played duets together she was so happy that her bow hold seemed to improve almost instinctively as her bow sailed musically across the strings. In his letters, John had many things to say about Vita's musical education that I wished I had had the courage to show to her teacher. In one, he wrote,

It is very important that Vita should think of her violin as an instrument to fool around on, to experiment on, and to improvise on. This improvisation can take three forms: (1) playing on the violin, by ear, tunes she already knows; (2) making up tunes on the violin as she plays it, that is, trying to play on the instrument the tune she is making up in her head; (3) still a freer kind of improvising, which is moving her fingers around on the strings to see what will happen, like a little child chanting. I do a lot of the third, make a big jump up or down the string and then try to deal, musically, with whatever I have got.

I think it will be very important for Vita, as for any beginning string player, child or adult, to get used *from the very beginning* to the idea that she/he can play *anywhere* on the instrument, low strings, high strings, low positions, high positions. As tactfully as this can be managed, she should be encouraged to play tunes she knows on all the strings and in a variety of positions, even way up at the tippy top high notes. The thing to avoid is the trap that most beginning string players fall into, of thinking that the higher positions are "harder." In some ways they are easier, since, when your ear is good enough, you can make a very quick adjustment for a slightly out-of-tune note just with the tiniest roll of a finger—and by the way, even the greatest players do this, they correct the notes faster than we hear them.

In another letter John wrote,

Children learn *physical* motions best by imitation. For this and other reasons I think it would be a very good idea for Vita's teacher to *play* his violin for her some of the time during each lesson. Perhaps [he could] play a few simple tunes that she can work on, plus a little bit of fancy stuff from his own music just to let her know what goodies lie ahead. And, as you said, it's important for her to play for him. If I were giving lessons to a child of her age, particularly one who liked to play as much as she does, I would begin each lesson by having some musical fun together, the kind of stuff she and I were doing—some "conversations" or duets or follow-the-leader with her being the leader more than the follower. The lesson should begin with pleasure and end with pleasure.

Just had an idea for a game I will play with Vita next time we are together. I on my cello and she on her violin will do long glissandos (slides) on each of the four strings, sliding up and down, like a fire engine. When we are on the lowest string I will call it a Bob fire engine, or a John fire engine; on the next string it will be a Nancy fire engine; on the next, an Ishmael fire engine; and on the highest string, a Vita fire engine.

It would be lovely if Vita's teacher could get loose enough in spirit, and playful enough, to do this kind of musical play with Vita, and perhaps he will, but perhaps not, and if not, it's nothing to be too disappointed in or worried about. He has a great deal to offer her anyway, if only as an example of a good violin player, and Vita is likely to learn more from his example than from most anything he says.

Meanwhile, there's no reason why you couldn't have, on the piano, or later on the viola as well, the kinds of conversations, and jokes, and follow-the-leader games that she and I were having together. I never thought of doing that before, but I think it is a very promising idea. Not only is it fun, but it is a way to introduce a child to some of the technical possibilities of the instrument, which one day she will study intensively, without worrying her about how hard it is or about doing it right.

And this would be a good thing for you to do some of the time in your own piano playing. Imitate some of the things a good pianist does, big crashing chords and runs of keys and trills and what have you. Don't worry about how good the imitation is, what you want is the spirit. The spirit of play!

In still another letter, John wrote,

Vita's teacher thinks that unless he shows her how to do everything and keeps after her all the time, she will never learn to play, but will develop more and more "bad habits"—the great bugaboo of music teachers. It completely misses (as do most Suzuki teachers) the original point about children learning to play the violin the way they learn to talk. When children start to talk we don't talk to them about the proper tongue position and teeth position. They start talking, not very well, and they get their feedback by seeing and hearing what happens, and by comparing what they do with what we do. If Vita plays and has fun playing, she will get feedback from her own muscles, which will tell her when something is awkward, and from seeing and hearing other people play.

I agreed with most of the things that John wrote to me. I could see for myself that Vita grew musically in direct proportion to the amount of pleasure she had with her violin—and with the piano, too. But all the same, holding up a violin is completely different from just letting a cello rest between your knees. I continued to feel that the approach that Vita's teacher was taking, and that of the Suzuki method, did have some value.

John responded,

I don't think of my approach differing very much from Suzuki. I know they are concerned about getting children to do things properly, but to a large degree I share this concern. Where we might differ slightly is on *how* to get children to do things properly. I think, in the first place, that children want to do things as well as possible, and are very sensitive to the kind of instructions they get from their muscles, so that they tend to move away from doing things that are very awkward. It was very interesting for me to see how Vita's hand fell, almost by instinct, into a very good grip on the bow.

If I were teaching a child to play, let us say, the cello, and saw that he/she was using a cramped and awkward grip, I would, after a while, begin to think about tactful ways to get them to try a better one. Most children who sit down and begin to fool with the cello for the first time—and most adults too, for that matter—tend to use a grip that makes it easy for them to bow on the low strings. But with this grip it is very nearly impossible to bow on the high strings. So perhaps one way of getting a child, or an older person to change this would be to suggest that they do some playing on the top, or A string. Simply in the effort to do this they would have to make some kind of change with their hand. I don't know in exactly what way I might intervene here. Perhaps I would just show them my hand and say, "here is how I hold it, you might try something like that." Tact is important, and the true Suzuki people, like Suzuki himself, are extremely tactful.

After a couple of months, Vita's teacher became too busy concertizing to be able to continue with her lessons. No doubt that result came about partly because of the fact that the more demoralized she became, the more he felt that his time could be better spent on his own career. So, once again, I became her teacher. With John to give me ideas and to bolster my confidence, I decided to wait before going out to look for another teacher. I looked forward to having a respite from those long drives to violin lessons, and I realized that I first had to decide what I was really looking for in a teacher. I had a new bridge and a set of new strings put on my viola and started re-learning how to play it. Once I had a few Suzuki folk songs under my belt, Vita and I played duets, harmonized with each other, and had great fun improvising. I was still concerned about her faulty playing posture, but I thought that for the time being it would be best not to worry her about it.

During this time, many other things were happening to us on the musical front. For one thing, the kids had started making music together. Ishmael played songs by Gilbert and Sullivan or Rogers and Hammerstein out of two song books we had been given. Vita stood at the piano and sang along, feeling quite grown up because she could now read well enough to keep her place in the music and turn the pages at the right time. Sometimes, too, they got their "band" together, which was composed of numerous homemade drums, a zither strung with fishing line, a bamboo whistle, a washtub bass, a beer bottle xylophone, and many other instruments that they had made themselves. They somehow managed to play simple folk songs on those instruments, and (of course) they had much more fun when they could persuade their neighborhood friends to join in.

Vita and Ishmael were also obsessed with composing music. Ishmael even composed a series of short operettas that he and Vita performed. We could never figure out how Vita began writing music, since when she started she only had a glimmer of how to read it. I *think* that what happened was that Ishmael showed her how to write a middle C and then she wrote the rest of the notes by interval. Through the process of writing music, she taught herself, with only a minimum of help, many of the fundamentals of reading music. While Bob and I were amazed at this seemingly backwards approach to music reading, Vita took it for granted. Once, when she had sight-read several pieces from her *Look and Listen Reader*, Bob congratulated her heartily. All she said in response was, "I write music, so of course I can read it!"

At about this time, Bob Fraley suggested that Vita and Ishmael might like to play a few pieces along with some of his other students at a local nursing home. This was a big event—their first concert! In order to prepare, we began having our own family concerts in the evening. The kids practiced announcing the pieces they were going to play—"The first piece I am going to play is Minuet in G by Bach"—and then bowed to applause after they finished. I played at these private concerts, too. Although I wouldn't have *dared* to play at the nursing home, I still felt I needed the experience of playing before others, and Bob and the kids made a good practice audience. Bob, who had recently taught himself to play the recorder, brought it out and played a few solos and then some duets with me—always being careful to announce his pieces and bow, just like the kids. What fun we had!

Vita and Ishmael played beautifully at the nursing home. When I asked Ishmael afterwards if he had been nervous, he said, "Yes, terribly. I was afraid I wouldn't bow properly."

From then on, we continued to have family concerts as often as we could. The first half was usually pretty formal, with all of us playing specially prepared pieces. As we got warmed up, though, we found that there were all kinds of other things we wanted to try. Perhaps Vita had a violin piece that she wanted to perform, but she needed a piano accompaniment. Would Ishmael see if he could play it? Or perhaps Ishmael had some Rogers and Hammerstein songs that he wanted to play for us, even though he was only just learning them. Or Bob might want to see if we could play a recorder trio with him, with Ishmael and I playing recorder parts on the piano. John Holt visited us a few times when we had our concerts, and he made a wonderful addition to our group with his cello. He used to play some of the Bach cello suites and excerpts from the pieces he was playing with his string quartet in Boston. He and Vita also improvised a series of silly violin-cello "sonatas," which added a whole new dimension to our get-togethers. Soon we were all jamming, often trading instruments—and Vita's giggles seemed like an instrument in themselves. Since we played in our music room, which doubled as a guest bedroom, we called ourselves the "Bedchamber Players." We even made recordings of ourselves that John took back to Boston and played for the people who worked in the *Growing Without Schooling* office.

More than music, it was our pleasure that pervaded those tapes. You could feel our joy emanating from them. Sometimes, though, that very joy hung over me like a cloud. This was because although the kids had neighborhood and home-schooling friends who would occasionally join their "band," they had no real musical friendships—except for John, who was a very busy man and could only visit intermittently.

Not surprisingly, then, when Bob Fraley told us about a Suzuki Institute that was being held in Maine during the summer, we leapt at the chance to go. Suzuki Institutes are, so far as I know, an unusual occurence in the musical world because, unlike summer music camps that only music students attend, the Institutes are designed for both students and their parents. In fact, one parent is required to attend for each child enrolled. Since they are recognized as the children's primary teachers, the parents need to be involved in every step of their children's musical training.

This particular Institute interested me because it included classes for children studying either violin, cello, or piano, and I was anxious to learn more about the orthodox Suzuki approach to teaching strings. Also, the fact that the brochure we received said that children could only sign up for instruction in one instrument implied something wonderful to me about many Suzuki-trained children. It suggested that they, like Vita, loved music enough to want to play more than one instrument. Vita, though, was upset because she couldn't take violin *and* piano classes. In the end, although I recognized that in many ways she preferred her violin to the piano, I signed her up for piano. I was afraid that otherwise she'd have to spend the whole week learning how to stand and hold her bow.

The Institute was a milestone in our lives. It taught me a

great deal about music and music teaching, and about children and their musical perceptions. Even more, it taught me many things about Ishmael and Vita that I had been slow or perhaps unwilling to see. Throughout the whole week I found myself feeling a wonderful contentment with being surrounded by at least a hundred parents who were all actively involved in the pleasures and pains of teaching their own children. The Institute wasn't by any means unmitigated joy, however. I found much about the Suzuki approach to music that disturbed me, too. In my journal, I kept a detailed account of our activities and feelings during that week, and some selections from it follow.

SUNDAY.   I am sitting out in the hall of a college dorm at the University of Maine. Vita is in our room trying to go to sleep. Since the only light in the room is huge and glaring, I am letting her sleep in darkness and using the hall for light.

The campus here is much nicer than I expected. The buildings are old brick and there are vast lawns planted with interesting trees and bushes. When we drove up to the music building to register, the first thing we noticed was a whole colony of swallows' nests built in the eaves. All the birds were chattering away and working hard to feed their families. It reminded me of a row of crowded city tenements.

I felt nervous as soon as we entered the building. I guess I was afraid of getting lost or being disorganized or forgetting something. As we registered, I was given a huge packet full of stuff. I felt like a freshman at college on her first day. But despite the anxiety, I felt a thrill at seeing so many tiny children all carrying violin cases around. And I will admit to a hovering feeling of jealousy too—they all have violin teachers, unlike Vita.

In the packet was a schedule for the week. Vita and Ishmael both have a theory class at 8:30 each morning. At 9:30, Vita has a private lesson. At 10:30, both kids have a repertoire class in which they will play with other kids who are about at their level. From 11:30 until lunch there are various lectures that Bob and I can attend. After lunch, the kids have to go to a "piano play-in" which involves more group playing, but this time with all the piano students at the Institute. At 2:30, Ishmael has his private lesson. Finally, at 4:30 there are recitals, in which some of the best children are asked to play.

So much music! In the music building while we registered we saw glimpses of some videos of Japanese children playing the violin. I looked for the stiffness in the bow arm that John H. had mentioned noticing in Suzuki students. I didn't see it, but I did notice that the kids played very mechanically. Still, it was amazing to watch a tiny four-year-old play a difficult Bach minuet in perfect tune on a violin.

We found our "dorm" on the map, drove over, and moved in. It's worse than a chain motel, but I guess I'll survive. Unfortunately, the bathroom is a mile down the corridor. I have to get used to the "group life." At 5:00 we went to eat at the dining hall. Standing in line waiting for a tray and a plastic plate full of food reminded me vividly of my junior high school days, but at least here, the food was pretty good. There was a salad bar with some raw vegetables and some whole wheat bread, but even so, I was terribly homesick for a salad straight out of the garden.

At 6:30 we went over to the big concert hall for the Welcoming Ceremony. The woman who organized the Institute began by warning us to look after our children at all times. She had a bunch of other equally demeaning things to say— all spoken with the deliberateness of a woman who has taught kindergarten for too many years. I would have been disgusted and perhaps even would have walked out, but I was too busy watching a fascinating sight. About thirty children in the audience were fooling around with their violins—making little plucking sounds or quietly bowing, all impatient to really play. The vitality of a room full of musical children!

At 7:00 we went to a "play-in" with the two piano teachers. Each child who wanted to got up and played a favorite piece. Vita was upset because she wanted to play her violin, so she pouted on my knee. Ishmael played the Kuhlau sonatina and it was beautiful. I felt as though I was hearing it for the first time. I was a little disappointed, though, because I expected to hear some breathtaking playing. Where are all those four-year-olds who play Beethoven sonatas? Out of the thirty kids who played, only five or six really impressed me, and while they played confidently and musically, they mostly seemed to punch at the piano—to slap it, as my grandmother would say—and it seemed to me that they must have been taught to play that way. Well, I'll try to be open-minded . . .

The piano teachers are two gushy middle-aged women. They kept asking the children teacherish questions, which got on my nerves. But when one of the teachers looked out at the audience after a child had played and asked, "Now who knows what that piece was?" and a child of about seven answered, "Sonatina, by Beethoven," I felt totally forgiving. Another thing that was impressive was that all the children bowed before they played and afterwards, and—except for Ishmael—they bowed with poise and grace. Hopefully he'll get some practice during the week. I just can't get over all these little kids, with their parents, all so deeply involved in music.

3 P.M. MONDAY.   I'm out in the hall again. What an incredibly depressing day. Maybe I'm just exhausted. The poor kids had one class after another without any breaks, and we had to dash to meals so that the dining hall wouldn't lock its doors before we got there.

"Theory" class was first. Vita was immediately overwhelmed, as she entered, by all the tall ten- and eleven-year-olds in the class. I think she was grouped with them because she is playing such advanced music, but she spent most of the class on my lap. The teacher, Michiko Yurko, was delightful to watch. First she had everyone stand in a circle and bow to each other—the Japanese greeting. Then she asked them to tell each other their names—there were perhaps ten or twelve kids in the class. Whenever I hear that many names I just automatically blot them out, but not Mrs. Yurko. You could see her mind focus on each one. When the kids were done she went around the circle and repeated each child's name (good practice for memorizing music, or anything, for that matter) with only one slip. Then she asked the

kids to scramble themselves up so she could really test her
skill. She had a much harder time—there were long pauses
as she thought, and many times the kids tried to help her—
but she always said, "Don't tell me. This is *my* test, not
yours." When she had named each child correctly, it was
time for the class to begin. They spent the first half hour talking about all the instruments in a large symphony orchestra.
They learned all about the conductor's score and practiced
the conducting patterns for 4/4, 3/4, and 2/4 time. Then Mrs.
Yurko produced a big board with black lines depicting a staff
and placed a felt treble clef on the left-hand edge. She played
groups of four or five notes on the piano and asked the children to put little round bean-bags in place on the staff to rep-
resent the notes she had just played. That was tough! I tested
myself on the sidelines, but the kids were invariably faster
and more accurate than I was. At the end everyone bowed
good-bye. Ishmael enjoyed the class and was looking forward
to the rest of the day. For poor Vita, though, it was a bad
start, and she freaked out when it was time for her lesson at
9:30. It's hard for her to be about the youngest child here.
Now I know where all those fabulous four-year-olds are—
they are at home napping in their cribs like civilized children. Finally, I just dragged Vita to her lesson and we sat
around (Vita on my lap again) Suzuki-style, while the three
other children in her group had their individual lessons.
Suzuki feels that children learn just as much from observing
other children's lessons as they do from lessons of their own,
so he encourages this kind of group class, in which the children take turns with the teacher. It would have been valuable for Vita, but she just seemed too tired; so I took her out
to skip and do cartwheels until the teacher called her in for
her lesson. She played the second Bach minuet quite well,
although she forgot her first repeat. The teacher didn't mind,
but I did—we had been working on that repeat for a month!
The teacher asked Vita to try moving her arm rather than
stretching her fingers on all the broken chords at the beginning of the piece, and Vita enjoyed working on that. Then
she asked Vita to play the minuet hands separately. Vita did
fine with the right hand, but she botched up the left. Some-

how we have to find a few minutes to practice it before her next lesson. I think Vita feels good about her teacher and good, too, about the way she played the minuet.

At 10:30 the kids had their repertoire class. Once again, we sat and sat while about fifteen children each played a piece. Vita played another Bach minuet (perfectly!) and Ishmael played the Beethoven *Eccossaise*. Throughout, the teacher initiated discussions about the composers that the kids were playing, and Ishmael had a lot of fun. He's such an encyclopedia!

Then we went to a lecture on "motivation." It's the last lecture I'll go to while I'm here. The two teachers who lectured seemed completely divorced from the realities of families and children. Their advice was that "success is the best motivator." Their keys to success were: (1) only let children go a step at a time, (2) make sure children practice every day, (3) don't let them play ahead since they may work in mistakes that they'll have to unlearn later, and (4) praise children often. I mentioned that in our family what motivates the kids most is the fact that we try to have as much fun with music as we can. When we play a lot for pure pleasure and don't worry about mistakes, we get the boost we need to work on hard pieces without freaking out. Often the kids are inspired this way to play for two or three hours a day. I would have elaborated about the kind of fun we have, but the teachers seemed completely uninterested.

After a terrible lunch the kids had a "play-in" class in which all thirty piano students took turns playing. Ishmael played the first movement of his Clementi sonatina and Vita played Schumann's "Happy Farmer," with many mistakes. Then, while Ishmael had his private lesson, Vita went off with Bob to get some exercise. This class has four boys in it—the most advanced pianists here. They all seem nice and rather studious, like Ishmael. When it was his turn, Ishmael played his Clementi again. Although it wasn't his most inspiring performance, it was graceful, smooth, and musical. The teacher, though, wasted no time with praise. Instead, she told Ishmael that he had to relax his wrist more and she encouraged him to jab at the piano—just the way many of the little kids had jabbed last night. Finally, she told him to forget about forearm rotation (the fast roll Bob Fraley taught him to make with his wrist in order to play the runs quickly, yet smoothly) and to use his individual fingers instead. Tears welled up in my eyes so that I couldn't speak. She was telling Ishmael that he should unlearn his beautiful playing and poke at the piano instead. I felt like packing up and going home, and we may just do that if things don't get better.

MONDAY EVENING.   At 4:30, we went to the student recital. Two violinists and a cellist played breathtakingly. Then another little girl played a jerky version of "Go Tell Aunt Rhody." It *had* to be jerky because she had so many "bow tapes" to tell her exactly where to stop and start as she bowed. Worrying about whether her bowing was exactly right, she lost all sense of the piece as a song. Am I just jealous and being unreasonable? I don't think so.

We were so tired that we ate supper and took baths and decided not to go to the evening concert. The kids lay around and read while I went back to the music building to practice, which was heavenly. When I came back, Vita was playing her violin, accompanied by Bob on the recorder. I kept feeling sad, because the kids actually have had very little chance to play today.

TUESDAY EVENING.   We got up at 6:30 this morning and ate a quick and yucky breakfast so that we could get a little practicing done this morning. Vita was quite good about it. I think she was feeling better since she played so well yesterday. She was even willing to work on raising her pinkie in the second minuet. At 8:30, we went to the theory class. Michiko Yurko is a super teacher, unlike any other teacher I have seen. Her goal is, unabashedly, to have everyone in her class learn everything. She absolutely discourages competition. For example, with her winning smile, she asked everyone to sit cross-legged on the floor and put a hand on each knee. "Alright now, I want you all to think of four brass instruments, and when you can name them to yourself, put your hands in your lap." When everyone had put their hands in their laps, she asked someone to name the brass instruments aloud—"horn, trombone, tuba, and trumpet." Then she said, once again with a smile, "Alright, I want you to think of four brass instruments, and when you can name them, put your hands in your lap." The kids were already busy thinking when they realized that she had asked them the same question. But "No," she said, she hadn't made a mistake. She kept asking it until she could be certain that everyone could come up with the right answer quickly and easily. Because of her enthusiasm, no one felt bored. In fact, they felt challenged.

Mrs. Yurko is preparing them to play a board game called "Orchestra Odyssey." It has game cards with questions on them that the kids will have to answer if they land on certain squares. Slowly, in the course of the week, she plans to go over each question (like "What are the four brass instruments?") to make sure that the kids know all the answers. I really enjoyed watching Ishmael sitting happily with that bunch of kids, all animatedly trying to answer Mrs. Yurko's questions. "At what time should you arrive before a concert?" "Early enough to find your seat, go to the bathroom, and read your program." "Who tunes up the orchestra?" "The oboe, or sometimes the concert master (or mistress)—unless they are playing a piano concerto, in which case everyone tunes to the piano."

At 9:30 Vita went to her lesson, this time voluntarily. The kids were video-taped as they played. Then they watched themselves on a television screen and talked about how each of them felt about their playing posture and overall performance. Vita played the second minuet again. She was concentrating so hard on her pinkie that she forgot her first repeat and played the second half over three times. The teacher gently tried to stop her, but she played on with fierce concentration.

At 10:30, there was a group class for kids in Suzuki books 2 and 3. The teacher brought out her "bagful of tricks," as she called it—about fifty index cards with tricks written on them. The kids each had to pick a card and then perform the given trick: "Play a scale with the right hand legato and the left hand staccato," "Play your favorite piece with your hands crossed," or "Play your favorite piece but clap the rhythm of the right hand and play the left hand." They had a great time and really amazed both the teacher and the parents with their skill. In the middle, Bob had to take Vita out—but she seemed to have enjoyed herself while she was there.

Afterwards, I skipped the lecture and Ishmael and I went out on the grass to meet Bob and Vita. We found them sitting with one of the smallest cellists I'd ever seen. He was playing duets with Vita, who was happily sawing away on her violin. He knows a harmony part to "Twinkle" that is just lovely. Seldom have I seen Vita so happy as while they played together. Zack told us that the month before his two-year-old sister had taken a hammer and a screwdriver and had tried to chop his cello down to violin-size. She wanted to play the violin, but her mother had told her that she had to wait until she was three. I guess she just got impatient. Anyway, Zack had to go for three weeks without his cello while it was being repaired. He and Vita were really drawn to each other. They agreed to meet tomorrow at 11:00 for more music.

We had to hurry with lunch so that Ishmael could practice before his lesson. While Bob and Vita went off to do cartwheels, we walked over to the practice rooms to work. He was wonderful working on the Clementi—trying to follow the teacher's instructions, and yet doing his best to retain his musical integrity. He also played a bunch of other things for fun—he's hardly had a chance to touch a piano while we've been here. After a while, William, a really nice boy in his advanced class, came in with his little sister, a violinist, to watch Ishmael play. Then two other boys arrived, and soon they were having a free-for-all at the keyboard. So rowdy and so musical!

At 1:30, Ishmael went to his advanced class for his private lesson. Like the kids in Vita's class, Ishmael and the three other boys were video-taped. This time I liked the teacher a lot more. She made some very legitimate criticisms of Ishmael's playing, which we can work on tomorrow; but she was also genuinely pleased with his overall performance. It was as though it had taken her a while to understand his style of playing, or perhaps she had been tired and nervous yesterday, like the rest of us. What I enjoyed most about the class was that the four boys really admired one another's playing and made nice comments to each other as they watched the video-tape. All four were recommended by the teacher to play in a special recital tomorrow. Once more, thanks to Suzuki, competition is downplayed. It would have been awful if only one or two of the boys had been chosen to play.

After class, Ishmael went out to play on the grass and I watched a violin class. I was horrified. A small boy walked up on stage, bowed to his teacher, and then went through the "checkpoints"—proper foot position, proper posture, proper this, proper that, bow laying on strings right at the red tape, first finger placed on yellow tape on the fingerboard, ready, set, go. From then on it was stop, start, stop, start, as the teacher corrected the boy and he tried to fight her off in order to play. And since he had a million things to think about, and most especially his multicolored bow tapes, his playing was extremely choppy. At the end of his allotted time, the boy complained, "I wanted to play the whole song." His teacher responded, "You are only supposed to be playing the first line, and only when you play it perfectly will you be allowed to go on." The boy bowed and walked off stage.

We had dinner tonight at Philip Burns' house. Philip is an outstanding pianist—one of the boys in Ishmael's class—and his younger brother plays the violin. Ishmael managed to learn a thing or two about boogie-woogie from Philip, and Vita played violin trios with little Bobby Burns and his father, who is also studying Suzuki violin. Later, Bobby took his violin out on the lawn and just played away—partly to attract the attention of the girl next door, and partly just because he loved playing. After a while, I asked his father how much he practiced a day. I'm not sure why I used the word "practice." Most likely it was because it is the conventional term and I thought he'd misunderstand me if I said "play." Anyway, Bobby's father laughed and said, "He seldom practices, in fact he hates to, but since I don't want to battle with him, I don't push it."

So then I rephrased the question. "What I meant was, how much does Bobby play?"

"Well, quite a bit," he answered, "but it is just playing. His feet aren't right and his hand position isn't good. I wish he would settle down and practice more. Of course, I am just like he is. I love to play my violin but I hate to practice, since that involves worrying about my bow tapes and having to play segments of pieces over and over again."

WEDNESDAY 8:25 A.M.   I am sitting here waiting for the theory class to begin. Four or five kids are hanging around the piano playing rags, Beethoven's *Für Elise*, be-bop, and just plain kid stuff. They can't seem to get enough of it. I can't get over how they all take turns and really listen to each other.

8:35 A.M.   The kids are busy playing Musopoly, a board game in which you earn money for correctly naming musical symbols, performing pieces, clapping out rhythms, and so on. Everyone is helping everyone else—particularly Ishmael, who is always a bit dazed—and there is so much laughing and smiling. If your marker lands on a certain square, you have to get up and play a piece for everyone else. You have a choice of just playing it, and earning three coins, or of deciding to try to play it perfectly and either earning a gold coin if you do or losing all if you make a mistake. "Who decides if you played perfectly?" the kids all wanted to know. "You yourself do," said Michiko Yurko, flashing one of her lovely smiles. Before each of the kids played, they always bowed, to a respectful, encouraging audience.

9:00 P.M.   Just got Vita to sleep. She's exhausted! Let's see. What happened today? After theory class, Vita went off to her private lesson and Ishmael went over to the practice rooms with William. I like the way William seems to look after Ishmael. Vita played well. The teacher spent the whole time going over the dynamics in Vita's minuet, but she responded happily. At the end of the lesson, she played a song that she had made up. The teacher actually listened and seemed interested.

During the group class the kids played tricks again, but this time they were tricks brought in by the students themselves. William played a passage from the first Bach minuet and asked the class if they could guess which of the other minuets had the same passage in it—only written a third lower. Vita shouted out, "Minuet Two!" Everyone was amazed. She went up to the piano, and sure enough, in the left hand of the second section the passage was right there, just as William had said, a third down. Those kids not only know their music backwards and forwards, but they all seem to have incredible dexterity and coordination. At 11:00, Bob took Vita out to play duets with her little cellist friend. Later, he told me that he had tried to join in with his recorder but that he had screwed up the rhythm so much that he had had to quit.

At 11:30, we ate lunch and then took baths and rested a bit before Ishmael and I went to the practice rooms to go over his Clementi again. I'm a bit concerned that with so many little points to remember he'll begin intellectualizing too much and lose his feel for the music, so basically I tried to get him to relax. Although he didn't perfect every point that his teacher wanted him to, he did fix up a lot, and of course I thought it was lovely.

Then Bob took the kids bowling while I sat in on a group violin class. What upset me, once again, was that the teacher treated the music so mechanically. She would squat when she wanted the children to play softly and would go up on her toes when she wanted them to play louder. She insisted on short jerky bows. Despite the fact that the violin teachers keep harping on posture and position, many of the kids slouched and played badly. Others, though, played just beautifully.

At 2:30, to was time for Ishmael's private class. It is way too short. Each of the four boys gets only fifteen minutes, and the teacher is left rather breathless. Today Ishmael had a chance to play the second and third movements of the Clementi sonatina, which aren't a part of the Suzuki literature. The teacher was pleased enough to ask him to play them in the group class tomorrow. Ishmael seemed very tense during his lesson, but she was quite nice about it.

At 3:30, he went off to buy himself an ice cream cone (such independence!) in preparation for his recital at 4:30, and Vita bought herself some juice. Eight or nine kids played in the recital. Some were *so* good. I am very impressed with many of the more advanced violinists. They have obviously outgrown their early jerkiness and show no signs of the mechanical playing that is so prevalent with the beginners. Ishmael played the Clementi beautifully. He was called back to the stage to take a second bow. Afterwards, many, many people congratulated him. Fortunately, he has learned to say thank-you, although he is still quite awkward in the face of praise.

We ate a quick dinner, and then Vita dressed in her best to play in her solo class at 7:00. She even made me take out her pony tail so that she could play with her hair down. Then I took her over to the practice rooms. Since she was planning on playing the fourth Bach minuet, I had her play it through three or four times. I don't think that I've ever mentioned that up in the practice rooms there is almost always a parent with each child. In different circles, one would accuse the parents of being pushy, but Suzuki was a genius for encouraging parents and children to work together.

The solo class was a mixture of violin, cello, and piano students. Little Zack played "Lightly Row" beautifully. Vita, who announced that she was going to play the fourth minuet, sat down and proceeded to play the second instead. Everyone broke into smiles, but at least she did a good job. She never noticed her mistake until she was in bed. Ishmael played the Kuhlau sonatina. Someone in the audience exclaimed "Wow!" when he finished, but I could tell that he was having quite a bit of trouble. Later he explained that the action on the piano was too heavy. Anyway, we all felt elated and it was difficult to get everyone to sleep.

All day, I've been wondering how the advanced Suzuki violinists can play so beautifully after being given such (what I consider) disastrous starts at their instruments. And why do so many of them continue to play and work when their teachers do so little to inspire them? I wonder if the secret doesn't lie with Suzuki's emphasis on group playing and family togetherness. Never does a Suzuki child have to go off for a half an hour to practice alone—he always has a parent to keep him company. Suzuki also encourages teachers to have weekly group classes where the children can play for and with each other. This musical sociability is what I have been watching all over the place—from kids' fooling around together in the practice rooms and before class, to the formal group sessions in which, instead of being competitive, the kids seem to get real pleasure from one another's playing. Having a shared and beloved repertoire is also helpful in getting children to feel that they aren't alone with their instruments. You can actually see the younger children's excitement when the older ones play. Someday soon, they are saying to themselves, we'll be able to play those pieces too! Looking back at Vita's lessons on the violin, I can see that if she'd had other children to play with in a group class—and incidentally to improvise with before and after class—she would have retained much more of her enthusiasm.

SATURDAY.　Home again and totally exhausted. I couldn't believe the change in this place over the last five days. The garden is like a jungle. The flowers all grew at least a foot, the blueberries are hidden in the weeds, the pea vines are heavy with peas, and I picked ten quarts of strawberries. Bob made a strawberry cake and the kids and I made jam.

Last Thursday, our last day at the Institute, I was just too tired to write. Bob took Ishmael to the theory class, and Vita played hooky so that she could play more duets and practice the piano. At the repertoire class, two of the older boys and Vita brought their violins and played with the pianists so that they could begin learning how to accompany soloists. Vita and Ishmael played "Lightly Row" together, Philip and Matthew played the first movement of the Seitz Violin Concerto beautifully—Matthew on violin and Philip on piano. Then Joshua, Matthew, and Vita played "Long, Long Ago" on their violins while two other kids accompanied them on the two pianos. Ishmael and Matthew played the Kuhlau sonatina together on the piano. Finally, Joshua and Matthew played the first Bach minuet on their violins while two other kids played the second minuet on one piano and another team played the third minuet on the other piano. They had all three minuets going at once, and they actually fit together! It was terrific!

During the "play-in" class at 1:30, the kids rehearsed for the final concert which was to be that evening. They lined up according to size, and then each played the piece that he or she had been preparing. Vita played her Bach minuet and Ishmael played all three movements of the Clementi—although in the actual concert he was only supposed to play the first movement. After he had played, he did one of his usual awkward bows. The teacher, with the friendly help of the class, taught him a foolproof method for bowing.

At 2:30, it was again time for Ishmael's private lesson. Of the four boys in the class, two played just perfectly. Perhaps I should say spotlessly. One is a little less coordinated than the others, although he really improved over the week. Ishmael is the one who plays most beautifully, yet he lacks the precision of the first two. His dynamics are never quite right, and his trills aren't brilliant. He plays from the soul, not from the printed page. The teacher spent the most time with him, going over his concert piece for that night. At the end of the class, she hugged each boy. She was genuinely sad that it was the last day.

At 3:30, we dashed up to one of the big rooms where Vita was to meet Zack for a final session of duets. She was tired and grumpy, but Zack was his usual cheerful self. They played together for a bit, and then an older girl asked if she could join in. I said sure, but then Vita refused to play. Finally, I asked the girl if it would be alright if she let Vita and Zack play by themselves. She was very nice about finding something else to do.

Afterwards, Bob took the kids bowling while I went to listen to the student recital. Michiko Yurko, the theory teacher, played her own "Twinkle Variations" at the end. She walked up on stage, bowed, made herself comfortable on the piano bench, and then just meditated for thirty seconds or so. After that long silence, she put her hands on the keys and really let loose. Imagine "Twinkle" played as boogie-woogie, as a polka, and in a super jazzy rhythm. Her fingers just danced across the keys. Fortunately, Vita and Ishmael had lost interest in bowling and were in the audience to watch her play. Ishmael was just thrilled.

Next we dashed to dinner, dashed back to the dorm to dress, and dashed to the auditorium again for the Final Concert. Vita and Ishmael went backstage while Bob and I found good seats. It was a large audience—the largest by far that the kids had ever played for. It was an "educated" audience, too, which made it all the more exciting. The pianists played first. They were seated on stage according to height, so that the shortest ones played first. Each child walked out when it was his turn, faced the audience, introduced himself and the piece he was going to play, and then bowed to encouraging applause. Then, after being helped by one of the teachers to get comfortable at the Steinway grand (equipped with pillows and footstools for the smaller ones), the child would play. Afterwards he would bow again, with as much poise as ever, and go back to his seat.

Vita played third, after two even tinier children of about four or five. She looked lovely and composed as she announced her piece, "Minuet #2 by Bach," and then she bowed. During the first part of the second section she goofed up momentarily; but she kept her cool, and it was really gorgeous. She put her whole self into her pinkie, and lightened up with her thumbs just as the teacher had asked her to do. Afterwards, I could hear people in the audience whispering about her. Ishmael played towards the end. He was as nervous as I was and forgot to bow, but he put everything he had into his playing. Technically, he did many things wrong. He forgot some of the fortes and pianos, he skipped a few rests in his left hand, and so on, and yet it was very moving to hear. The audience loved it, and he got a huge ovation. Actually, all the pianists played exceptionally well. Somehow, being dressed up and having such a large audience really inspired them. I felt great pride for all of them, particularly since their playing had improved dramatically over the week.

Next, the older violinists played—Bach's Double Concerto, and some pieces by Dvorak, Handel, and Schumann. Then it was the cellists' turn. Most of them were very young, like Zack, and they carried along their own little stools. One cellist, who was two, played a full-sized viola. The more advanced among them played "Happy Farmer" by Schumann, a Bach minuet, and then a piece by Purcell. Then the rest joined in for some folk songs from the Suzuki repertoire. Afterwards, the older violinists played some more. As they gradually moved to easier pieces, other violinists joined them until the stage was literally full of string players. When the smallest child of all had toddled on stage, they all joined forces for "Twinkle, Twinkle Little Star." Tears welled up in my eyes. You could tell that they were all playing it with love, despite the fact that they had heard and played it hundreds of times. To me, and to the whole audience, really, it represented so much of what we had had a taste of at the Institute, but needed so much more of—the chance to play and share music with others.

Afterword

Less than six months after going to the Suzuki Institute, we moved to Ithaca, New York—home of Cornell University, Ithaca College, and Ithaca Talent Education, a respected Suzuki music school. We had sold our dear old house, had bought a homely cottage across from a park in a charming old-fashioned Ithaca neighborhood, and had enrolled Vita and Ishmael at the music school. Amazed? So were we. In fact, after a year, I still often wonder if the whole thing isn't just a dream.

Despite our mixed feelings about the Institute, our delight at meeting so many great kids there made us face up to just how isolated Vita and Ishmael had been at home. We finally had to admit to ourselves that their isolation wasn't just an inevitable and unfortunate aspect of home-schooling. There *were* other kids out there that they could relate to and have fun with. But how could we find more opportunities for Vita and Ishmael to meet them? And was there any way that they would be able to form ongoing friendships and not just have to make do with sporadic chance meetings at places like Institutes? Moving to a town with an organized Suzuki music school and other types of cultural and social activities available for children seemed to be the obvious solution.

Although our first thoughts about moving were motivated by

our concern for the kids's social well-being, the more Bob and I talked about the idea the more we realized that we had unspoken desires of our own. The thought of living in town began to look attractive even from a merely selfish point of view. How I longed to be able to go to concerts without driving for hours, and how Bob longed for a really good library to work in—one that he would perhaps even be able to walk to. And my idea of heaven, I had to admit, was being able to walk to the grocery store, not to mention piano lessons.

It seemed as if we were always in the car, and the endless driving was wearing us all down. Besides, our interests had really shifted during the past few years. I wanted to write without feeling guilty about neglecting the chickens or letting the blueberries run wild. Bob wanted to spend what free time he had with us, not thawing out frozen pipes or hassling with the chain saw. Even Ishmael and Vita, I couldn't help noticing, now spent most of their time performing plays in the attic, flopping on their bedroom floor with their dolls, or composing, improvising, and practicing at the piano. I felt like I had to nag them to climb trees, pick berries, and generally act like country children, which seemed pretty ridiculous. In any case, after much serious reflection, it began to seem clear that we weren't cut out to be the farmers we thought we had been. Although there were aspects of country life that we knew we would miss, we all began to look forward to a life in town—"as long as there's space for a theater in the new house," Vita and Ishmael insisted. So, after the usual traumas of moving, here we are.

Our house is a lovely fifteen-minute walk from the Cornell library. We live within two blocks of a grocery store, a Chinese grocery, a bagel shop, and a bookstore, and we can walk to concerts and movies at Cornell. Ithaca has not only a music school, but also a couple of ballet schools and a community arts school which offers music, art, and language classes. There are also numerous drama classes and many other interesting things for the kids to do, all within a mile or two of our house. And because we will never be entirely city people at heart, we are delighted by the wild gorges that cut through town, the large expanses of wild and cultivated land owned by Cornell, and the state parks—all only a short drive away.

I have to admit, though, that the actual process of moving was awful. It wasn't exactly a nightmare, since everything went as we planned it to, but practically so. First, of course, there was the real estate worry—buying and selling houses, dealing with realtors, bankers, and insurance salesmen, the intervening hours of showing glum, disappointed prospective buyers around our house, and the dreary days spent desperately looking for a place we could stand to live in here in Ithaca and still afford. Then there was the dark day when both Vita and Ishmael burst into tears when they realized that we were seriously considering buying this house. "The park is too small," wailed Ishmael. "I hate the way the house smells," cried Vita. It was an even worse day when, after a month of packing books and dishes, after the misery of disposing of the chickens and saying good-bye to our friends and neighbors, we finally left for Ithaca—in a car with three desperately car-sick cats, two bunnies, two exhausted kids, and every other available space filled with half-frozen house plants. How we ever managed to get here, I'll never know. Fortunately for all of us, the house smelled better and the park looked bigger when we arrived.

But perhaps the most worrisome and upsetting part of the entire moving process was the whole problem of home-schooling. Despite the fact that Ithaca's schools have a good reputation, we were determined to continue teaching the kids at home. The thought of having them spend so much time in school when there were so many more interesting things going on right in the community seemed absurd. Although we were eager to indulge ourselves in the cultural and social life of Ithaca, we knew that as home-schoolers we weren't free just to pick up and move here without checking out the situation to the last detail. We were too involved with the kids' learning to want to even think about wasting time fighting with school officials about it.

It was a really scary thing to face up to the fact that we might risk being labeled criminals or child abusers by moving casually into a state which might, for all we knew, prohibit home-schooling or have such stringent regulations that we couldn't possibly meet them. As I anxiously researched New York State's education laws and court precedents, I had visions of Peter and Brigitta Van Daam, home-schoolers in Rhode Island. Thanks to the TV screen at a neighbor's house, I had watched them bravely waving good-bye to their children as a policeman drove them off to jail for failing to comply with the state's compulsory attendance law. I thought, too, of the Sessions family in Iowa, in and out of court for years while fighting to keep their boys out of school, and of John Singer, the father of seven children in Utah, whose battle with school authorities ended tragically when he was shot to death in a battle with some sheriff's deputies.

All of our troubles with our own school authorities must have really traumatized me, because I still felt anxious even after it became clear that getting permission to home-school in New York State wasn't going to be nearly as problematic as it had been in New Hampshire—and not even remotely like what the Sessions, Van Daams, and Singers had experienced. The first good sign was in the state's compulsory attendance law. "Instruction given to a minor elsewhere than in a public school shall be at least substantially equivalent to the instruction given . . . at public schools." Granted, the word "equivalent" was pretty vague, but it looked far better to us than "manifest educational hardship." Reading our back issues of *Growing Without Schooling* was also encouraging. I discovered several letters from home-schoolers in New York—even one from a family living near Ithaca. It not only seemed like they had all had an easy time of getting initial permission, but none of them mentioned the kind of frequent and unpleasant type of evaluations that we'd had to go through.

Still, feeling jittery and afraid to leave any stones unturned before we made a definite decision about moving, we visited the New York State Department of Education in Albany to talk directly to the people there. Unlike New Hampshire's Department of Education, which is located on the second floor of a cut-rate clothing store, New York has a massive marble building that takes up a whole city block. As we parked and walked toward it, I prepared myself for the worst, imagining the vast faceless and unfeeling bureaucracy inside. But from the moment the doorman flashed Vita a warm smile, I felt that everything would be all right. The Assistant Commissioner of Non-Public Schools—the only person who knew much of anything about New York's home-education policies—was equally friendly and seemed delighted to have the kids in her office.

Home-schools, she explained, are treated in New York much the same as private schools, except that home-schools don't need health or fire inspections. Like private elementary schools, they don't even have to go through any formal approval process. All we had to do, she said, was to notify our local superintendent of our intent to teach Vita and Ishmael at home and to explain that we planned to meet the equivalency requirements by teaching the minimum courses required by law for five hours a day, by keeping attendance records, and by "*having* the kids tested" annually. Everything sounded better than we'd ever dreamed possible, except for the testing. When I asked her just what she meant by the phrase "*having* the kids tested"—she was vague and uncertain. Finally, she suggested that we try to work something out with our superintendent.

You can imagine the state I was in until we managed to meet with him. "I'll just put my foot down," I would yell at Bob. "There's no way I'll let them test the kids. I'll take it to the Supreme Court it I have to! I mean," I would plead, "I'm already experienced at giving these tests. Surely no one, certainly not a judge, could object if I explained that I wanted to test the kids at home. After all, their school *is* home."

Bob was relieved, probably for a number of reasons, when we finally did get to meet with the superintendent in Ithaca. "Fine, fine," he said, when we told him that we planned to teach Vita and Ishmael at home. "There are about five other families right here in town who are also home-schooling, and they all seem to be doing quite well." He was so nice that I really felt I ought to say something flattering about his school system. So I began by explaining, almost apologetically, that it was our idiosyncratic ideas about education, not his schools, that made us want to continue home-schooling. With my first breath, though, he cut me off. "Look," he said, "How parents choose to educate their children is their own business. If you have the guts to take on the responsibility of teaching your kids yourself, I think I can assume you are doing a good job. All we ask is that you send us a quarterly attendance form with a few paragraphs about how each child is doing. Our Director of Pupil Personnel is in charge of administering our home-education programs, so if and when you move to Ithaca you should write him a letter notifying him of your intentions. But don't be in a rush. Give yourselves a chance to settle in first."

"But what about testing?" I persisted, unable to really take in his relaxed attitude.

At first my question seemed to confuse him. Then he must have figured that we had a money problem, because he said, "Oh, don't worry, we'll provide the tests. In fact, we are obligated by law to provide you with textbooks and art materials as well. And if you need any other materials, just let us know and we'll see what we can do." When we left his office, we knew for sure that Ithaca was the town for us! (Later we discovered that despite the favorable attitude toward home-schooling at the state level, not all New York superintendents are as amenable as Ithaca's. Some families have had real trouble at the local level. We feel that it is a real credit to the Ithaca school system that the superintendent and his staff are so willing to tolerate alternative methods of education in their district.)

Within a week after we had moved here, I had practically signed Vita and Ishmael's lives away. For Vita, I'd scheduled violin and piano lessons, with group classes on Saturdays, and weekly gymnastics, ballet, and art classes. Ishmael got piano lessons, also with group classes, and ballet and drama classes. As if that weren't enough, we soon found ourselves attending a couple of concerts a week, visiting art galleries and museums, and even going to lectures at Cornell.

One reason for this seemingly mad frenzy was a natural desire to make up for lost time—twelve years on Bob's part and really a whole lifetime for me, since I'd moved to the wilds of New England when I was only eighteen. Of course we wanted to indulge Vita and Ishmael, too, after their hermetic life, by sending them to every class in which they expressed an interest. Even more importantly, we wanted them to start making friends.

Socially, though, things didn't turn out as we planned. Vita and Ishmael didn't meet any kids at their piano group class that they liked well enough to invite home, and, in any case, none of the children seemed to be as serious about music as they were. And although there were some serious little students in her violin class, Vita didn't make any instant friendships. Her art class was full of bigger boys, Ishmael's ballet class had only younger girls, and the one girl that Vita attached herself to in ballet lived thirty miles out in the country.

Meanwhile, Ishmael was enjoying his drama classes at a small local theater, The First Street Playhouse, which specialized in producing original plays by children as well as adults. Where he found the time, I don't know, but he was so inspired by the thought of having one of his plays produced in a real theater that he wrote a musical play called, *Love's Path Is Lumpy, or Eat Your Spaghetti*, and handed it in to Carolyn Fellman, the director of the playhouse.

My parents always told me that you can never expect to start at the top. The people who succeed, they would lecture, are those who are willing to perform menial tasks at the bottom— like my mother, who used to empty wastepaper baskets in the offices at the *New York Times* with the hope of getting a job as a reporter there someday. Although I never thought that I had taken their lectures too seriously, I now found myself giving Ishmael the very same speech as we all waited for Carolyn's judgement on his script. "You can't expect her to produce the first real play you've ever written," I kept telling him, "but what you should do is to ask her if you can work as an usher or help with scenery or lights. By just making yourself generally useful around the place, and learning how a real theater works, you'll not only gain Carolyn's respect, but you'll get a better idea of how to write plays." (A few months later, during a newspaper interview right before the opening of his play, Ishmael told a reporter that at first he'd had "high hopes of being an usher." She was incredulous, but he was quite serious.)

After a week or so of suspense, Carolyn finally called and asked Ishmael to come down to the theater to play the music for her. When he came home he seemed to be practically in a state of shock. "She says that if I make it longer and put in more adventures, she'll take it!" he told us dreamily, letting the words linger on his tongue as if their sounds would finally convince him that this was all true. For the next two weeks, we practically tiptoed around the house as Ishmael rewrote his play. I went over his drafts and gave him a little critical advice, but mostly I just took care to see that he had as much uninterrupted time as he needed. He added some pirate scenes and a spy scene, wrote more songs, and even wrote an overture in the style of Gilbert and Sullivan. Carolyn was delighted with the additions. To our astonishment, she announced auditions for the following week.

Greater than Ishmael's ambition to be a playwright was his ambition to be an actor, and fortunately Carolyn understood this well enough to give him some small parts. Vita, of course, was also desperate to act in the play. Although Carolyn was dubious, since Vita was only six, she did give her a tiny role. Later, as she saw what a wonderful little actress Vita is, she gave her other, more important parts.

For the next six weeks, both kids were far too busy for me even to think about worrying over their lack of friends. Acting in the play, I soon realized, was Ishmael's chance to acquire the kinds of social survival skills that he'd missed out on by not being in school. I don't really think he would have learned these things there anyway, as he would have been too traumatized. The theater, on the other hand, was a nice, congenial place for him to begin learning to deal with noise and confusion, and there was plenty of it. At home, the phone used to ring constantly as Meg, the production manager, called to change the time of a rehearsal, or as Carolyn wanted to discuss a line change or to ask who wrote the lyrics to a certain song. Ishmael, who had never successfully managed to get his coat, boots, and mittens on and off in school, now had to be responsible for changing his costume four different times. He even had to help with publicity by giving interviews for the local newspaper and television. He couldn't afford to be his old dreamy self; he had to be alert!

Vita, as I guess we knew beforehand, was an entirely different kettle of fish. Despite her obviously limited experience, she made arrangements over the phone like a real little businesswoman; she learned her lines like a professional; she managed her costumes efficiently; and she made her fair share of the noise and confusion that Ishmael had to learn to tolerate. She even made a point of helping him keep his costumes straight.

Love's Path Is Lumpy was a terrific success. The theater was filled to bursting at practically all of the eight performances, and many people came back two or three times. The woman who operated the theater lights said later, "I think I laughed harder each time I watched the show. I was still picking up on new jokes at the last performance." I knew what she meant. But it wasn't just Ishmael's writing that was so successful. Carolyn makes a practice of casting both children and adults in her productions, with little regard for realism in terms of age. In *Love's Path Is Lumpy* it was easy to see that the adults really inspired the kids in their acting. Yet the influence of the kids helped the adults to feel loose and relaxed enough with their parts that they often improvised new aspects to their characters during each performance. The combination of professionalism and fun gave the show much of its liveliness, and the absurdity of the character's sizes in contrast to the seriousness with which they were played really won over the audience.

Bob and I could never seem to keep away from the show, although staying at home would have given us a chance to get some work done in complete peace and quiet. It seemed as if every night Vita would ask plaintively, "What will we ever do when the play is over?"

"Sleep," I would say. But we knew how she felt.

Although Vita, and Ishmael too, enjoyed gossiping and goofing off backstage with the other kids, the only long-term friendships they made were with adults—Carolyn, and Laurel Guy, the playwright she shares a house with. It wasn't long, however, before other children came into our lives in a big way. The snow melted, Easter vacation arrived, and Bob innocently hung a rope swing on a "climbing tree" in the park across the street. By the next afternoon the park was swarming with kids, swinging, climbing the tree, and fooling around in the mud while waiting for a turn on the swing. Everyone was curious to meet the "new kids" in the neighborhood. Vita and Ishmael seemed to be popular from the start—not only because it was their swing, but because almost everyone had seen *Love's Path Is Lumpy*.

Vita found three or four girls her age to play with, and Ishmael found a couple of boys (although I think he preferred playing with one of the older girls). From what I could observe from a distance, and from what Vita and Ishmael told me, the boys and girls seemed to play happily together and everyone made a point of helping the younger kids get on the swing or climb the tree. Finally, I thought, Ithaca has given us everything we ever dreamed of!

Within a day or two, though, Ishmael grew tired of playing. Perhaps he would take a few turns on the swing, or skate around the block once or twice, but he preferred to sit on the porch swing and read about famous composers or study scores of symphonies.

Vita, on the other hand, couldn't get enough of the other children. She dashed out into the park early in the morning and just hung about, waiting for her little friends to appear. I had to practically drag her in at night. Once inside, she was consumed with desires. "Mommy, you should see the doll Carey has. Can I have one?" or "I wish I had a necklace like Esme." On rainy days, when the park was empty, she was bored. It was the first time that we'd ever seen her at such a loss for things to do by herself. As I watched the ever-busy, self-sufficient side of Vita disappearing, I began to regret that all these kids had ever appeared in the park at all. Fortunately, for my peace of mind as well as Vita's, the Easter vacation was soon over. It took Vita three or four days to become her old self again, but then we really did seem to have the best of both worlds: peace and quiet until 3:30, and then—*plenty of kids*.

Meanwhile, although Vita and Ishmael didn't seem to be making any close musical friendships at the music school, Bob and I were becoming much clearer about the kind of musical educations that they wanted and needed. Although I had often been appalled watching Suzuki violin instruction at the Institute, it never struck me as odd until we moved to Ithaca that I seemed to be willing to put Vita through that kind of training just for the sake of her social life. How did I ever expect her to relate happily to her fellow violinists at the school if she was wilting under the rigors of her violin instruction?

As it happened, though, and quite by chance, we found the directors of the school to be a delightful couple. They were interested in John Holt's ideas about learning and full of enthusiasm for music and children. They assigned Vita to a teacher who, although strictly Suzuki-oriented, is gentle and respectful of Vita's music. The proper violin posture and bow hold *are* important to her, but she just quietly molds Vita's hands and body to her instrument—never making a big deal out of it. And although she is old enough to have grown children of her own, she spends a great deal of the lesson time on her knees so as not to tower over Vita. The combination of the time Vita spent learning to play her violin with me, improvising and experimenting, and now the new but sensitive structure offered by her teacher and the frequent opportunities she has to watch the more advanced students play at the school has really helped her to flourish musically. I never would have imagined that already she'd be studying music by Beethoven and Boccherini, playing long notes with a wobbly vibrato, and bowing with such a smooth, flowing legato.

Unfortunately, piano lessons didn't go as well. Ishmael found it difficult to relate to the teacher. Although she was a fine musician, she was not interested in his composing and didn't share his passion for music theory and history. Vita got along much better with her, but Ishmael grew more and more unhappy, occasionally even crying after lessons. As his playing began to reflect his unhappiness, the situation became so tense that I thought it would be best if both kids found new teachers. Besides, Vita was anxious to spend more time reading music—not just playing the Suzuki literature by ear—and Ishmael was eager to have lessons on the romantic and modern music that he was always sight-reading.

Really taking the time to seek out the right piano teachers for Vita and Ishmael was an exhausting business. Interviewing teachers and then having to explain to them that they "wouldn't do" was embarrassing. After our last experience, however, I was as cautious as if I had been trying to arrange marriages for the kids. I had learned that music was too important to them for me to expect that they could have just casual relationships with their music teachers.

After what seemed like ages, we found a dear piano teacher for Vita. She is a Suzuki teacher, so she understands Vita's background; but she (like many Suzuki teachers, actually) also stresses music reading and theory. Even more important, she is warm and kind. For Ishmael, we found a teacher who is not only a wonderful pianist, but who acts like his colleague. She is always delighted to talk with him about the music he is writing, eager to show him far-out modern pieces that she often performs (including compositions by her husband), and always ready to help Ishmael analyze the pieces they are working on or to discuss alternative ways of interpreting them. Since he has been studying with her, he has really opened up at the piano —not so much because she has given him lots of technical advice about playing, but because through her friendship she has helped him to express himself through his music.

After we had been here for a few months Ishmael wisely dropped ballet for lack of time and interest, and Vita dropped gymnastics. He now takes lessons in music theory and solfeggio with a woman up the street who studied at the Kodály Institute in Hungary, and he studies composition with a composer and organist who recently earned his doctorate at Cornell. These teachers, along with Carolyn and Laurel, his "theater friends," are the people Ishmael feels most at home with. In fact, through him, they have become regular friends of our whole family. Vita is especially close to Carolyn and Louise, Ishmael's theory teacher. She likes to spend her Friday afternoons with Carolyn, who is an art teacher in one of the local schools. Tuesday afternoons are reserved for Louise, who directs a little girls' chorus. When Vita isn't giggling with Louise and the others, she is happily learning "solfege" and improving her accompanying skills at the piano.

I now realize that it was foolish to think that Ishmael and Vita needed other children, as such. What they really needed were a few friends, of whatever age, who share their interests. They are fortunate to have found them.

Still, when Ishmael sits out on the porch swing and reads thick tomes about obscure composers, I feel a certain sense of security in knowing that there are children out in the park with whom he could be playing if he wanted to. I really do enjoy the little friends that Vita brings home, although these days she, too, often prefers to read or draw rather than play. I am pleased, too, that while they don't see her too often, Vita and Ishmael have befriended a little girl, also a home-schooler, who composes music, plays Mozart sonatas, and adores listening to Ishmael tell stories. Less frequently, they see the children of two other home-schooling families with whom we have become quite friendly. At those times, even Ishmael indulges in some pretty rough-and-tumble play.

Because our school authorities have given us so much freedom, and because Vita and Ishmael's musical and dramatic activities take up so much time, the purely academic side of our home-school has become far more casual. At the same time, the kids constantly amaze me with their self-imposed rigor and dedication to learning. Only today, for example, when Vita was so quiet that I suspiciously asked her what she was up to, she surprised me by explaining that she was writing a report on weather. She wasn't kidding! She had already written three pages and she wasn't nearly done.

Bob continues to read science and history to the kids at night, and I work on music with them all morning. They joined a German class, so we often attempt to speak a little German together, especially when we take walks. This past fall, Ishmael spent hours every day working on a new and much more ambitious musical which he calls, *I Love You More Than a Grapefruit Squirts, or Confusion Compounded*. During that time, we not only let everything else slide, I even tried as much as possible to keep him away from his regular school work so that he would have time to get outside during his spare moments. But when he picked up math again, we were all surprised to find that not only had he not forgotten anything, he seemed to have "grown into" math in much the same way that Vita "grew into" reading. He finally seems to be competent with numbers, and he definitely picks up on new mathematical ideas more quickly that I do. Now It's me struggling to make sense of decimals and percents, not him, and I love it.

Looking ahead, rehearsals start for *Confusion Compounded* in a few weeks, and both Vita and Ishmael have small parts.

They are busy with rehearsals for a musical play they are doing with their German class, in which Ishmael will accompany the singers on piano. Vita is preparing for a piano recital in which she will perform two sonatinas and some shorter pieces, and she is looking forward to singing on TV with her chorus. Ishmael is submitting three pieces to a national composition competition. He will be having two of his pieces performed at a concert of Ithaca composers. And he is hoping to begin studying Hungarian this summer with Louise, with the far-fetched notion of studying at the Liszt Academy in Budapest someday.

In bed at night, Bob and I often wonder how Vita and Ishmael will fare in the more distant future. It's really hard for us to make any guesses. Certainly high school, with its long hours, seems out of the question, since both kids would then have so little time for their music. Even Ithaca High School, with all its "frills," would, I'm pretty sure, seem dreary and boring to them after all the interesting things they've been doing these past years. At some point, though, if only for practical reasons, they may very possibly decide that they need some sort of formal schooling or training. But I'm not sure that even college will be the answer. It seems probable that Ishmael, who is pursuing so many interests in such depth already, and who is already eager to audit classes and attend lectures at Cornell and Ithaca College, not to mention ransack their libraries, will have gotten the most he wants to out of a liberal arts education by the time he's eighteen. It is conceivable that he'll want to pursue a more specialized academic interest like history or writing at a college, or more likely, a graduate school. In terms of his present interests, though, it is easiest for us to picture him attending a music school—maybe even the Liszt Academy. Who knows?

Vita is too young even to try to make guesses about. Will she end up favoring the violin or the piano? Will she drop music and become a dancer or an actress? What will she do with her art? For all we know, she will become a short-order cook or a laundress like she threatens to. I imagine, though, that she will have read so widely and will have made such good use of the resources available here by the time she reaches college age that a conventional liberal arts education may not seem important to her, either.

If she or Ishmael do decide that they want to go to college, or if they find that they need a college degree for some reason, we are certain that their unusual educational backgrounds will, if anything, be an asset—as long as they do well on their College Boards. I read somewhere, not too long ago, that the admissions director at the University of California said he gets six or seven applicants a year who have been educated at home. "We give them proficiency tests," he explained, "and if they pass we go ahead and take a chance on them. Usually they do very well." Music schools, on the other hand, like ballet and art schools, traditionally accept students on the basis of merit, regardless of past school attendance. My mother told me recently that she sat next to the head of a prestigious music school at some kind of benefit dinner. When she asked him provocatively whether he would admit someone like Ishmael, "who had never been to school," his reply was, "We have only one criterion for admissions. You have to be a good or potentially good musician."

Meanwhile, like most other parents, we are appalled at how quickly Vita and Ishmael are growing up. As fast as I let down Vita's dresses, she seems to obstinately outgrow them. And yesterday, while Ishmael and I were buying winter boots at the shoe store, we discovered that our feet are the same size only his are wider! Every day seems to be a constant reminder to us that the kids won't be around the house forever, that soon they won't need us to tuck them in at night or to make hot cider after an afternoon of sledding. Naturally Bob and I love it when Vita and Ishmael swear that they'll never leave us, but we don't expect that. And actually, although we are totally wrapped up in the kids, we don't expect to find an unfillable gap in our lives when they are gone—although naturally we *will* miss them. They have set us such inspiring examples through their industry, self-confidence, and creativity that I can't imagine a time when our lives won't be full to bursting. There are just too many things that we want to do. Bob, who has just taken up the cello, wants to get good enough so that he can play real chamber music with friends. I want to re-learn the viola and get halfway decent on the piano. And we both have books that we want to write.

We play music and write now, but not nearly as much as we would like. It seems as if we can never expect long enough periods of peace and quiet to really concentrate. There's always some apologetic child interrupting us to ask what a congruent triangle is or wanting to know how to make script "J"s. One friend of ours, although she is totally supportive of our desire to keep the kids out of school, thinks I am crazy to give them so much of myself. She once wrote me a well-meaning letter to that effect:

> Be *sure* to make time and commitments for yourself and your own interests. The kids don't need a martyr/chauffeur for a mother. Why are they entitled to do fifty million interesting things and you not one? They have long lives ahead of them, and they will always have time to learn and sing in choruses or whatever. I think you should do something entirely for youself. If need be, put it to the kids that way— i.e., "Look, it's a choice between you doing X or me doing Y." They're not heartless monsters, they'll understand.

I appreciated her concern. What she failed to understand, though, was that I, too, spend most of my time doing what interests me—namely, being with my kids. True, it's aggravating to go to a movie and have Vita asking constantly, "Now what's happening?" But on the other hand, movies give me a chance to hold her on my lap, and I like to hear her impressions afterwards. It's also true that often I practically have to steal time to read or write, but as John Holt would say, "It's never too late." I have years ahead of me to read and write and play music, but I only have a few years left to spend entirely with my children. No matter how crazy it might seem, I plan to make the most of them!

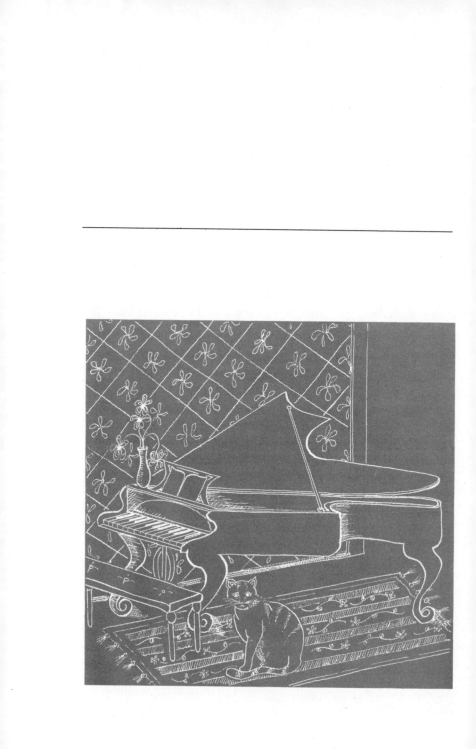

Resources and Suggestions for Potential Home-Schoolers

Growing Without Schooling

For those of you who are seriously considering home-schooling but are unsure how to begin, and for anyone who is interested in learning more about home-education, I strongly recommend subscribing to John Holt's newsletter, *Growing Without Schooling* (729 Boylston Street, Boston, MA, 02116).

First, and most important, for home-schoolers or potential home-schoolers, GWS gives you the comfortable feeling of being part of a growing movement rather than merely being an isolated family with weird ideas. It provides a national forum for parents writing about the experiences they've had teaching their children at home. I not only learn a lot from these other parents, but they help me to reinforce my own ideas about education and child-rearing.

In addition, GWS has articles about subjects as various as math, art, music, reading, writing, and home curriculums; it has book reviews by John Holt; it provides information about recent court rulings and legislation; it provides solid advice about strategies for dealing with school authorities and, if necessary, with the courts; it has a directory of correspondence schools and private schools that enroll home-schoolers; it lists friendly lawyers and friendly school districts; and best of all, it has a lengthy directory of home-schooling families from all fifty states and Canada who are happy to help others in any way they can.

Teach Your Own by John Holt

Teach Your Own, by John Holt (New York: Delacorte Press/ Seymour Lawrence, 1981) is the most in-depth book I know about home-education. Much of the book is drawn from material in *Growing Without Schooling,* but much is new, too. Like all of John's books, it is well worth reading.

How Do I Go About It?

Before actually taking your children out of school or deciding not to send them there in the first place, be sure to acquaint yourself as thoroughly as possible with your state's compulsory attendance laws and with any applicable regulations—including whatever home-schooling regulations may be in existence. With this kind of information under your belt, you will be able to decide what approach to take in your dealings or non-dealings with your local or state authorities. Will you go ahead and try to seek permission from your superintendent or local school board? Will you enroll your children in a private school that allows for home-based study? Will you form your own private school and register it with the state? Will you try your luck "underground"? All of these options, and perhaps others, will become much clearer when you understand just how restrictive the laws in your particular state are.

Perhaps the most pleasant way to find copies of these documents is by writing or calling one of the families listed in the *GWS* directory under your state. If they don't have the information themselves, they'll most likely be able to steer you to some sympathetic person who does.

Another way is to contact your local state representative and ask him to get the State Department of Education to send you everything you need. If you aren't in a hurry, write to the Department of Education yourself. Sometimes the folks there are prompt, but often not. A quicker and more interesting way would be to pay them a visit, as we did.

If you are sure from the beginning that you want to be above-board and try to get permission from your local school authorities to teach your children at home, there is no harm in asking your superintendent to show you all the rules and regulations pertaining to non-public education and home-education that he may have in his files.

Once you have all the information you need, you will quite likely decide that you really do want to try your luck at the local level. Unless you have an unusually progressive or receptive superintendent, it will be wise to prepare a lengthy written statement for him (and/or your school board). Outline your educational philosophy and goals and show how what you propose to do with your children is consistent with the state law and regulations. GWS has printed many such statements written by families across the country. Reading them can be very helpful in getting you started with your own writing. In fact, you should feel free to crib as much of them as you like.

Many school districts, in fact most, will expect you to provide them with a home curriculum. Once again, GWS can be of invaluable help, but so can your school districts themselves. They usually have curriculums of their own for each grade level, and it is important that you ask to see these. They will give you an idea of how detailed you ought to be and will also help to keep you in touch with what all the other kids are supposedly learning. In addition, most schools have a "resource room" for teachers which is crammed full of sample textbooks. Ask your superintendent if you can look these over. Who knows, you may find some that you think are worthwhile, and they will make your curriculum look more impressive.

A more interesting place to go hunting for learning materials is your local library. And don't overlook the other resources in your community—museums, art galleries, theaters, concert halls, factories, workshops, government agencies, artists, musicians, writers, teachers, etc. Remember, the whole world is at your fingertips.

Good luck.